DR. TOM MALONE
PREACHES ON
FAITH

DR. TOM MALONE
PREACHES ON
FAITH

SWORD of the LORD
PUBLISHERS
P. O. BOX 1099, MURFREESBORO, TN 37133

Copyright 1993 by

DR. THOMAS L. MALONE, SR.

ISBN 0-87398-175-8

Printed and Bound in the United States of America

Introduction

The apostles said unto Jesus, "Lord, increase our faith." The reason they made this request unto the Lord was that the challenge at hand was greater than their faith. Our faith should be equal to or greater than the test we face.

In the forty-five years I pastored Emmanuel Baptist Church, my faith was constantly being tested. Many times there was the need for large sums of money to build buildings for Emmanuel Baptist Church and Midwestern Baptist College. I needed increased faith for the healing of the sick and for winning the lost to Christ. I often found that the need was much larger than my faith, and I had to ask the Lord to increase my faith. God does this for us through His Word as He leads us to the precious promises. My search for an increased faith was the motivation for many sermons on faith during those forty-five years, and when I preached those sermons I preached more to my own heart than the great church family. My preaching on faith was my way of saying, "Lord, increase my faith."

God gave me many wonderful experiences as a church family trusted God for unusual blessings. I am happy to share these simple sermons with you, and I would be grateful to God if they help in some way to increase your faith.

Dr. Tom Malone, Sr.

Table of Contents

   I. *What Constitutes a Great Faith*............9
  II. *What Faith Believes*......................23
 III. *Living by Faith*..........................41
  IV. *Have Faith in God*........................55
   V. *The Importance of Faith*..................69
  VI. *The Kind of Faith We Need Today*..........83
 VII. *Faith Abiding*............................97
VIII. *Faith for Slaying Giants*.................113
  IX. *A Faith That Wins*........................129
   X. *The Measure of Your Faith*................141
  XI. *The Expansion of Faith*...................159
 XII. *Faith Defeating Our Fears*................171
XIII. *Faith for Living on High*.................199
 XIV. *Rahab's Faith and the Scarlet Cord*.......215
  XV. *"According to Your Faith"*................235
 XVI. *Trusting in the Lord*.....................249
XVII. *Faith for Miracles*.......................261

Chapter I

What Constitutes a Great Faith

(Preached in the Emmanuel Baptist Church, Wednesday evening, January 19, 1966)

READ: Matthew 15:21-28

"Then Jesus answered and said unto her, O woman, great is thy faith: be it unto thee even as thou wilt. And her daughter was made whole from that very hour."—Matt. 15:28.

I want to condense our text to just four words, tremendous words that fell from the lips of our Lord Jesus Christ, the blessed Son of God: "...great is thy faith...."

I speak to you on "What Constitutes a Great Faith." What does it mean for a Christian, a believer, young or old, new convert or mature Christian, to have a great faith? What constitutes a great faith? Jesus saw here a woman who had great faith.

It is interesting to see a great contrast in the Bible, in this book of Matthew especially, between unbelief and faith, two opposites described in the Bible.

It is interesting in the Bible to see the various types of unbelief. There is more unbelief than just the unsaved man or woman, boy or girl, who does not believe in Jesus Christ as his or her personal Saviour. In fact, Jesus talked more to Christians about unbelief than He did to unsaved people about unbelief.

There are great verses in the Bible, such as Matthew 13:58, "And he did not many mighty works there because of their unbelief." You will see in the Bible that unbelief was one of the most damaging sins in the hearts and lives of the people of God in both the Old and New Testaments. Unbelief kept Israel out of Canaan for forty years. Unbelief is a damaging sin. And Jesus talked about it often.

Now in chapter 16 of Matthew, unbelief expresses itself in a strange way. Jesus said to these religious people, "A wicked and adulterous generation seeketh after a sign; and there shall no sign be given unto it, but the sign of the prophet Jonas," or the sign or miracle of the resurrection (vs. 4). Jesus is saying to these people, "It is wicked of you to ask Me to perform a miracle, something tangible, visible and physical, that you can see, in order to make you believe."

A type of unbelief found in the hearts and lives of many of God's people demands tangible evidence.

That is what Thomas wanted. He said to the other disciples after the resurrection, "Except I shall see in his hands the print of the nails, and put my finger into the print of the nails, and thrust my hand into his side, I will not believe" (John 20:25). But Jesus said to him, "...blessed are they that have not seen, and yet have believed" (vs. 29). Wicked unbelief demands tangible evidence before trusting the promises of God.

There are many other types of unbelief in the Bible. There is indifference to God's past blessing. It is so easy to forget what God has done for us before.

I read in chapter 16 of Matthew a strange thing. Jesus was talking to the disciples about some spiritual matters, but they didn't understand Him at all. They got in a boat and started across the sea and forgot to take bread. When Jesus said, "...beware of the leaven of the Pharisees and of the Sadducees," they reasoned,

WHAT CONSTITUTES A GREAT FAITH

"It is because we have taken no bread." But that was not what Jesus was talking about. When Jesus perceived their attitude, He said, "O ye of little faith, why reason ye among yourselves, because ye have brought no bread?" He said, 'Don't you remember how I performed one miracle by feeding five thousand men, besides women and children, with just a little bit of bread? Don't you remember another miracle where I fed four thousand and provided bread for everyone?' They had already forgotten about that. Isn't that strange?

Many times, when a Christian at a crucial moment ought to believe, he forgets all the past victories, all the answers to prayer, all the evidence of the reality of God in his life.

Many times unbelief lays hold on the heart of the Christian.

Unbelief manifests itself in so many different ways. Unbelief manifests itself in indifference to the Person of Jesus Christ. Then there is unbelief in His atoning work. John 3:18 says, "He that believeth on him is not condemned: but he that believeth not is condemned already, because he hath not believed in the name of the only begotten Son of God." Keep this one picture in your mind for a moment.

Then there is this other wonderful contrast—faith, that faith that lays hold upon God against all odds and believes and trusts God to do the miraculous.

There is what I call the "scale of faith" in the Bible. It is very plain and evident.

In Mark 4:40 we read, "...how is it that ye have *no* faith?" Most people have "no faith"—that is, no real Bible saving faith.

In Matthew 6:30 He said, "O ye of *little* faith."

There is the scale. You start at the bottom—"no faith"; then move up just a little bit to "little faith." But of the woman I speak about, Jesus said, "...*great* is thy faith...." That is what people need in this difficult hour—"great" faith.

This woman had a great faith. Why? It was great for five reasons. It was great, in the first place,

Because of Who She Was

This woman was not religious. She was not one of the chosen ones, not of the elect of the house of Israel. She lived over in Tyre and Sidon. She is a Canaanite, a Syrophenician woman. She was outside the race of people to whom God had said would come the blessing, the word, the truth. She, a heathen, had absolutely no right—none whatsoever—to ask God for anything. God had declared in Romans 1:16, "I am not ashamed of the gospel of Christ: for it is the power of God unto salvation to everyone that believeth; to the JEW FIRST, and also to the Greek." Here is this woman, even before Calvary, before the age of grace, demanding something of Jesus Christ. Oh, you don't realize what faith that took!

She had great faith because of who she was.

The Samaritan woman at the well even said to Jesus, "How is it that thou, being a Jew, askest drink of me, which am a woman of Samaria? for the Jews have no dealings with the Samaritans" (John 4:9). In the thinking of the people, it could not be reconciled that one other than a Jew would ever come to God for anything.

But here comes a mother, a heathen Syrophenician woman, saying, "Jesus, I want something from You." Not one who stood around that day ever believed she would get it.

Because of who she was, it took great faith. Jesus talked so plainly to her. "It is not meet to take the children's bread, and cast it to dogs [the Gentiles]." This woman readily admitted she was a dog, so to speak: "Yet the dogs eat the crumbs which fall from their masters' table." She was saying, "I am going to believe that I can get the mercy of God until I get it."

It was a great faith because of who she was.

WHAT CONSTITUTES A GREAT FAITH

One great thing has to happen before God honors faith, and that is an absolute unbelief and distrust in one's self. You can't believe in yourself and believe in God and have faith at the same time. You have to believe that it is "not I, but Christ." There must be an absolute resignation from self. This woman admitted she was just a dog, but 'yet dogs get the crumbs.'

I read a little story years ago of a German prince who visited the prison of Toulon. When he came to the outer gate, he said to the keepers, "I am going to release one prisoner today."

"Prince, whom will you release?" they asked.

"I do not know yet," he replied.

It is said that the German prince walked up and down and talked to the prisoners as they came up to the bars. He asked one, "Why are you here?"

He answered, "I have been wronged and mistreated. I didn't do anything wrong, and I don't deserve this punishment."

He walked on. He asked another prisoner, "Why are you here?"

"The trial was rigged. There were false witnesses, and I don't deserve this."

He walked on. He asked another prisoner, "Why are you here?"

"I am here because I deserve to be here. I am guilty. I am far more wicked than any of them know. And I am here because I deserve to be here."

The German prince called the keepers and said, "Unlock this door. Here is the man who is fit to go free."

No one can have his faith honored until there is an absolute distrust in self, and a trust and faith in the power of God alone.

And so, her faith was great because of who she was.

"Then Jesus answered and said unto her, O woman, great is thy faith: be it unto thee even as thou wilt. And her daughter was made whole from that very hour."

Notice a little further. Her faith was great

Because It Came From the Right Source

Faith is not something you work up. There is only one definition of faith that I know of in all the Bible. In Hebrews, chapter 11, "faith" is mentioned exactly two dozen times. The chapter begins with a definition: "Now faith is the substance of things hoped for, the evidence of things not seen."

Mrs. Malone said to me the other day, "I believe we need faith to help some of our seminary students who are going through trials and whose faith is weak and who sometimes surrender to situations and circumstances."

Like one Christian asked another, "How are you?"

"Fairly well, under the circumstances," he answered.

I say, no Christian ought ever be under the circumstances. Faith does not live under circumstance. Faith lives on a higher plane. And faith can come from only one source—from the Word of God. We see it right here. Her faith was great because it came from the right source.

Not in this account in Matthew, but in the account of the same thing in Mark 7:25 we read, "For a certain woman, whose young daughter had an unclean spirit, HEARD of him, and came and fell at his feet." She "heard of him." That goes right along with Romans 10:17: "So then faith cometh by hearing, and hearing by the word of God."

You will never have a strong faith apart from this Book. Make light of it, leave it out of your life, disregard it, do not emphasize it—and you will be weak in faith. But you meditate on it and, like Mary of old, sit at His feet and hear His Word—and you will have a strong faith. It won't come any other way. I know by experience. When I needed a strong faith and didn't have it, I knew I could come to the Bible. As I read the promises of God, everything became brighter. Yes, "faith cometh by hearing, and hearing by the word of God."

John 5:24 says that, too: "Verily, verily, I say unto you, He that heareth my word, and believeth on him that sent me, hath everlasting life, and shall not come into condemnation; but is passed from death unto life."

Her faith was great because it came from the right source.

In the third instance, her faith was great

Because It Demanded the Salvation of One of Her Children

Here is a woman who came asking for something for one of her children. I am amazed at the emphasis in the Bible placed on what I call "household salvation." I hear a lot in this day about various types of evangelism: mass evangelism, personal evangelism, child evangelism, church evangelism, etc. But the Bible mentions household evangelism more than any other kind.

When the Philippian jailor said, "Sirs, what must I do to be saved?" Paul answered, "Believe on the Lord Jesus Christ, and thou shalt be saved, AND THY HOUSE" (Acts 16:30,31).

A man said to me only a few days ago, "I don't believe that promise that your family is going to be saved." I do. "Believe on the Lord Jesus Christ, and thou shalt be saved, **and thy house**." There is a faith that not only leads to your salvation but a faith that reaches out and embraces every member of your household.

What a sweet and mighty heavenly revival would come to our churches if our families would become burdened about the members of their own household who are lost!

Here is a woman whose faith was great because it demanded the salvation of her child. How many times household salvation is taught in the Scriptures! In Acts 16:15 we read about Lydia, a seller of purple, who was holding a prayer meeting down by the riverside. But she was untaught in pure salvation. The Lord opened her heart as she heard Paul. "And when she was baptized, **and her household**...." Not a thing is said about her husband. Whether he was dead or alive, we don't know. But one thing we do know: another woman got every member of her household saved and baptized.

Think about Cornelius. One whole chapter (Acts 10) is about the salvation of a man's family. I took the Bible today and underscored some things it said about Cornelius, this man who sent for Simon Peter to come to his home and preach to his family and get them saved. "A devout man, and one that feared God with all his house...."

If you have the kind of religion that makes you happy and lets you come to church while your family is going to Hell, you do not have the kind that I have. The Bible says, "...with all his house."

Notice again. When the messengers came to Peter, they said, "Cornelius the centurion, a just man, and one that feareth God, and of good report among all the nation of the Jews, was warned from God by an holy angel to send for thee INTO HIS HOUSE, and to hear words of thee." If you do not press your Christianity across the threshold of your home, you haven't gone far enough.

Notice again. "Cornelius waited for them, and had called together his kinsmen...." He wanted his kinfolk saved.

Some folks say, "I can't be bothered with the kinfolks." Bible converts didn't say that. "Cornelius waited for them, and had called together his kinsmen and near friends." He said, 'I want my kinfolks and close associates saved.'

Now notice verse 30: "I prayed in my house...." What do you do in yours? A house without prayer is apt to be a home where some of the children lose their souls.

I will never forget hearing a preacher friend tell about a man who was a sot drunkard in his town. His name was often men-

WHAT CONSTITUTES A GREAT FAITH

tioned. People had said, "If we can get So-and-so saved, we will have done the greatest piece of work we could have ever done."

One day while he was preaching, this alcoholic rose to his feet, marched down that aisle like a soldier, fell on that altar, wept, opened his heart and took Jesus as his Saviour.

A few days later when the preacher was arranging baptism and church membership for him, he asked him, "Fred, what is it about this church, its ministry and its preaching that brought you to the Lord?"

Fred Hall replied, "I don't want to hurt your feelings, preacher. You are a great preacher, and you preach the truth. I have confidence in you and love you. But I'll tell you. The other morning about three o'clock, I rose from a gambling table and staggered on my way home. As I walked across the living room, I heard a groan. I stumbled around in the darkness until I found on the floor my sobbing, brokenhearted, gray-haired mother." He said to that preacher these exact words: "I could have gone to Hell over your church, I could have gone to Hell over your preaching—but I couldn't go to Hell over a praying mother!"

The kind of faith that this woman had is household salvation. She came to God saying, "O God, my child is being destroyed. Help him to turn from his wicked way."

"O woman, great is thy faith: be it unto thee even as thou wilt. And her daughter was made whole from that very hour."

In the fourth place,

Her Faith Did Not Leave Her in the Face of Difficulties

It is very easy to trust God right now, isn't it? We are sitting in church, we are in good health, our needs are supplied, the sun shines in our life. But wait until the tempestuous winds blow, wait until the trials come—then where is your faith?

The faith of the Syrophenician woman did not waver in the face of difficulties. Let's look at some of the difficulties.

First, one statement would have thrown most of us: "But he answered her not a word" (vs. 23). He didn't even speak to her when she spoke to Him. That would have sent most of us on the run. Not this woman. She just kept hanging on.

Something else, and we will always have it. The disciples said, "Send her away...." That would have been it for most of us. But if you keep your eyes on people, you will not have any faith, and you don't deserve any. There will always be people who will not encourage your faith. These disciples said, "Send her away." They didn't care what she wanted—"get rid of her."

The silence of Christ, the attitude of the disciples; now notice the Lord's words: "It is not meet to take the children's bread, and cast it to dogs." Even these words of the Lord sounded discouraging.

Three things discouraged her faith: (1) the silence of Christ; (2) the stoicism of the disciples; (3) the selection of the Jews to be blessed before the Gentiles.

My faith is not what I wish it were. People have said to me, "Preacher, I wish I had the faith you do." My wife has said, "I wish I could have the faith that you have." I would give anything if it were ten thousand times more than it is.

But here is a woman with great faith. Here is a woman that, in spite of all obstacles, said, "I'll not quit believing." Right at the very time when most would have quit, she hung on. She said, "Lord, help me" (vs. 25). Not very oratorical, is it? But it got results. Try it yourself sometime!

What did Simon Peter say when he was about to go down? He didn't say, 'Oh, Thou great God, who sitteth upon the realm of the universe....' He just said, "Lord, save me," coming right to the point and coming to the right place. Such gets results. "Lord, help me" will always move the Master.

WHAT CONSTITUTES A GREAT FAITH

I read of a woman some years ago, a Mrs. Carter. She had a boy named Tom. She was saved but had an unsaved husband. The boy went the way of the father for years. He finally wound up in prison.

(I preached a week in Jackson Prison. You wouldn't believe the type people who are there. I met every kind you could think of. Some came to me and said, "Preacher, I'm a member of such-and-such a fundamental church." Some said, "I'm saved and know it." One young man came to me and said, "I was saved in Emmanuel Baptist Church [our church] and baptized. I'm a member there. I'm ashamed for you to find me in prison.")

Tom Carter wound up in prison. The aged mother would take the Bible every day and go yonder to the secret place—like godly mothers will do when their children are on their way to Hell—and stain it with her tears. She stayed upon her face before God and prayed, "O God, somehow or another, in that prison bring my boy to Christ."

One day she got a telegram. It was not good news: TOM CARTER WAS FOUND DEAD IN HIS BUNK THIS MORNING.

She took that telegram, went back to the secret place, took this good old Book filled with promise after promise, and again prayed: "Lord, I don't believe it. I have prayed, believed Your Word and stained it with my tears. I have waited upon You. I wanted my boy saved. This telegram says he's dead. I don't believe it. I am still going to claim Your Word and still believe You will answer my prayer. I will never waver in my faith."

In about twenty-four hours she got another telegram, which read:

WE MADE A TRAGIC ERROR. ANOTHER TOM CARTER IN THIS PRISON WAS FOUND DEAD IN HIS BUNK. YOUR TOM IS ALIVE AND WELL.

Not long after that, the story in the *Sunday School Times*

magazine said that Tom Carter had been gloriously saved.

Now, listen! That is faith. Faith cries, "It shall be done."

Jesus said to this woman, "O woman, great is thy faith: be it unto thee even as thou wilt." Jesus told her, 'It will be just like you want it. Write your own ticket.' That kind of faith God wants us to have—a faith that laughs at impossibilities and cries out, "It shall be done."

The faith of the Syrophenician was great because it did not waver in the face of difficulties. "And her daughter was made whole from that very hour."

There is always a good "quitting place" for Christians. Perhaps God made it that way. He wants us to have some trials that will make us believe.

Her faith was great in the fifth place,

Because It Was Rewarded

Jesus walked fifty miles from the early part of this chapter to where He met that woman. And can you show me any other reason why He went there? He knew what was going to happen all the time. When He said, 'I can't give the bread to the dogs,' I think Jesus said, "I hope she won't take Me at face value right now. I've come fifty miles to meet this poor soul."

And He rewarded her. He complimented her. Compliments may not mean much, and they are as passing as time itself. But Jesus said, "O woman, great is thy faith...." She was rewarded by Him because she got her girl saved and cured. That is reward enough, isn't it?

I would like to have seen that mother and that little girl going home! No doubt that child walked, maybe for the first time, normally. Mother kept looking at her and squeezing her hand as they both wept. I think they vowed, "When we get home we'll get on our knees and thank Jesus." As the mother walked along, surely her thought was, *I got what I went after.*

It takes faith to get what you go after.

Years ago I knew a great man of faith and prayer, but he still had two unsaved brothers. For many years he prayed for God to save them. One was saved before he died, and one was not. When he died and left an unsaved brother, the old Devil might have said, "See, God does not honor his faith." But shortly after he went to Heaven, the other brother was gloriously saved.

Let me encourage you with two verses. Hebrews 10:35: "Cast not away therefore your confidence, which hath great recompence of reward." Don't quit believing, dear people. And then Hebrews 11:6: "But without faith it is impossible to please him: for he that cometh to God must believe that he is, and that he is a rewarder of them that diligently seek him."

Sometimes your faith will be tried, just as surely as you are sitting here right now. Sorrow comes to everyone. Remember the story of the man whose son had died. He said to the preacher, this unbelieving man, "You talk so much about God. Where was He when my son died?" The preacher wisely answered, "The same place He was when His Son died."

God loves you. Let that encourage your faith. You are in the hollow of His hand.

"Then Jesus answered and said unto her, O woman, great is thy faith: be it unto thee even as thou wilt. And her daughter was made whole from that very hour."—Matt. 15:28.

Chapter II

What Faith Believes

(Preached in the Emmanuel Baptist Church on Sunday evening, June 27, 1976)

READ: Psalm 116; II Corinthians 4:1-15

"I believed, therefore have I spoken...."—Ps. 116:10.

"We having the same spirit of faith, according as it is written, I believed, and therefore have I spoken; we also believe, and therefore speak."—II Cor. 4:13.

My subject may seem a rather strange one: "What We Believe." There is no question about in whom we believe. Different ones have asked me, "Just exactly what does this church believe?" No one could give his whole creed or all that we believe in one service. But tonight I speak on "What We Believe."

The psalmist said, "I believed, therefore have I spoken...." Paul said: "...we also believe, and therefore speak."

Your believing is the most important thing that can happen to you. It is a life-changing experience. Your belief affects your behavior. We read: "...they trusted in thee, and were not confounded" (Ps. 22:5). The most important thing that can happen is to come to the place where one really believes.

Years ago when I was on the radio every morning, one day I came down out of the Riker Building, where WCAR radio station was at that time; and I found a Pentecostal preacher out on the sidewalk slapping his thighs and laughing. He was by himself. He and I were friends even though we both knew we differed in what we believed in many instances.

I walked up to him and said, "What are you laughing about?"

"I just talked to a man I met on the street. When I asked him, 'What do you believe?' he said, 'I believe what my church believes.' I said to him, 'What does your church believe?' He said to me, 'My church believes the same thing that I believe.'"

Now that Pentecostal preacher was slapping his thighs and laughing at that. He said to me, "Don't you think, Brother Tom, that fellow does not really know what he believes?"

I said, "I think that is true."

The psalmist declared, "I believed, therefore have I spoken."

In 1935, the second week of August, I had an experience that perhaps nearly everyone in this room has had. I believed, and my life and whole future were changed. My past was even changed because, in God's sight, it was blotted out.

To believe is the most life-changing experience a person can ever have. Belief is absolutely essential to successful living.

A person should know what he believes. I do. There is a system of truth I believe. I may be speaking out of turn, but no power on earth could change what I believe because it is based on what God said! Believing is essential to successful living.

A man came to Jesus bringing his lunatic, demon-possessed son, saying, "I brought him to thy disciples, and they could not cast him out." Jesus looked at that man standing at the foot of the Mount of Transfiguration and said, "If thou canst believe, all things are possible to him that believeth" (Mark 9:23). You will never please God until you, by faith, believe Him.

Belief determines your relationship to God and man: "But without faith it is impossible to please him: for he that cometh to God must believe that he is, and that he is a rewarder of them that diligently seek him," says Hebrews 11:6. It is more than that. That is what the psalmist and Paul are talking about. The Bible says that, without this belief, it is impossible to please God, because he that comes to God must believe that He is. Watch that last phrase: "...and that he is a rewarder of them that diligently seek him."

I believe everything that affects my life is going to be all right with me. I believe God will reward me as a Christian.

These things we believe for certain. We are not "wishy-washy" about them.

Luke, in chapter 1 of Luke, says something about what we believe.

"Forasmuch as many have taken in hand to set forth in order a declaration of those things which are most surely believed among us, Even as they delivered them unto us, which from the beginning were eyewitnesses, and ministers of the word; It seemed good to me also, having had perfect understanding of all things from the very first, to write unto thee...."—Vss. 1-3.

In verse 3 he is saying, "...having had perfect understanding of all things from above." He is saying, 'What we believe came from above! It is not traditional, not man-made; it is not a decree of man nor creed of man. What we believe came from above!'

That is true tonight of those who are born again. We believe something that is not earthly, but heavenly.

On these seven things hangs the important faith, the important belief, that we share tonight.

I. I BELIEVE IN A SACRED BOOK—THE BIBLE

I never believed anything any more in all of my life than I believe that the Bible that I am reading from and preaching from is the Word of God. I believe in a sacred Book. "All scripture is given by inspiration of God, and is profitable for doctrine, for reproof, for correction, for instruction in righteousness'' (II Tim. 3:16). The Bible says that all Scripture is given by the Spirit, is God-breathed. The Book that lies before me is the infallible, inerrant, indestructible, indivisible Word of Almighty God.

Whether one believes the Bible or not, makes a difference. It sets a guideline for our lives. Whatever it says is so. I may not agree with some person on what it says, but one thing we agree on is that whatever it says is true because this is the Word of God. We believe in the sacred Book—the Bible.

I believe the Bible is a perfect Book. Psalm 19:7: "The law of the Lord is perfect, converting the soul." I could give you several hundred reasons why I know the Bible is a perfect Book. Each Christian sitting here is a testimony that the Bible is a perfect Book. "The law of the Lord is perfect, converting the soul." Every time a soul is saved, God is saying, "My perfect Word did it all!" The Word of God is a perfect Book.

I saw *Look* magazine's lengthy article quite a few years ago on "Is the Bible a Myth? The Bible—50,000 Errors?" How that stirred my soul. I wrote the editors of *Look* magazine. I sent them every kind of letter—from a penny-postcard to a registered, airmail, mule-mail letter. But I could never get an answer. Finally, I did receive a halfhearted acknowledgment. Not one person would dare accept the challenge of a Baptist preacher that the Bible was a perfect Book! Do you know why? We have irrefutable proof that God's Word is without a flaw and without an error. "The law of the Lord is perfect, converting the soul."

The Bible is eternal. No other book has, in the annals of human history, suffered the fierce, satanic attack that the Bible has suffered. The scholarly man has sought to extinguish it. The fool in his folly has bombarded it with his little pebbles of thought. But the Bible still stands because it is an eternal Book. That is what Jesus meant when He said, "Heaven and earth shall pass away,

WHAT FAITH BELIEVES

but my words shall not pass away'' (Matt. 24:35).

I thank God as a preacher, whose whole life is given to preaching the Bible, that I preach a Book of which Jesus said, 'It shall never pass away!' When mountains have crumbled to dust and the stars from Heaven have fallen, this Bible will still be. I believe the Bible is eternal.

I believe that it is indestructible, for Jesus said in John 10:35, "...the scripture cannot be broken." You cannot break this truth. This is divine truth, the unbreakable sword of God Almighty. There are so many evidences of it in the Bible itself.

The Lord Jesus was crucified between two thieves. Crucifixion was not just a matter of nailing someone to a cross. The Roman law demanded that, before one could ever be removed from that cross, there had to be certain proof that the person was dead. The Roman custom was, with a big, long Roman ax, to break the legs of the one hanging there. They would chop into the thighs and literally almost sever them from the human body. By doing so, they were making sure that not a drop of blood remained in that body. This made sure that the person on the cross was dead before he was ever brought down.

There were two thieves, one on either side. The Scripture said of Jesus like it said of the Passover Lamb, "Not a bone of that Lamb shall be broken." Here is Jesus on the cross, God's eternal Lamb. The Bible prophesied of Him, "He keepeth all his bones: not one of them is broken" (Ps. 34:20). His brow shall be pierced; His side shall be opened; His hands and feet shall be nailed; but not a bone of Him shall be broken!

Here comes the Roman soldier. He comes to one thief and breaks his legs. He comes to the other thief and breaks his legs. Here is the important figure, the One who stirred the whole Roman Empire. The soldier stands with his ax raised. I watch that ax raised, that Roman soldier standing there. The Word of God hangs in the balances! If that Roman soldier can swing that ax and break a bone in the body of the Lord Jesus Christ, this Bible will be broken. But he lowers his ax and walks away, "that the scripture should be fulfilled" (John 19:36). All the power of Roman legions could not break a bone of the Son of God after the Bible had said, "Not one of them is broken."

We believe in a sacred Book that is indestructible and is lifegiving. It gave life to me. In John 6, when the multitudes turned away, Jesus said to the disciples, "The words that I speak unto you, they are spirit and they are life." He said, "...the flesh profiteth nothing: the words that I speak unto you, they are spirit, and they are life" (vs. 63).

There is life in this Book. So many times when I hold it to my heart, I can almost feel it breathing. God says it is a living Book.

No book written by human hands gives such peace as does this Book. "Great peace have they which love thy law: and nothing shall offend them" (Ps. 119:165). When you hide this perfect, this eternal, this indestructible, this unbreakable, this life-giving Book in your heart, it means you have a peace that passeth understanding.

When Sir Walter Scott lay dying, he said to his nephew by his bedside, "Bring me the Book!"

Since Sir Walter Scott had many books, his nephew said, "Uncle Walter, what book?"

Sir Walter Scott replied, "There is but one Book—the Bible!"

"I believed; therefore have I spoken...," declared the psalmist. I too believe in this sacred Book.

II. I BELIEVE IN A SACRED SON—A SECOND MAN

We read in I Corinthians 15:47, "The first man is of the earth, earthy: the second man is the Lord from heaven." The first is speaking of Adam, who came from the fall. He was sinful and a sinner. Then God sent another Man, the Lord from Heaven. He is above sin.

Jesus is divine. You ask me, "What do you believe?" I believe that Jesus is the Son of God. I believe He was born of a virgin, with no human father like you and I had. I believe as Peter said, "Thou art the Christ, the Son of the living God" (Matt. 16:16).

He lived a perfect life and said, "Which of you convinceth me of sin?" (John 8:46). He died a supernatural death for the sins of the world. The veil was rent in twain. The earthquake broke the rock. The resurrection took place, and people came out of the graves. They stood back and saw it all and said, "Truly this was the Son of God" (Matt. 27:54). He arose from the dead. He saves, He keeps, He satisfies. I believe in a sacred, divine Son.

Back some years ago, down in a little coal-mining town called Salem, Kentucky, fifteen miners were entrapped down hundreds of feet below the surface of the ground, all from twenty-five to thirty-five years of age. It was a historic meeting, an impromptu meeting, held underground. No one ever planned it. That meeting lasted 153 hours—impromptu, unadjournable. When they reached them, all dead, they found written on the walls of their tomb these words: *"If we are dead when you find us, we're all saved."*

People knew that only two or three of those fifteen men were Christians. During those 153 long and crucial hours, those two or three led the other dozen to Christ. They trusted in a sacred Son and went out into eternity saved.

III. I BELIEVE IN A SECOND BIRTH

I do not believe there is any substitute for what the Bible calls the "second birth." Jesus said to a religious man named Nicodemus, "Except a man be born again, he cannot see the kingdom of God" (John 3:3). He said, "Except a man be born of water and of the Spirit, he cannot enter into the kingdom of

God'' (vs. 5). Water here does not refer to baptism. It is explained in Ephesians 5:26: "By the washing of water by the word." Water is a symbol of the Bible. Being born of the Word of God and of the Spirit—except a man be thus born, "he cannot enter into the kingdom of God."

He first of all says, "You can't even see it." That is why a man should not expect to understand it **before** he is saved. And a lot of things you are not going to understand **after** you are saved.

I say more to you. There are a lot of things about a lot of other things you do not understand. Some of you men don't understand how you can eat the cooking you have been eating for thirty years and still live! I never could understand how a brown cow could eat green grass and give white milk and have it turn into yellow butter! I do not understand electricity, but I am not fool enough to sit in the dark until I can explain it.

You will never understand the new birth. Jesus said, 'Until you are born again, you cannot even see it!' Then He said, 'Except you are born of water [the Word] and of the Spirit, you cannot enter into the kingdom of heaven.'

Dear soul, search your innermost being and ask yourself life's most important question: "Have I been born again?" Jesus said, "Marvel not that I said unto thee, Ye must be born again" (John 3:7). You just can't understand it before you are saved, and even after you are saved, you will marvel at it. Unless you are born again, you cannot see the kingdom of God.

The new birth proves many things. First, it proves that you were born wrong the first time. The new birth assumes the total depravity of the human heart. If you had been born right the first time, you would not have to be born the second time. The first time, you were born with a sinful nature. That is why the psalmist cried out, "Behold, I was shapen in iniquity: and in sin did my mother conceive me" (Ps. 51:5).

Children don't become sinners after they sin; they are sinners by nature, born sinners. I used to marvel at the accuracy of the verse, "...they go astray as soon as they be born, speaking lies" (Ps. 58:3).

I once heard some women discussing that verse. If you want to learn about the Bible, listen to a bunch of women discussing it in a women's missionary meeting or at a Bible study! One lady said, "I don't see how that could be true, 'They go astray as soon as they be born, speaking lies.'"

Neither did I understand it until I became a father; then I believed it. Those little rascals will tell you at three o'clock in the morning, "I'll die unless somebody holds me and rocks me! I'm breathing my last breath! I'm hurting; I'm in great pain!" All you need do is pick the little one up, rock him and sing to him, and he will go back to sleep. Just as the Bible says: "They go astray as soon as they be born, speaking lies."

Man is totally depraved. Nothing makes me any sicker than to hear these modernistic, liberal, ecumenical preachers preach there is something good in everybody! The opposite is true. There is something rotten in everybody—sin. The new birth is God's sure remedy and God's cure.

We believe in a second birth.

IV. I BELIEVE IN A SECOND DEATH

I am going to tell you why I am including this tonight. We believe in the eternal punishment of sinners, as the Bible says. We believe in a second death. Revelation 20:14 says, "And death and hell were cast into the lake of fire. This is the second death." When someone dies physically, we think what a tragedy it is, especially when it is somebody who has not lived his expected life span. What a tragedy it is—physical death! But that is not the tragedy. Physical death is not even permanent. Spiritual death is tragic! Spiritual death is soul death! It is being cut off from God. It is separation! It is alienation from the face of God forever! That is Hell!

Anybody who deliberately refuses Jesus Christ dies without God and without hope, and suffers such an eternity as that. There is a second death.

Speaking of people who will be raised when the Lord comes, the Bible says, "On such the second death hath no power" (Rev. 20:6). The Bible teaches it does have power over people who are not saved: "But the fearful, and unbelieving, and the abominable, and murderers, and whoremongers, and sorcerers, and idolators, and all liars, shall have their part in the lake which burneth with fire and brimstone: which is the second death" (Rev. 21:8).

This verse is the roll call of Hell. I talk to a lot of people who say, "Preacher, I guess I should be saved, but I don't want to walk down that aisle with all those people looking at me." That means that they are fearful. The Bible says "the fearful, and unbelieving" will have their part in Hell. With all that other motley crew of Revelation 21:8 is that one who is afraid to trust Jesus Christ! He will go just as deep in Hell and stay there just as long as the liar, idolator, sorcerer or murderer.

God says the fearful shall burn in Hell forever. Why? Because fear is of the Devil. People are afraid to be saved because the Devil puts fear in their hearts and causes them to gamble with their souls and be separated from Jesus Christ forever.

The unbelieving say, "I'm going to believe sometime, but I'll believe when I get ready." You don't know that you can believe when you get ready. The Bible warns, "Seek ye the Lord while he may be found, call ye upon him while he is near" (Isa. 55:6). You never know but that, when you do want Him, it might be too late.

This actually took place in England years ago. The fire department received a **postcard** from a man (unthinkable), saying, "My house is on fire!" They went to the address and saw the smoldering embers and the house gone.

You say, "What a fool he was to delay such a critical thing by sending a postcard! That's unbelievable!" Yes, and it is just as unbelievable that a man, a woman, a boy, a girl would gamble with his or her soul that is as eternal as God! Why do people wait until it is too late and they are burning in Hell?

I believe in a second death. "I believed, therefore have I spoken...." As a preacher I use the word *Hell* because the Bible teaches that "the wicked shall be turned into hell, and all the nations that forget God" (Ps. 9:17).

"I believed, therefore have I spoken...."

"We having the same spirit of faith, according as it is written, I believed, and therefore have I spoken; we also believed, and therefore speak."

V. I BELIEVE IN A SECOND COMING

I am looking for the Lord Jesus to come. When I said to a man the other day, "I'll see you tomorrow if the Lord tarries," the most puzzled look came on his face. That good, sweet man knows nothing about "if the Lord tarries." I said, "The Lord who came the first time is coming a second time."

Two messengers came from Heaven when He walked that invisible, golden stairway back into Glory. They said, "This same Jesus, which is taken up from you into heaven, shall so come in like manner as ye have seen him go into heaven" (Acts 1:11). Jesus said, "If I go and prepare a place for you, I will come again, and receive you unto myself" (John 14:3).

The second coming makes you a soul winner.

There are those here tonight who do not really believe that the Lord is coming. To some in this house tonight the second coming is nothing but a doctrine—an obscure, impersonal doctrine of the

Bible! But the coming of Jesus is a reality. The Lord is coming. He said He would. Angels from Heaven said He would. Those who really believe in the coming of the Lord want to get people saved.

I shall never cease to thank God for what the reality of His coming did for me. God laid it upon my heart when I was in Ohio some years ago. For two days and nights I could do nothing but read the Bible, pray and search my soul. Then the next few days after that, I led to Christ some of the most important people in my life.

Believing in the second coming makes one a soul winner.

It does something else. It separates people. The second coming of the Lord Jesus Christ is a separatist doctrine. You can't possibly believe in the coming of Christ and not be a separated Christian. Read Titus 2:12,13:

"Teaching us that, denying ungodliness and worldly lusts, we should live soberly, righteously, and godly, in this present world; Looking for that blessed hope, and the glorious appearing of the great God and our Saviour Jesus Christ."

John put it this way:

"Behold, what manner of love the Father hath bestowed upon us, that we should be called the sons of God...Beloved, now are we the sons of God, and it doth not yet appear what we shall be: but we know that, when he shall appear, we shall be like him; for we shall see him as he is."—I John 3:1,2.

I ask you a question tonight: "Are you ready for the second coming of Jesus Christ?" Yes, I know you are saved, but are you ready for the Lord to come? "And now, little children, abide in him; that, when he shall appear, we may have confidence, and not be ashamed before him at his coming" (I John 2:28).

Would you be embarrassed if the Lord came tonight—if you

were caught up, raptured away to stand in His presence at the marriage supper of the Lamb? Would you have confidence at His coming? I ask again, "Are you ready for the second coming of the Lord Jesus Christ?"

VI. WE BELIEVE IN A SANCTIFYING SPIRIT

It would take many pages to thoroughly define the word *sanctification* as used in the Bible. One of the difficulties is that the word must be viewed scripturally as being past, present and future in its divine operation. The definition becomes even more difficult when we are clearly taught in Scripture that all three members of the blessed Holy Trinity are credited with being the source of the believer's sanctification.

However, the Scriptures teach that the Holy Spirit is the one most effective in the experimental phase of sanctification. The word and its New Testament synonyms came from the root Greek word *hagiasmos* and other New Testament Greek words taken from the same root word. It means "to render or declare sacred," "to be set apart as holy," "to be purified and dedicated to God."

God the Father is said to be the Source and Author of sanctification: "And the very God of peace sanctify you wholly: and I pray God your whole spirit and soul and body be preserved blameless unto the coming of our Lord Jesus Christ" (I Thess. 5:23).

God the Son is also said to be the author of our sanctification: "Unto the church of God which is at Corinth, to them that are sanctified in Christ Jesus, called to be saints, with all that in every place call upon the name of Jesus Christ our Lord, both theirs and ours" (I Cor. 1:2).

The Holy Spirit is given great prominence in the New Testament as the Sanctifier of the saints: "But we are bound to give thanks alway to God for you, brethren beloved of the Lord, because God hath from the beginning chosen you to salvation through sanctification of the Spirit and belief of the truth'' (II Thess. 2:13).

Paul makes reference to "the Gentiles...being sanctified by the Holy Ghost" (Rom. 15:16).

Peter makes reference to the saints of God as being "Elect according to the foreknowledge of God the Father, through sanctification of the Spirit..." (I Pet. 1:2).

Sanctification is immediate, progressive and ultimately consummated to perfection. It can be truthfully said that we are immediately sanctified or set apart when we are born again and saved by the Lord Jesus Christ. We are continuing to be sanctified by the constant work of His indwelling Spirit, and we shall ultimately be rid of this fleshly body and be sanctified holy as He is holy.

We believe that every believer has the Holy Spirit: "What? know ye not that your body is the temple of the Holy Ghost which is in you, which ye have of God, and ye are not your own?" (I Cor. 6:19).

Every believer has the baptism of the Holy Spirit: "For by one Spirit are we all baptized into one body, whether we be Jews or Gentiles, whether we be bond or free; and have been all made to drink into one Spirit" (I Cor. 12:13).

No believer yet has reached sinless perfection, which is impossible while living in a body of enfeebled flesh. Every believer is being progressively sanctified (II Cor. 3:18) and will experience entire and complete sanctification at the second coming of the Lord Jesus Christ. "And not only they, but ourselves also, which have the firstfruits of the Spirit, even we ourselves groan within ourselves, waiting for the adoption, to wit, the redemption of our body" (Rom. 8:23).

Every believer may now have the power of the Spirit (Eph. 5:18).

Yes, we believe in the sanctifying work of the Holy Spirit.

VII. I BELIEVE IN A SECOND HEAVEN AND A SECOND EARTH

"And I saw a new heaven and a new earth: for the first heaven

and the first earth were passed away; and there was no more sea. And I John saw the holy city, new Jerusalem, coming down from God out of heaven, prepared as a bride adorned for her husband.''—Rev. 21:1,2.

A brief and outlined history and future of the heavens and the earth is given in II Peter, chapter 3.

1. The earth that was: "Whereby *the world that then was*, being overflowed with water perished" (vs. 6).

2. The heavens and earth which are now: "But the heavens and the earth, *which are now*, by the same word are kept in store..." (vs. 7).

3. The heavens and earth *which shall be*: "Nevertheless we, according to his promise, look for new heavens and a new earth, wherein dwelleth righteousness" (vs. 13).

The "earth that was" was destroyed. It was the world of mankind. The earth that "now is" will be renovated by fire, and God will make a new earth and new heavens. This will be the heavens and earth of the millennial reign of our Lord Jesus Christ. That reign will last a thousand years. The term "thousand years" is found six times in Revelation 20. That thousand-year reign of Christ on earth will be characterized by five great things:

1. Satan is bound in the bottomless pit (vss. 1-3).

2. The saints of God will reign with Christ for a thousand years (vs. 6).

3. The longevity of man is restored (Isa. 65:20).

4. Jerusalem will be the capital of the world in which God will rejoice with His people Israel.

5. The earth shall be filled with the knowledge of the Lord (Isa. 11:9).

We are on the winning side, and some glad day we shall help the Saviour rule the world. Oh, happy day when we fixed our choice upon Him! Oh, happy day when He teaches us completely what a wise choice that was!

VIII. I BELIEVE IN A SECOND CHANCE

I do not believe, as the universalists, that in the finality of things God is going to save everybody. The Bible does not teach that. I didn't get saved the first time I heard the Gospel. If there were no second chance, I would not be saved today because I missed out on my first chance. It is not the same with everyone. Some don't get to hear the Gospel for the first time, and I am sure there are some who have heard or will hear the Gospel only one time. Others have heard it many times. However, God is the God of the second chance.

Nicodemus was a Pharisee and a ruler of the Jews, says John 3:1. The Pharisees had the Old Testament Scriptures which spoke again and again of the coming of Christ as the Lamb of God to take away the sin of the world.

Nicodemus had the truth; in fact, he was supposed to be a guardian of the truth, but he failed to see Christ in the Old Testament Scriptures. Many had been saved before Nicodemus, but he had missed out on his first chance. God gave him a second chance when the Lord Jesus talked to him one night. It was to Nicodemus that John 3:16 was spoken: "For God so loved the world, that he gave his only begotten Son, that whosoever believeth in him should not perish but have everlasting life." Nicodemus believed and was saved and became a friend of Jesus.

John Mark had a second chance. He was already a believer when he went on the first missionary journey with Barnabas and Paul, but he failed. "And when they were at Salamis, they preached the word of God in the synagogues of the Jews: and they had also John to their minister" (Acts 13:5).

However, John did not finish the journey. He gave up the mission and left two great men of God and went back home: "Now when Paul and his company loosed from Paphos, they came to Perga in Pamphylia: and John departing from them returned to Jerusalem'' (vs. 13).

What a beautiful thing is seen in Paul's last words before he died! He wanted John Mark to come to him in prison. Paul had refused to take Mark with him on a second missionary journey. John Mark's failure at Perga was a matter of conflict between Paul and Barnabas. The contention was so sharp that it separated the two; then Paul and Silas went on the second missionary journey.

Now Paul's ministry has come to its closing days; soon he is to be martyred for Christ, and he wants to see John Mark. Read about it in II Timothy 4:11: "Only Luke is with me. Take Mark and bring him with thee: for he is profitable to me for the ministry."

God gave John Mark another chance.

Peter had a second chance after so emphatically denying the Lord on the night of His trial and betrayal.

"And after a while came unto him they that stood by, and said to Peter, Surely thou also art one of them; for thy speech bewrayeth thee. Then began he to curse and to swear, saying, I know not the man. And immediately the cock crew. And Peter remembered the word of Jesus, which said unto him, Before the cock crow, thou shalt deny me thrice. And he went out, and wept bitterly."—Matt. 26:73-75.

Never did anyone deny Christ more emphatically, but never did one repent so completely.

Peter was one of the first to the empty tomb and one of the last to whom Jesus spoke before His ascension. Peter was the preacher on the day of Pentecost and the first to officially preach the Gospel to the Gentiles. God gave Peter a second chance to be a man of God and a witness to the saving power and grace of our Lord Jesus.

God gave Thomas a second chance, and he cried, "My Lord and my God" (John 20:28).

God gave Jonah and Samson and Demas and many others a second chance to surrender to His will for their lives.

One Sunday morning after I had preached in Emmanuel Baptist Church, a man, weeping, said to me, "Will God give a fifty-five-year-old man a second chance to preach the Gospel?" I said, "Yes, He will. God gives people a second chance. I believe in the God of a second chance."

"I believed, therefore have I spoken...."—Ps. 116:10.

"We having the same spirit of faith, according as it is written, I believed, and therefore have I spoken; we also believe, and therefore speak."—II Cor. 4:13.

Chapter III

Living by Faith

(Preached at Emmanuel Baptist Church, Sunday night, January 22, 1961)

"...*the just shall live by his faith.*"—Hab. 2:4.

This great life-changing verse is found four times in the Bible. I would like for us to see the four books of the Bible where this verse is found and the central theme of each of these four books.

Location:	*Central Theme:*
Habakkuk 2:4	The Consistency of God
Romans 1:17	The Righteousness of God
Galatians 3:11	The Superiority of Faith
Hebrews 10:38	The Superiority of Christ

Habakkuk means "wrestler." The prophet of God wrestled with the Lord about the sin of the people and the justice of God.

God had told the prophet that the wicked and cruel Chaldeans would be used to punish the backslidden nation of Israel. The Prophet Habakkuk was perplexed as to how God could look upon such a sinful nation as Chaldea and use them to punish His own people Israel.

God gave him the answer in Habakkuk 2:4:

"*Behold, his soul which is lifted up is not upright in him: but the just shall live by his faith.*"

The hearts of the proud Chaldeans and many of Israel were puffed up, lifted up against God. They were self-relying. There were those, however, who trusted God and leaned on Him for their salvation and deliverance. They were self-renouncing. God is simply saying in Habakkuk 2:4 that justification by faith will solve the problem.

Notice this great verse as it is found four times in the Word of God. In Habakkuk it has seven words, *"the just shall live by his faith."* In the other three uses of this statement there are only six words, *"the just shall live by faith."*

This great truth, justification by faith, was used as the basis for Paul's great argument in all of his epistles for the righteousness and mercy of God. God rules out every hope or effort to obtain God's righteousness, except by faith. He used this great foundation truth against those who hoped to be saved by the Law. This truth eliminates the possibility of being saved by works and rules out all hope of salvation through the observance of sacraments. This verse points men to the cross and the sacrificial work of Christ thereon. It points men to the empty tomb.

"The just shall live by his faith."

There is not a greater verse in the Bible than this one on how to be a Christian, what it means to be a Christian, and how God can make of you a Christian if you want to be one.

This is the verse that revolutionized the life and saved the soul of Martin Luther. I am sure you are all familiar with how he was saved. Martin Luther was climbing the so-called "Sancta Scala" or the sacred stairs. In the city of Rome—right now and all day today—people are climbing those stairs. Mrs. Malone and I had the privilege some years ago to stand at the foot of the stairs and watch people climb up them on their knees. Then we walked up to the top another way. There we saw a silver star. It had a piece of glass in the middle, on which church officials claim are some drops of the blood of Jesus Christ.

Those stairs, supposedly and according to the Roman Catholic church, are the ones taken out of Pilate's judgment hall, the stairs up which Jesus climbed on the night He was judged by Pilate and betrayed by Judas. It is said that those stairs were moved from Jerusalem and placed in Rome.

People have believed that, and for hundreds of years they have been climbing those stairs, called the "sacred stairs." Confessing their sins step by step as they climb up on their knees, as they reach the top, they bend over and kiss the spot supposedly where the blood of Jesus was shed.

There is supposed to be something efficacious about their climbing those stairs, something that would cause them to get forgiveness of their sins.

Martin Luther, a Catholic monk and a scholarly man, a student of the Bible who memorized every single word in the book of Romans, was one time climbing those stairs on his knees, confessing his sins, longing to be free and delivered from the guilt of sin. About the middle of the way up, all of a sudden Romans 1:17 flashed across his mind: "The just shall live by faith." He then descended the stairs and was born again by the Spirit of God—saved by believing in Jesus Christ. From that moment on, Luther put no confidence in the law or good works to save his soul from sin. That verse revolutionized the life of Martin Luther, the father of the Protestant Reformation.

I would to God tonight that out of this verse there will come to us some truth that will grip the hearts of both saved and lost.

As I have already said, this verse is found four times in the Bible—here in chapter 2 of Habakkuk and three times in the New Testament. Each of the three times in the New Testament (in Romans, in Galatians, in Hebrews), there are just six words—

"The just shall live by faith."

Just imagine that these six words are written across the front of this church in blazing fire: THE JUST SHALL LIVE BY FAITH. I want us to see tonight the emphasis God puts upon this great salvation verse.

There are six words, found in three books, each book emphasizing two words. Romans emphasizes the first two: "the just." Galatians emphasizes the middle two: "shall live." Hebrews emphasizes the last two: "by faith."

"The Just"

In Romans 1:17 is this phrase, "THE JUST shall live by faith." Romans emphasizes those first two words—"the just."

When you read in the Bible of a just man, you are reading of someone God looks upon and sees as righteous. In fact, throughout the Bible "just" and "righteous" are almost synonymous. So to be just before God is to be righteous before God.

Let's see what the Bible teaches in the book of Job. In chapter 9, verse 2, Job pondered this question: "How should man be just with God?" or, "How can a man be righteous?" All of us have pondered that question. You wouldn't have to convince any Christian that he has sinned against God. Any saved person knows he was saved from sin, knows that he has been guilty before God of breaking His law, of rejecting His Son, of grieving His Spirit, of counting the blood as an unholy thing. People know that they have sinned. Knowing that, Job asked, "How can a man like me ever be righteous in the eyes of God? What can God do with my sin? How can a holy, righteous God ever make me holy and righteous in His sight?"

Some men in the Bible were just and righteous. In Genesis 6:9 we read that "Noah was a just man and perfect in his generation." The verse before that says, "Noah found grace in the eyes of the

Lord." Because of the grace of God and Noah's believing faith, God said, "There is a righteous man."

Noah was not righteous because he built an ark and believed that it was going to rain. Noah was righteous because he found grace in the eyes of the Lord and, believing God's Word, he put his faith in God. We know that the ark was a type of Christ, and I think it safe to say that Noah believed in a Saviour yet to come. When one believes in Jesus Christ, the righteousness of God is imputed unto him. "For what saith the scripture? Abraham believed God, and it was counted unto him for righteousness" (Rom. 4:3).

Six times in Romans 4 God uses the word *impute*, meaning "to put down to a person's account." Three times in the chapter we find the word *reckon*, meaning the same thing. Twice in the same chapter we find the word *count*, which also means the same thing.

Eleven times in one chapter God says He imputes His righteousness or puts to our account the righteousness of Christ when we believe upon Him. God imputed our sin to Christ on the cross, and He imputes His spotless righteousness to us who believe.

If I were to examine or talk to you tonight with no light from the Scripture, I would say this next man was not such a good fellow. His name was Lot. Lot was a Christian, but a poor one. He left the fellowship of his sweet and godly Uncle Abraham and moved into the sinful city of Sodom, in which city he lost his family and testimony. He did not win one single soul to Christ except his two daughters. He even let his sons-in-law go to Hell, as well as his wife and all the other people of that city. So I would say he was not a good Christian, wouldn't you?

But in II Peter 2:7 we read, "...And delivered just Lot, vexed with the filthy conversation of the wicked." Looking back into the Bible, back into the book of Genesis, II Peter calls Lot a "just" man. Why? When we look back through this Word of God—from

II Peter back to the book of Genesis—we see the cross of Calvary and Jesus dying on the cross for Lot's sin, as well as yours and mine. Looking through the cross, through the blood and through the atoning work of Christ, God said Lot had been declared righteous in the eyes of God.

Now, if you have trouble accepting that Lot was righteous in the eyes of God in spite of his sins, then you who are saved first examine your own lives to see whether you within yourself could be righteous in the eyes of God. Because of the righteousness we have received from Jesus Christ, we have been made just.

Dr. H. A. Ironside used to tell a most amazing and fantastic story. It seems almost unbelievable, but it is true.

Dr. Ironside was visiting a sheep ranch in Texas years ago. He saw a little lamb that looked deformed. He said that, instead of having four legs, it looked like he had eight. He couldn't figure it out.

Dr. Ironside said to the sheep rancher, "That is a funny-looking thing. It looks like it has two heads and four front legs and four back legs. It looks like a freak of nature. Can you explain that to me?"

The ranchman said, "This is a strange thing. When that little lamb was born, its mother died. Another ewe lamb gave birth to a little baby lamb, and the little baby died. So we had a little lamb without a mother and an ewe without a baby." He went on to explain: "We decided to take that little baby and give it to that mother. She would nurse it, and that would make everything all right." He said, "We put that little orphan lamb in with that mother lamb. She butted it away and wanted no part of it. We went out there where the little dead lamb's body was, took off its skin and tied it around this little body. Its little legs now look like they hang down just with skin and the hoof. Then we put it back with the ewe. She loves it and has adopted it. She is raising it, and it is healthy, and it is hers."

What a picture! God could not tolerate one of us tonight without the righteousness imputed to us from the Son of God. Every Christian has had a covering for his sins. *Atonement* in the Old Testament means "a covering over," a looking forward to the coming of Jesus when He died to take away our sins.

That leads me to this wonderful Bible truth: God looks upon a Christian—upon me and every other believer—as if we had never sinned one time.

A wonderful statement is I John 4:17: "Herein is our love made perfect, that we may have boldness in the day of judgment: because as he is, so are we in this world." Jesus is righteous; and "as he is, so are we" because we are in Him. His righteousness is placed to our account in Heaven.

That literally teaches that, as He is, so are we. When God looks upon me, He sees Jesus. When God looks upon me, He sees me as righteous. When God looks upon me, He sees me as just. Why? Because of the righteousness of Jesus Christ.

When Jesus stood before Pilate, recorded in chapter 27 of the book of Matthew, Pilate got a note from his wife, which said, "Have nothing to do with that just man." After awhile Pilate washed his hands and said, "You see to it. I will have nothing to do with the innocent blood of this just man."

Jesus was just in the eyes of God. And God the Father, through the salvation plan, has made you and me as Jesus in His sight.

The hardest truth to get a Christian to see is the truth of justification. A lot of people have a problem with it. They think justification takes place within you, but it doesn't. Regeneration, or the new birth, is a miracle of grace that God performs within me, but justification is not within me, but within the mind of God.

Yonder on His throne God declares righteous everyone whom He sees in Jesus Christ—the just. If you are saved, thank God that the past is all gone and you now stand in the eyes of God as clean as if you had never sinned.

My wife was reading the obituary. A lady 92 years of age had recently died in a little town where we had our first church more than twenty years ago. What a sweet lady she was—72 years of age then, and a widow. I will never forget this dear lady and two others. All three have gone to be with Jesus. A lady was saved in our church who had not lived a good life. (And I don't know anyone who has, do you? Looking down your nose at other people and talking about their past is bad business.) This lady got saved and wanted to join the church. These three sweet widows—God bless them—came to me, and that one whose obituary Mrs. Malone had read said, "Brother Tom, this lady has a past! I don't think she should be taken into our church."

God bless her! She was as sweet as any Christian who ever walked on earth. But I looked at her and said, "Mrs._____, so do you, and you, and you—and so do I."

Those three sweet widows, who had lived in that old country town where you would have to look for something bad to do with a spy glass, a little bitty hick country town, looked at me as though I were the meanest man that ever lived!

I continued: "All of us have a past. That dear lady who has just been saved has had all her sins blotted out just like yours were and yours and yours and mine; and we are going to take her into the church." And we did!

When one gets saved, everything is fixed up right then—and fixed up forever. When you are justified in the eyes of God, you are as clean as if you had never sinned.

"As he is, so are we." God looks upon us and sees us in Christ Jesus.

"Shall Live"

The second time this text is found is in Galatians 3:11. The same six words—*"the just shall live by faith."*

LIVING BY FAITH

You have already heard that the theme of the book of Galatians is faith. A distinction is made between trying to be saved by keeping the law of God's Book and believing in Jesus Christ. That is true in a sense, but the whole burden of the book of Galatians is about how we have life in the Lord. So, actually, this verse in Galatians, *"The just shall live by faith,"* gives prominence to the emphasis in that book which is put on those two words: "The just SHALL LIVE by faith."

It seems that a key verse in the book is Galatians 2:20: "I am crucified with Christ: nevertheless I *live*; yet not I, but Christ *liveth* in me: and the *life* which I now *live* in the flesh I *live* by the faith of the Son of God, who loved me, and gave himself for me."

"Life" or "live" is mentioned five times in this one verse. The book is teaching us that we are not justified by the keeping of the law, neither are we made perfect or righteous by the law. We are justified and have eternal life through Jesus Christ our Lord. The law sentenced sinful man to eternal death, but Christ gives to the believer eternal life. "The just SHALL LIVE by faith." That is where the emphasis is.

The Bible teaches two wonderful truths along this line.

First, it clearly teaches that by sin man lost his relationship with God. That happened in the Garden of Eden when Adam sinned. When God said, "But of the tree of the knowledge of good and evil, thou shalt not eat of it: for in the day that thou eatest thereof thou shalt surely die," that did not mean physical death. When you read, "The wages of sin is death," that is not physical. The best Christian in this house is going to die just like the worst sinner in this city. When God said, "Ye shall not eat of it, neither shall ye touch it, lest ye die"; when the Bible says, "The wages of sin is death"; when Ezekiel says, "The soul that sinneth, it shall die," this means spiritual death, which is alienation, separation, being cut off, put away, separated eternally from a holy God. That is the "wages of sin."

Now, how can one under such a curse and condemned and without life, have life? Galatians tells us how. "The just SHALL LIVE by faith."

Thank God for life tonight in Jesus!

I really believe that one just begins to live when he gets saved. We hear, "Life begins at forty," but not so. Life doesn't begin at forty. Life begins when Jesus comes in. Life really began for me twenty-five years ago when I received life from Jesus Christ.

I am amazed how much Jesus talks about the spiritual life He gives to those who trust Him. For instance, John 10:10 says, "I am come that they might have life, and that they might have it more abundantly." Jesus said to two brokenhearted sisters of Lazarus when He met them coming from the grave, "I am the resurrection, and the life: he that believeth in me, though he were dead, yet shall he live: And whosoever liveth and believeth in me shall never die" (John 11:25,26).

Jesus gives eternal life. "The just SHALL LIVE...." It means we are going to live forever with God in Heaven.

Jesus spoke so often about life in Him. Eternal life is not found in religion or good works or creeds or catechisms, but in the Lord Jesus Christ.

"For God so loved the world, that he gave his only begotten Son, that whosoever believeth in him should not perish, but have ***everlasting life***.*"*—John 3:16.

"Verily, verily, I say unto you, He that heareth my word, and believeth on him that sent me, hath ***everlasting life****, and shall not come into condemnation; but is passed from death unto* ***life***.*"*—John 5:24.

Eternal life is yours by believing in Jesus Christ.

In chapter 6 of the book of John, He said, 'I am the bread of God come down from heaven that you might have life.' In chapter

14 He said, "I am the way, the truth, and the life." All three of these things man lost in the Garden. He lost the life. Jesus said, "I am life." If you don't have life, you are dead! You have never started to live until you get saved. I don't mean get religion, either; I mean get saved.

Most everybody you ask in this day and time, whether they are Christians or not, will say, "Yes, I'm a Christian." Don't let them off with that, for sometimes they mean, "Yes, I learned the catechism"; or, "Yes, I've been baptized"; or, "Yes, I have my baptismal certificate"; or, "Yes, I've joined the church." I made a covenant with God a few days ago that I was going to ask somebody every day, "Are you a Christian?" One man said, "I don't know." Everyone else I have asked lately has said, "Yes, I'm a Christian." But the more I talked, the more I knew they didn't know what I was talking about.

Mrs. Malone and I parked the car the other day down at the parking lot. She got out and went ahead while I paid the attendant. When I asked him, "Are you a Christian?" he nearly fell!

He said, "I used to be a Christian."

First, he had been discussing the weather, but I wasn't interested in the weather. There will be weather tomorrow like there is today. But he was so friendly while we were talking about the weather. That was very important to him. Then when I asked, "Are you a Christian?" did he get busy! I couldn't catch him going around the car. But he did say, "Yes, I used to go to church."

He was not saved. I have seen people in this church that, when someone went to them and asked, "Are you a Christian?" their necks tightened, their faces got red, and they lost their tempers. I have had them say to me right here in this church, "What do you think I am—a heathen?" Yes! No Christian, when asked that, will ever become indignant. If one has life in Christ, he doesn't get mad when some concerned person asks, "Are you a Christian?'' When you get *life*, others will know it. Don't you think I know whether I am alive or dead? "The just SHALL LIVE..."; and you only begin to live when you have Jesus in your heart.

I keep thinking of a couple who came forward in this church who had visited here some years ago. One Sunday morning while others were coming, this man came to be saved, and his wife was a few steps behind him. Someone went immediately with him into the prayer room. His Christian wife tarried and said, "He has spent $6,000 in recent months trying to find peace from a guilty conscience. O Brother Tom, today God has done in a moment what $6,000 couldn't do in months!" He got life! It is real living when you know Jesus. I really enjoy being a Christian, reading the Bible and preaching. I have been *living* twenty-five years. And every now and then it grips my soul that I am going to live forever!

They broke into the news today announcing that Russia had sent a missile to Venus. I don't know where Venus is, but I'm going higher than Venus someday because I have eternal life.

"The just *shall live* by faith."

"By Faith"

The third time that wonderful truth, "The just shall live by faith," is found is in Hebrews 10:38: "Now the just shall live by faith: but if any man draw back, my soul shall have no pleasure in him."

Actually Hebrews 10:38,39 introduces the great "faith" chapter—Hebrews 11—where the word *faith* is found no less than twenty-four times. It appears that, in this use of the statement, "The just shall live *by faith*," the emphasis is on the two words, *"by faith."* Every person, from Abel, who "by faith offered a more excellent sacrifice," to the very last person to get saved, is saved by faith. There is no other way. Jesus said to the sinful woman who came to Him in the Pharisee's house, "Thy faith hath saved thee; go in peace." That is so simple that it is hard to get people to see it. That is the thing people stumble over. That is the reason I said to a man last Sunday in this church something that I have not said to many people since I have been preaching: "I believe, because of your faith, you are a Christian, whether you believe it or not." He said that he couldn't see it, and he wasn't sure that he understood it; but everything else he agreed with, accepted and believed.

It is by faith. Ninety-nine times in the Gospel of John alone we have the words, *believe, believed* or *believing.* Ninety-nine times in one book God says the only way one can be saved is to believe in Jesus Christ.

If someone should say a truth to you ninety-nine times, wouldn't you get to believing it? Ninety-nine times in one book God says one cannot be saved without faith, without believing in the person and work of the Son of God on the cross.

The most wonderful illustration of faith I ever read happened to John G. Paton, missionary to the New Hebrides Islands. He was translating the Gospel of John. He couldn't find a word in the New Hebrides language for *believing* or *trusting* or *faith.* He wrestled with it, he prayed about it, and he went to God with this problem. "Lord, if I can't make these folks know what believing is and what faith is, I can't ever get them to be saved. Lord, will You answer this thing?"

Under his tent he worked translating the Gospel of John into the New Hebrides language. A tired native came into the tent and, seating himself upon a chair, said, "I'm casting all my weight upon this chair." The missionary thought, *That's the word I want—casting—*casting all your weight upon Him to save your soul from *sin.*

A preacher friend asked 200 people in a group one night, "Suppose tonight we could take away every dollar you have ever given to the cause of Christ. Suppose tonight we could remove every prayer you ever prayed. Suppose tonight we could remove your baptism and church membership. Suppose tonight we could eliminate every time you have gone to God's house and listened to His Word. Suppose tonight we could strip you of every religious thing you have ever done. Now how many of you believe you are saved?''

Out of 200, six people lifted their hands. Do you know why so few? Because so many people do not believe it is by faith. They think that it is what we do that helps God save us. That is not true! It is like that thief on the cross dying and, in his closing moments, saying, "Lord, remember me." He never did one good thing for God; yet Jesus looked at him and said, "This day shalt thou be with me in paradise."

I do not mean to be a braggadocio, but I would throw everything away that I have ever done for God. For twenty-five years I have tried to serve Him. I would throw it all overboard. If you ask me tonight, "Tom Malone, are you a Christian?" I would answer, "Yes," because "the just shall live by faith." I am saved tonight because of Him.

Oh, it is wonderful to rest in a truth like that!

"The just shall live by his faith."

Chapter IV

Have Faith in God

(Preached at Emmanuel Baptist Church, Pontiac, Michigan, Sunday morning, April 25, 1954)

"And Jesus answering saith unto them, Have faith in God."—Mark 11:22.

The disciples had seen Jesus perform a miracle. Something out of the ordinary had just happened. Jesus had approached a fig tree looking for fruit for His breakfast, but had found none. He had pronounced a curse upon the tree, saying, "No man eat fruit of thee hereafter for ever" (vs. 14). In a short period of time the fig tree, once green and vigorous, died and dried up from the roots.

The disciples were amazed at this strange miracle and indicated their amazement to Jesus. He challenged their hearts with this word: "Have faith in God."

Do you want to see things miraculous and extraordinary happen? Have faith in God!

Do you want to see actual miracles wrought? Have faith in God!

Do you wish to be lifted out of the routine, the usual, the commonplace? Have faith in God!

The importance of faith is seen in a conversation Jesus had with Simon Peter, one of the twelve. One day Jesus said to Simon:

"Simon, Simon, behold, Satan hath desired to have you, that he may sift you as wheat: But I have prayed for thee, that thy faith

fail not: and when thou art converted ["converted" in the Bible does not always mean to be saved], *strengthen thy brethren."*—Luke 22:31,32.

He was saying, "When thou art turned again, when once more your faith is again strong, you shall strengthen your brethren and be a blessing to others."

I am so glad that Jesus said to Peter, "I have prayed for thee, that thy faith fail not." Faith of the people of God is so important in God's sight that, in the heavenlies, Jesus is faithfully praying at God's throne that our faith might not fail.

I say unto you this morning, have faith in God. May God give you Christians—and myself—an unusual and extraordinary faith.

I have never been able to define faith. There is only one attempt made in all the sixty-six books of the Bible to define faith, found in the opening statement of chapter 11 of Hebrews, where we read, "Now faith is the substance of things hoped for, the evidence of things not seen."

But I know a little about faith. Faith means believing God against all odds. Faith means seeing the unseen. A Christian can see by faith what no one else has ever seen except another Christian. In so many instances in the Bible men saw the unseen, saw the evidence, saw the substance of things not seen. In fact, Paul said, "We look not at the things which are seen, but at the things which are not seen: for the things which are seen are temporal; but the things which are not seen are eternal" (II Cor. 4:18).

Everything you can see, including this body in which the soul and spirit abide—everything you can see, every object, animate or inanimate, everything you can see with a physical eye, is temporal—that is, it is related to time. But God tells us that with the eye of faith we can see the unseen, which is related to eternal things, things which will live as long as God lives.

I think of the Prophet Elisha and his servant when he had fled to Dothan, pursued by the wicked armies of a Syrian king. There, as he looked out across the mountainside, he saw the host of some 800,000 soldiers. His servant trembled with fear, but as Elisha looked out, he saw something which the servant did not immediately see:

"And when the servant of the man of God was risen early, and gone forth, behold, an host compassed the city both with horses and chariots. And his servant said unto him, Alas, my master! how shall we do? And he answered, Fear not: for they that be with us are more than they that be with them. And Elisha prayed, and said, Lord, I pray thee, open his eyes, that he may see. And the Lord opened the eyes of the young man; and he saw: and, behold, the mountain was full of horses and chariots of fire round about Elisha."—II Kings 6:15-17.

Thank God, faith pulls aside the curtain of obscurity, and faith sees the unseen. O God, give the people today a vision to see that which the naked eye, the unconverted eye, could never look upon.

Jesus said in these four words, "Have faith in God." The greatest tragedy that could happen to a Christian is to lose faith and have confidence in the flesh. But "have faith in God," not in preachers, not in deacons, not in churches, not in church members, not in Christians, not in things you can see, not in circumstances, not in the brilliance and talents of man.

Never shall I forget hearing Dr. Joe Henry Hankins tell of a boat crossing the English Channel one stormy night. As the boat crossed the choppy waters and stormy channel, the winds blew, the waves rolled high like mountains, the thunder roared, the lightning flashed. It looked like God was angry at the world. While the boat plowed its way across the English Channel, the people screamed with fear. Some dropped on their knees and prayed.

But a little girl on that boat sat as calm, quiet and serene as if she were in the rocking chair in the living room of her home.

Someone said to her, "Little one, when it looks as if at any moment this boat will go down beneath the waves, why are you so calm?" The little girl looked at the one who had inquired and answered, "Because the captain of this boat is my father. And he has crossed this channel many times, through every kind of wind and storm. I know he will reach the other side tonight."

"Have faith in God."

It's like when Jesus said to His disciples, "Let us go over to the other side." I can see Him now standing along the beautiful, blue, quiet waters of the Sea of Galilee. He lifted that omnipotent finger that created worlds and said, "Let us go over to the other side." They got in the boat and started out. In the midst of the sea, a storm arose. His disciples began to cry, "Master, save us, or else we perish." Jesus arose from His sleep, lifted His head from His pillow, for He was tired and weary with toil, went to the little deck of the boat; and when He waved His hand across the sea, the waves lay down like little lambs at their mother's breast.

From the place where He found us bound in chains, steeped in iniquity, lost and undone and without God, Jesus points to the shores of Heaven and says to all Christians, "Let us go over to the other side."

"Have faith in God."

There are not enough demons in Hell or stormy winds to blow that can sink the boat of the child of God!

I have found seven different instances in the New Testament where tremendous emphasis is placed upon the faith of God's children.

I. FAITH IS ESSENTIAL TO GETTING PRAYERS ANSWERED

Jesus taught that here: "What things soever ye desire, when ye pray, BELIEVE [faith] that ye receive them, and ye shall have them" (Mark 11:24).

The prayer of faith raises up the sick, as we see from James 5:15: "And the prayer of faith shall save the sick, and the Lord shall raise him up; and if he have committed sins, they shall be forgiven him."

The prayer of faith removes mountains of difficulty and solves problems and relieves heavy burdens, says Matthew 21:21,22:

"Verily I say unto you, If ye have faith, and doubt not, ye shall not only do this which is done to the fig tree, but also if ye shall say unto this mountain, Be thou removed, and be thou cast into the sea; it shall be done. And all things, whatsoever ye shall ask in prayer, BELIEVING, ye shall receive."

In no realm of Christian living does the Devil put up a greater battle than in the realm of faith. He fights hard to shake the faith of the people of God.

God never meant for prayer to be a last resort measure for the believer. Prayer is not what we do when everything else has failed. Prayer is the believer's spiritual breath, our constant contact with divine omnipotence.

Jesus says, "...men ought always to pray, and not to faint." Paul admonishes, "Pray without ceasing." James declares, "The effectual fervent prayer of a righteous man availeth much." David tells us, "Evening, and morning, and at noon, will I pray, and cry aloud: and he shall hear my voice."

Ralph Cushman said:

**I met God in the morning
When my day was at its best,
And His presence came like sunrise—
Like a glory in my breast.**

**All day long the Presence lingered,
All day long He stayed with me;
And we sailed with perfect calmness
O'er a very troubled sea.**

> Other ships were blown and battered,
> Other ships were sore distressed,
> But the winds that seemed to drive them
> Brought to us a peace and rest.
>
> Then I thought of other mornings
> With a keen remorse of mind,
> When I, too, had loosed the moorings
> With the Presence left behind.
>
> So I think I know the secret,
> Learned from many a troubled way:
> You must seek God in the morning
> If you want Him through the day.

Oh, the sweetness and joy of answered prayer! When we come to God in prayer, we must come believing His wonderful promises. Faith is the great essential if we expect to get things from God.

It goes without saying that a clean and holy life and a constant study and meditation in the Word of God are also necessary. Sin and a strong, unwavering faith can never dwell in the same heart. Apart from the promises of the Word of God, there is no basis, no foundation for such a faith.

"Have faith in God."

II. FAITH IS A FRUIT OF THE SPIRIT

"But the fruit of the Spirit is love, joy, peace, longsuffering, gentleness, goodness, faith, Meekness, temperance: against such there is no law."—Gal. 5:22,23.

In chapter 5 of Galatians, the fruits of the flesh and the fruit of the Spirit are listed. The flesh is more prolific. And there are seventeen wicked fruits of the flesh enumerated here.

There is a ninefold fruit of the Spirit, and one of these is faith. Every Christian has the Holy Spirit in him, but every Christian does not have the fruit of the Spirit in evidence in his life.

If you are saved, your body is the temple of the Holy Ghost: you have Him, but so much depends on whether or not He has full control of you. When one is surrendered to the wonderful Person of the Holy Spirit, when there is nothing within to grieve or displease Him, then, and then alone, is He able to produce this ninefold wonderful fruit of the Spirit, one of which is faith.

Do you want to be strong in faith and mighty in prayer? Then surrender absolutely and completely to the Holy Spirit. A great and dynamic faith is the result or fruit of a Spirit-filled and Spirit-directed life.

Being filled with the Spirit and having a strong faith are joined together in the Word of God. This is illustrated in the life of Stephen, one of the first deacons—"And Stephen, full of faith and power, did great wonders and miracles among the people" (Acts 6:8).

This "faith and power" in the life of Stephen was the result of being a Spirit-filled man. The Scriptures state that a deacon in the church at Jerusalem was to be full of the Holy Ghost: "Wherefore, brethren, look ye out among you seven men of honest report, full of the Holy Ghost and wisdom, whom we may appoint over this business" (Acts 6:3).

A strong faith is the result of being filled with and yielded to the Holy Spirit so that He might produce His fruit in us. Sin, unconfessed and unrepented of, weakens the faith of the child of God and grieves the Holy Spirit, whose presence in us and control over us produce faith.

"Have faith in God."

III. FAITH IS A PART OF THE CHRISTIAN'S ARMOR

"Put on the whole armour of God, that ye may be able to stand against the wiles of the devil. For we wrestle not against flesh and blood, but against principalities, against powers, against the rulers

of the darkness of this world, against spiritual wickedness in high places. Wherefore take unto you the whole armour of God, that ye may be able to withstand in the evil day, and having done all, to stand. Stand therefore, having your loins girt about with truth, and having on the breastplate of righteousness; And your feet shod with the preparation of the gospel of peace; Above all, taking the shield of faith, wherewith ye shall be able to quench all the fiery darts of the wicked. And take the helmet of salvation, and the sword of the Spirit, which is the word of God: Praying always with all prayer and supplication in the Spirit, and watching thereunto with all perseverance and supplication for all saints."—Eph. 6:11-18.

Here are seven distinct parts of the Christian's armor which he must have at all times if he is to stand against the wiles of the Devil:

1. "loins girt about with truth";
2. "breastplate of righteousness";
3. "feet shod with the preparation of the gospel of peace";
4. "shield of faith";
5. "helmet of salvation";
6. "sword of the Spirit";
7. "prayer."

Notice that God says, "ABOVE ALL, taking the shield of faith...." Nothing is more necessary, more essential, than the shield of faith. Friend, are you dressed up in the armor which God, through His infinite grace, has provided for you? Go down this list of seven pieces of armor and see if there is any one of them missing in your equipment.

And notice that "faith" is a part of the Christian's armor. Faith is tremendously important in our battle against Satan. The purpose of the shield of faith is to quench the fiery darts of the Devil. Old-time students of the Word of God have pointed out that, in the description of the Christian's armor, God shows the Christian as "having" the loincloth of truth, the breastplate of righteousness, feet shod with the preparation of the Gospel of peace; but he is to "take" the shield of faith. It is available to the child of God in his battle against Satan, but he must "take" it up and use it.

Faith is important also in overcoming the world: "For whatsoever is born of God overcometh the world: and this is the victory that overcometh the world, even our faith" (I John 5:4).

The Bible does not state it in such terms, but evidently David took the shield of faith when he slew the giant Goliath. He was obsessed with the cause of God. He refused the armor of Saul and had no other armor, not even a sword. He remembered past victories over the bear and the lion, animals that would destroy his father's sheep. He believed that God gave him those victories and would give him this one also. David believed God. His faith was not in the armor of brass and steel but in the invisible armor of the Lord. He took the shield of faith, and God protected him from a superior foe.

No shield on earth will turn back the fiery arrows of Satan but the shield of faith. In the smoke and fire of spiritual conflict, we must "have faith in God."

IV. FAITH WILL PUT YOU ON GOD'S HONOR ROLL

Hebrews 11 is the great "Faith Chapter" of the Word of God. The word *faith* is found in the chapter twenty-four times. Faith is defined in this chapter as being "the substance of things hoped for, the evidence of things not seen."

By faith, Abel was saved, Enoch was translated, Noah saved his family, Abraham did the will of God and claimed the promises! Isaac and Jacob, Joseph and Moses, Joshua and Rahab, demonstrated under various circumstances and at different times, great faith in God and were all rewarded by being placed on God's Honor Roll.

But notice what a challenge is given to the child of God in verse 6: "Without faith it is impossible to please God." Think of it! No way to please God except by faith.

Do you wish to live a life that pleases Him? Then it must be a life of faith because God says, "Without faith it is impossible to please him." O God, increase our faith!

Chapter 11 of Hebrews proves that God keeps a record of those who have faith in Him. We are not dealing here with what might be called saving faith. We are talking about faith in the life of a Christian that overcomes all enemies, all circumstances, all trials, all tests. We are talking about a faith that sees victory when our eyes see all the symptoms and characteristics of utter defeat. The faith that pleases God is one that sees Him as a living God who delights to honor and reward that faith. Faith is confidence in God. Such faith gives us a "good report" (Heb. 11:39), or a good report card worthy of God's Honor Roll.

"Have faith in God."

V. THROUGH FAITH WE OVERCOME THE STORMS OF LIFE

"That the trial of your faith, being much more precious than of gold that perisheth, though it be tried with fire, might be found unto praise and honour and glory at the appearing of Jesus Christ."—I Pet. 1:7.

How important it is that we overcome the world! Worldliness robs the believer of power with God and with men. It brings certain defeat into the life of the Christian.

Worldliness made a weakling out of the mighty Samson; it stripped Lot of his possessions and cheated him out of his own family.

The world, the flesh, the Devil are set forth in God's Word as our three greatest enemies. These formidable foes can be overcome only as we "have faith in God."

This is a dark hour in the world's history. These are tempestuous and stormy times. But, thank God, my Father is at the wheel of this world and at the helm of my life. I shall not fear the stormy winds, for He has gone this way before and has never lost a passenger.

We sing precious words about going through the storm:

> **The winds and the waves shall obey My will,**
> **Peace, be still!**
> **Whether the wrath of the storm-tossed sea**
> **Or demons or men or whatever it be,**
> **No water can swallow the ship where lies**
> **The Master of ocean and earth and skies;**
> **They all shall sweetly obey My will;**
> **Peace, be still!**

God will honor the faith of the helpless when they must go through the storms of life. Faith is the means of a safe passage.

"Have faith in God."

VI. HAVE FAITH IN ORDER TO WIN THE LOST

That is the biggest job the world has ever known. You remember Jesus said, "Greater works than these shall ye do; because I go unto my Father" (John 14:12). God in His Word and through His Son has challenged the church of the twentieth century to do greater works than Jesus did when He walked the shores of this world two thousand years ago.

I remember that Jesus spoke to the dead, and they lived again. I remember that Jesus spoke to the blind, and they came seeing. I remember that Jesus touched the lame and crippled, and they were made whole again. Yet Jesus has said to me that I am to do greater works than He did.

We have a job to do that is greater than raising the dead, opening the eyes of the blind and straightening out the limbs of the crippled. "Greater works than these shall ye do." What work is that? The work of preaching the blessed Gospel of God's infinite, wonderful grace and mercy, and winning men from the jaws of Hell and judgment to a saving knowledge of Jesus Christ.

When you, with God working in your life, are used to win a soul, you have done a greater work than creating a world or hanging a star in the sky.

Four men brought the paralytic to Jesus, four who wouldn't quit, four who couldn't be defeated, four in whose vocabulary the words *quit* and *defeat* could not be found. They climbed up onto the roof of that house, tore up the roof and looked down through the opening. When they saw One standing down there who could make the man whole whom they had brought, they started letting him down through that hole.

Of all the miracles described in the Bible, I think I'd like to have seen that miracle more than any other. I wish I could have seen what Jesus saw when He looked up. The thing that impressed Him was not so much the crippled man borne of four being let down through the broken ceiling. What impressed Jesus most was their faith: "When Jesus saw their faith, he said unto the sick of the palsy, Son, thy sins be forgiven thee."

It takes faith to win the lost.

I have seen Christians believe God for the salvation of souls, pray right up to the time when God would save that loved one; then I have seen their faith waver and have then seen them fail to win that loved one.

I am preaching to people who carry a burdened and broken heart year after year. I am preaching to women whose husbands are on their way to Hell. I am preaching to husbands whose wives are lost. Some of your children are out yonder on the bleak mountainside of this world in sin, away from God, and are like sheep who have strayed from their shepherd. In God's name, have faith in God! Don't give up. Don't quit praying until God has saved your family.

"Have faith in God."

VII. HAVE FAITH FOR THE UNUSUAL

"And Jesus said unto them, Because of your unbelief: for verily I say unto you, If ye have faith as a grain of mustard seed, ye shall say unto this mountain, Remove hence to yonder place; and it shall remove; and nothing shall be impossible unto you."—Matt. 17:20.

Yes, the Bible tells how faith accomplishes the unusual. Sometimes people ask, "Mr. Malone, do you believe in miracles?" Yes, I do. I don't believe in miracles to the extent that I believe I can do anything Jesus or Peter, James, John and Paul did. I can't raise the dead. I don't have power in these hands of mine to heal the sick. If I could heal the sick and open the eyes of the blind, I would go all the way with God. The same Jesus who said, "Heal the sick and cast out the demons," said, "Raise the dead." Show me a man who can raise the dead. People who say, "I can heal the sick," but who do not raise the dead, only take part of what God said.

Have faith in God for the unusual!

I believe in miracles. My God can do things this morning that all the governors, senators, congressmen, even the President, cannot do. Many a time faith has accomplished the unusual, and the lack of faith has kept the unusual from happening.

You remember when Jesus took three of the twelve, went on the mountaintop and was transfigured, that Moses and Elijah appeared. There were six people on that mountaintop—Jesus and five men. When Jesus and the three came down from the mountain, Moses and Elijah did not come. When we are once in Heaven, we never leave His presence, never cease to be with Him.

Down in the valley something was going on. Jesus and the three went down into the valley and saw multitudes watching someone lying there writhing in the dust—a picture of the sin-cursed and lost of this world. There was a boy with twitching lips and glassy eyes, a boy foaming at the mouth, with limbs jerking. There he was lying unconscious, dust, sweat and blood all over him as he lay on the ground. There was his father, wringing his hands. Here are nine disciples standing around, nine men to whom Jesus had said, "I will give you power over demons [and that was what was wrong with the boy]; I will help you raise the dead, heal the sick, and preach the gospel."

Here this father stands with broken heart and wringing hands. He turns to Jesus and says, "I brought my afflicted son to these mighty preachers, but they could not heal him." The disciples couldn't cast out the demons. They turned to Jesus and asked, "Why could we not cast them out?" Jesus answered them: "This kind [the hard kind]"; "This kind [the unusual kind]"; "This kind [the unexpected kind]"—"This kind goeth not out but by prayer and fasting."

With faith in God and belief in prayer, you can do whatsoever has never been done before. Did not Jeremiah say, "Call unto me, and I will answer thee, and shew thee great and mighty things, which thou knowest not" (Jer. 33:3)?

No Christian will ever come to the place where his faith is not valuable. Christians should seek to face new worlds, conquer new continents, do new miracles, work new enterprises, until their faith is challenged, until they lean upon God to do the unusual. Have faith in God for the unusual.

What mountain needs to be removed in your life? What unusual thing do you need to have done in your life? Believe God for it. Nothing is impossible unto you if you will only believe God.

"Have faith in God."

Chapter V

The Importance of Faith

(Preached at Emmanuel Baptist Church, Pontiac, Michigan, Sunday morning, September 20, 1953)

"Now faith is the substance of things hoped for, the evidence of things not seen."—Heb. 11:1.

Hebrews 11 is called the Faith Chapter. The word *faith* appears no fewer than twenty-four times in this one chapter. The first two verses of chapter 12 also deal with faith. If we outline and divide the chapter, we find it falls into four great parts:

1. The Path of Faith (vss. 1-7);
2. The Patience of Faith (vss. 8-22);
3. The Power of Faith, or What Faith Is Able to Accomplish (vss. 22-40);
4. The Pattern of Faith (12:1,2).

In Hebrews 11:4-31 are mentioned several characters on God's Honor Roll of the faithful. We see what faith did in their lives and what it can do in our lives. Each demonstrates a different phase of the life of a Christian—his work, walk, witness, waiting, worship.

When we read what God has said in His Word, we realize how tremendously important faith is.

For instance, "Without FAITH it is impossible to please God."

God's Word also says, "This is the victory that overcometh the world, even our FAITH."

We read, "When Jesus saw their FAITH [the four men who brought the paralytic to Him], he said unto the sick of the palsy, Son, thy sins be forgiven thee."

We please God, win souls, overcome the world and get our prayer answers by faith.

Faith is total dependence upon God. Faith does not look at the seen but believes in the unseen, that which cannot be seen with physical eyes.

"While we look not at the things which are seen, but at the things which are not seen: for the things which are seen are temporal; but the things which are not seen are eternal."—II Cor. 4:18.

Faith is not overwhelmed by what appears to be overwhelming odds against us. Faith does not compare ourselves with the seemingly overwhelming circumstances, but compares the circumstances with God. In fact, faith closes its eyes to the things that are seen and makes no effort to walk by sight. "For we walk by faith, not by sight" (II Cor. 5:7).

We shall look at the lives of some of God's Old Testament people who lived by faith and pleased God.

I. ABEL—WE WORSHIP BY FAITH

"By faith Abel offered unto God a more excellent sacrifice than Cain, by which he obtained witness that he was righteous, God testifying of his gifts: and by it he being dead yet speaketh."—Heb. 11:4.

First, Abel shows that we worship by faith. I do not think we can dwell too much on these two brothers, Cain and Abel. In bringing their offerings to God, Cain brought the fruit of the ground, while Abel brought a lamb. Cain made the mistake of forgetting that God had pronounced a curse upon the ground. Anything this earth can produce is under the curse of God. When Cain brought fruit, he offered something that had God's curse on it.

Abel did not; he brought a lamb. The lamb speaks of the blood of Jesus. In the Old Testament the offering of lambs is most interesting. When an individual offered a lamb, he showed that he could be saved only by faith in the coming Redeemer. Exodus 12 shows a lamb offered by every family on the Passover night. The blood pointed toward the coming of Jesus. On the Day of Atonement (Lev. 16), the lamb was offered for an entire nation. A lamb for a man, for a family, for a nation. And in the New Testament, John said, "Behold the Lamb of God, which taketh away the sin of the WORLD" (John 1:29).

Abel believed in Jesus Christ when he brought a lamb. Every lamb slain upon a Jewish altar pointed to the death of Jesus at Calvary for the sins of the world.

Here are two brothers from the same family, with identical backgrounds. Both believe in a Supreme Being, both come to worship God. Yet one is to die in sin and go to Hell; the other is to be saved and have a home in Heaven. Both believed that they owed something to God, that they were duty-bound and obligated to Him; both came to discharge their duty and obligation. One brought a bloodless offering; one brought a blood offering.

Cain admitted there is a Supreme Being, but he was not going to get down into the dust of the earth and admit that he was a Hellbound sinner.

Abel, when he brought a blood offering, not only confessed he believed in a sovereign God to whom he was obligated, but also admitted he was a wicked and miserable sinner who could be saved no other way except by God's mercy and grace.

One can believe in a Supreme Being and still not be saved.

No man can get saved until he first gets lost. He cannot come to God until he realizes he is a sinner and under God's wrath. The Bible says, "He that believeth on the Son hath everlasting life:

and he that believeth not the Son shall not see life; but the wrath of God abideth on him."

By faith, Abel worshiped God.

There are literally hundreds of thousands, millions in America, who believe everything Cain believed. They believe in the fact of God, that Christ came to earth. They believe they are obligated to God, that there is a sovereign Supreme God to whom they owe something.

One can believe all that and not be a Christian. The only way to be saved is by faith in God's Son. By faith Abel was saved as he offered the bleeding lamb.

Martin Luther had the highest education that a man could acquire in his day. He was educated in the finest schools of his country. And some of the greatest schools ever in existence were the German schools of Luther's time. He was a Roman Catholic monk, deeply spiritual but not saved.

One day he decided to go deeper into the matter of religion, to study further along the lines of religious practice. He went to Rome, to the very center of the Roman Catholic church, to climb the Sancta Scala, the Sacred Stairs.

He started the long climb, one step at a time, on his knees, uttering prayers and penances. Shortly before, he had been reading parts of the Bible and had found the phrase, "The just shall live by faith," that man shall be made righteous in God's sight by faith in God's Son, not by works. As that brilliant monk climbed on his knees one step at a time, saying prayers, the Spirit of God flashed these words across his mind: "The just shall live by FAITH." He immediately arose and walked back down the stairs a saved man, praising God that one is saved through faith.

Man can never be saved until he has the faith to believe that the Word of God says he is a sinner.

"For all have sinned, and come short of the glory of God."—Rom. 3:23.

"All we like sheep have gone astray; we have turned every one to his own way."—Isa. 53:6.

"From the sole of the foot even unto the head there is no soundness in it; but wounds, and bruises, and putrifying sores: they have not been closed, neither bound up, neither mollified with ointment."—Isa. 1:6.

Twenty-three times in Isaiah 1, man is indicted as a sinner; twenty-three times in Romans 3 he is indicted as being a sinner. The whole chapter has only one theme: one can be saved by faith in the finished work of Jesus Christ on the cross. He can be a Methodist, Baptist, Jew, Gentile, Catholic, Protestant; but there is only one entry into the presence of God. Abel showed that way, worshiping by faith, faith in the shed blood of an innocent lamb!

II. ENOCH—WE WALK BY FAITH

"By faith Enoch was translated that he should not see death; and was not found, because God had translated him: for before his translation he had this testimony, that he pleased God. But without faith it is impossible to please him: for he that cometh to God must believe that he is, and that he is a rewarder of them that diligently seek him."—Heb. 11:5,6.

In Genesis 5:24 we read, "And Enoch walked with God: and he was not; for God took him." His was a walk of faith. Remember, Enoch lived in the antediluvian generation (Noah's generation), and he walked with God in that generation. He walked with God while all the rest of the world walked contrary.

Many say a man cannot live for God if he is the only one saved in his home. A man can live for God anywhere if he wants to. Here is one who by faith walked with God against his generation, against the leadership of the Devil. Here is one man who believed God. It takes faith to do that.

One of the greatest enemies of faith is feeling, one of the most confusing things in many a Christian's life. The Bible never says a good word about it. Not once in the Bible does it say that feeling has anything to do with our being saved.

Isaac had two sons, Jacob and Esau. When Isaac was ready to die and the time arrived for him to bless his firstborn, he was deceived and confused because he went by feeling instead of by voice or Word of God. Jacob the deceiver put hairy skin on his arms so they would feel like Esau's. Jacob comes first to blind Isaac, who reaches out to feel his arms. Jacob speaks, and Isaac says, "The voice is that of Jacob, but it feels like Esau." He must have pondered, *What shall I do?* Then he decided, *I will go by what I feel, rather than by what I hear.* He went by feeling, thus bestowing the birthright on the wrong son.

Christians, instructed by God's words, must walk with God by faith apart from feeling. The feeling comes after the faith, never before. Unless your faith is in Jesus Christ and you believe the voice of God in this Book, you will never have that assurance and God's blessing.

A man lost his way one night in a London fog. As he stumbled along, he bumped into another man. The man he bumped said, "I'm sorry."

The first man said, "I'm lost. I can't find my way home. I can't see in this fog."

"Where do you live?"

The first man told him.

"I know where that is. I will take you home."

He reached out, took the other's hand, led him through the dense fog, along narrow streets, across little bridges, until they arrived at the correct address. "Here is your home," he said.

"I don't understand how you did it," said the other. "I stumbled. I could not see. I held onto your hand, and you led me directly

THE IMPORTANCE OF FAITH 75

home. I don't see how you did it."

"Well, I am not able to see—I am blind—so I walk by faith. I know the landmarks. They never change. I walk not by sight but by faith."

How true this must be of a believer! We, too, must walk by faith, not by sight. We must believe that the God who holds our hand will lead us through every dark valley, every fiery trial, and lead us safely Home at last.

No matter how dark it may get, how crooked the path may become, how wicked the world may get, thank God, He will take me by the hand and lead me every step of the way!

III. NOAH—WE WITNESS BY FAITH

"By faith Noah, being warned of God of things not seen as yet, moved with fear, prepared an ark to the saving of his house; by the which he condemned the world, and became heir of the righteousness which is by faith."—Heb. 11:7.

Noah was a witness. There are several very interesting things in his testimony. By faith Noah was warned of things not seen. The things that mean the most to a Christian are things you can't see with the naked eye. Love, faith, prayer—you can't touch these things, take hold of them nor put them into containers. Paul said, "...we look not at the things which are seen, but at the things which are not seen: for the things which are seen are temporal; but the things which are not seen are eternal."

How does that apply to the faith of Noah?

One day God said, "I am going to destroy the world with a flood." It took a lot of faith to believe that. It had never rained before. How was the earth watered? With a mist. Man had never seen a drop of rain, a thundercloud, a flash of lightning or a flash flood. God said, "I am going to destroy the world with a judgment never seen before—a flood."

By faith Noah believed what God said; and he, moved with fear, prepared an ark to the saving of his house. Noah's generation laughed at his faith, as people laugh at ours; but, like Noah, we'll have the last laugh.

Noah was moved by fear, the Bible says. The whole existence of the human race is owed today to this one man who got scared. I would rather be Hell-scared than Hell-burned.

An old preacher scared me eighteen years ago. I saw Hell and God's wrath and the anger and hatred of God against sin. I would never have gotten saved had I not gotten scared.

Noah was moved by fear, not by love. He prepared the ark. If you are not afraid of sin, Hell and God's judgment, I fear for you.

Some years ago down South a mentally deficient young man wandered onto the highway one day. He didn't see the car coming around a curve. Brakes and tires squealed; the driver had all he could do to keep from hitting that boy.

The mentally deficient young fellow got a kick out of it. He thought it was fun. He tried it again and again. He would laugh as the brakes and tires squealed and cars skidded around the curve. He would hide in the bushes and dart out in front of the oncoming cars. The drivers would slam on their brakes and holler at him.

Some of the neighbors who caught him at it, warned him that someday one of those drivers would have bad brakes or be half asleep and not see him. But he laughed and mocked at the warnings.

One day after he'd done it several times with no fear in his heart, he said, "I can do it again; I can play the fool once more." But this time that car hit and killed him. That happened to a young man who had no fear and not enough sense to listen to warning.

I beg you people who are unsaved, who reject God's Son and live according to your own pattern, by faith trust the Lord Jesus and walk with Him and witness for Him.

IV. ABRAHAM WAITED BY FAITH

Books could be written on the faith of Abraham. He waited many years for Isaac, the promised heir. He was a hundred years old and Sarah, ninety, when Isaac was born. Sarah's faith staggered when she recommended that Abraham have an heir by Hagar. But Abraham's faith "staggered" not: "He staggered not at the promise of God through unbelief; but was strong in faith, giving glory to God" (Rom. 4:20).

There is no record that Abraham ever built a city. As far as we know he never built a home. He sojourned in the land of promise, living in tents. When God appeared to him in the plains of Mamre, he was sitting in the door of his tent (Gen. 18:1).

Lot built a house, only to see it destroyed in Sodom when the Lord brought judgment upon that city. Abraham was waiting for a city which God has built, a city which we call Heaven. ". . . he looked for a city which hath foundations, whose builder and maker is God" (Heb. 11:10).

Abraham was well endowed with this world's goods, but he was willing to wait for the heavenly city. The phrase, "looked for a city," means literally he "waited for a city." He never envied Lot for having a house because he was willing to wait for a heavenly home.

Some things the believer must "by faith" wait for. We by faith wait for the coming of the Saviour. We by faith wait to see our loved ones on the morning of the resurrection. By faith we wait for the day when we shall have a new body. By faith we wait for the glorious day when we too shall walk the streets of gold in God's new Jerusalem. Faith is patient and willing to wait on God.

"Now faith is the substance of things hoped for, the evidence of things not seen."

V. ISAAC WILLED BY FAITH

"By faith Isaac blessed Jacob and Esau concerning things to come."—Heb. 11:20.

Chapter 27 of Genesis is like a man reciting his Will to his two sons, Jacob and Esau. The record, found in that chapter, would seem to indicate that Isaac was confused when he blessed Jacob while thinking it was Esau, but the Word of God plainly says that "by faith Isaac blessed Jacob."

Many students of the Scripture believe that, before the process of blessing both Jacob and Esau had ended, Isaac finally discovered that it was Jacob he was blessing, not Esau. He had no doubt heard that Jacob had gained the birthright from Esau but felt that he must play his part in the drama until the blessing of both of his sons was resolved. In any event, he did bless Jacob "by faith" concerning things to come.

It seems that faith most always has to do with "things to come." Whether in the matter of salvation, answers to prayer or believing in the prophecy of the Bible, it has to do with "things to come."

Believing in Christ as our Saviour means that through faith salvation comes to pass immediately. Salvation is one of those "things to come" when we believe.

Isaac's faith in blessing Jacob and Esau did not rest upon anything he could see at hand. He had only heard what God promised to his father Abraham, and he believed it would come to pass. His faith rested upon God's Word to Abraham concerning "things to come." True faith always rests upon the Word of God. "...faith cometh by hearing, and hearing by the word of God."

VI. JOSEPH WAS WEANED FROM EGYPT BY FAITH

"By faith Joseph, when he died, made mention of the departing of the children of Israel; and gave commandment concerning his bones."—Heb. 11:22.

Hebrews 11 (the great Faith Chapter) does not mention the great and dramatic events of Joseph's life—his sorrows, afflictions, self-denials and sufferings. Neither does the great Faith Chapter mention his great exploits and triumphs in Egypt. God mentions his faith in the hour of his death. He requested that his bones not be left in Egypt when the children of Israel departed for the promised land.

He believed that the children of Israel would depart from Egypt because God had said it.

"And he said unto Abram, Know of a surety that thy seed shall be a stranger in a land that is not their's, and shall serve them; and they shall afflict them four hundred years.... And thou shalt go to thy fathers in peace; thou shalt be buried in a good old age."—Gen. 15:13,15.

His faith, as always, rested upon the Word of God. Joseph is saying to the children of Israel, "Egypt is not your final home, so don't get attached to her. Canaan, the land of promise, is to be your home." His dying request was that even his dry bones not be left in Egypt. He is teaching us that the child of God should not be attached to this world, because Heaven is our home.

VII. MOSES, BY FAITH, WOULD NOT BE KING

"By faith Moses, when he was come to years, refused to be called the son of Pharaoh's daughter."—Heb. 11:24.

Seven of the forty verses of Hebrews 11 are devoted to the faith of Moses and his parents. By faith his parents overcame the fear of man. By faith Moses overcame the friendship of men. His parents were not afraid to defy the orders of the Egyptian monarchy, while Moses was not afraid to refuse the monarchy itself. He "refused to be called the son of Pharaoh's daughter."

The faith of Moses is expressed in five active responses.

1. He refused—vs. 24.
2. He chose—vs. 25.
3. He esteemed—vs. 26.

4. He forsook—vs. 27.
5. He kept—vs. 28.

His refusal of the crown of Egypt is mainly what we want to look at, at this time. All the other active responses of faith followed his refusal of that crown. He refused to become a member of the Egyptian royal family by not being willing to be called the son of Pharaoh's daughter. He had the offer made to him, or he could not have refused it.

Many Bible students believe that had Moses accepted the offer, he would have been in line for the throne of Egypt. Moses knew that he was a Hebrew and that someday the Hebrews would be delivered from Egypt. God had made His plan for Moses' life clear to him. His helping a Hebrew brother by slaying an Egyptian indicated that God had raised him up to be a deliverer of God's people out of Egypt.

He refused! Faith refuses friendship with the world at the expense of fellowship with God and His people. Faith finds the will of God and carries out that will regardless of the cost. By faith we too must refuse friendship with the world. "Ye adulterers and adulteresses, know ye not that the friendship of the world is enmity with God? whosoever therefore will be a friend of the world is the enemy of God," states James 4:4.

Refusing the crown meant he was identifying himself with the suffering and trials of God's people. His choice was worth the cost. He saw these people delivered by the blood of the lamb. He talked with God on the mountaintop and one day came from Heaven and stood with Jesus on the Mount of Transfiguration, a mountain much higher than Pharaoh's throne.

VIII. JOSHUA WARRED BY FAITH

"By faith the walls of Jericho fell down, after they were compassed about seven days."—Heb. 11:30.

THE IMPORTANCE OF FAITH

This verse is speaking specifically of the faith of Joshua. Joshua had seen the miracle of the Red Sea; now he needs a miracle to bring down the strong walls of Jericho.

What a beautiful story is found in Joshua 5:13-15! Here Joshua meets the Captain of the unseen hosts of the Lord. The appearances of God in the Old Testament as He appeared here to Joshua are called the theophanies.

The Captain of the armies of Heaven gave Joshua direction as to how to take the city. His orders are found in Joshua 6. No mention is made of battering rams and implements of war. God speaks to Joshua about marching and blowing trumpets. How foolish these directions would sound to those who know not God!

Joshua's faith not only led him to believe what God said, but also to believe that what God said, He would surely perform.

It worked! Faith in God always works. Do you have any walls in your life which need to be torn down? What wall stands between you and victory? What wall stands between you and God's will? By faith the walls of Jericho came down. And by faith the walls of our lives can also come down. The plan of faith sounds like foolishness to the world, but God makes it work in the Christian's life.

IX. RAHAB, BY FAITH, WON HER FAMILY

"By faith the harlot Rahab perished not with them that believed not, when she had received the spies with peace."—Heb. 11:31.

Rahab was saved by faith. No one has ever been saved any other way. She identified her residence by letting down the scarlet rope from her window. This spoke of safety through the blood. She had heard how God had blessed His people and delivered them from Egypt by the blood of the lamb, so she, by faith, believed that the blood could cause her and her whole family to be spared when the city fell. They all were safe because of the scarlet line hanging from her window.

"And Joshua saved Rahab the harlot alive, and her father's household, and all that she had; and she dwelleth in Israel even unto this day; because she hid the messengers, which Joshua sent to spy out Jericho."—Josh. 6:25.

What faith did for Rahab! She was an harlot, but God saved her, and she won her family also. The grace of God in salvation is so greatly demonstrated in the life of Rahab. She is lifted from the life of a harlot to a place in the lineage of Jesus Christ.

"And Salmon begat Booz of Rachab; and Booz begat Obed of Ruth; and Obed begat Jesse" (Matt. 1:5). From whoredom to royalty! By faith sinners are saved. "And he said to the woman, Thy faith hath saved thee; go in peace" (Luke 7:50).

"Now faith is the substance of things hoped for, the evidence of things not seen."—Heb. 11:1.

Chapter VI

The Kind of Faith We Need Today

(Preached in Emmanuel Baptist Church, Pontiac, Michigan, October 17, 1954)

"By faith Noah, being warned of God of things not seen as yet, moved with fear, prepared an ark to the saving of his house; by the which he condemned the world, and became heir of the righteousness which is by faith."—Heb. 11:7.

Here in chapter 11 of Hebrews is the only attempt in all the Bible to give a definition of faith. Let us look at Noah's faith. His is the kind we need today.

The Word of God explains the kind of faith a Christian is to have before the coming of our Lord.

Noah's faith is described:

"By faith Noah, being warned of God of things not seen as yet, moved with fear, prepared an ark to the saving of his house; by the which he condemned the world, and became heir of the righteousness which is by faith."

Noah's faith is needed for these last days.

The Bible tells us that, before the coming of the Lord Jesus Christ back to earth, these times are to be like the times of Noah. Matthew 24 describes what it was like in those days and tells us that, just before the Lord comes again, the world is to be similar to those days in Noah's time.

"BUT AS THE DAYS OF NOE WERE, SO SHALL THE COMING OF THE SON OF MAN BE. For as in the days that were before the flood they were eating and drinking, marrying and giving in marriage, until the day that Noe entered into the ark, And knew not until the flood came, and took them all away; so shall also the coming of the Son of man be."—Matt. 24:37-39.

The Lord Jesus, the Son of God, Truth Himself, said these last days will be "like the days of Noe [Noah] were."

There seems no question that these are the last days. Read in the Bible the description of the last days; then read in your daily newspaper what is going on in the world: even one not claiming to be a Bible scholar would have to admit that we seem to be in the last days. In fact, strange as it may sound to you, we have been in the last days for two thousand years. The Prophet Joel in the Old Testament spoke of the "last days." He said two things would happen in the "last days": the Holy Spirit would come into the world, and there would be signs in the heavens:

"...upon the servants and upon the handmaids in those days will I pour out my spirit. And I will shew wonders in the heavens and in the earth, blood, and fire, and pillars of smoke. The sun shall be turned into darkness, and the moon into blood, before the great and the terrible day of the Lord come."—Joel 2:29-31.

The Holy Spirit coming into the world took place on the day of Pentecost. Two thousand years ago we began the period that the Bible speaks of as the "last days."

Jesus said that, in these last days, the world is going to be like it was in the days of Noah. Read the account of Noah in Genesis—that wonderful man who preached for 120 years one theme and one sermon; that man whom God allowed to live 950 years; that man who was successful in saving his family, though all the rest of the world went to Hell.

THE KIND OF FAITH WE NEED TODAY

Notice this about Noah's day. First, 'they were marrying and giving in marriage; they were eating and drinking; and knew not until the flood came, and took them away.'

There is nothing wrong with eating, nothing wrong with drinking—if you drink the right things. Jesus ate and drank. But Jesus here reprimanded and condemned the antediluvians for "eating and drinking." Jesus is teaching here that here was a generation of people who thought of nothing but the physical, the body, the natural, and that which you could see. "Eating and drinking" speaks of the material. Noah's age was characterized by the fact that it was a materialistic age.

People were thinking of eating, drinking, building houses and owning real estate—things material, things you could lay your hands on, to the exclusion of Almighty God. A materialist is one who emphasizes what he can see, what he can hold in his hands, to the exclusion of the unseen and the spiritual. That was the kind of people Noah lived with.

There is no doubt about it. Hear me this morning, friends. Both history and the Bible prove that every time a nation of people have become sexually insane, soon decay and dissolution have set in upon that nation. Then comes the judgment of God upon it.

Something else about them: they were "marrying and giving in marriage." Nothing is wrong when a man gives his daughter in marriage, if it's a scriptural marriage and of God. But here Jesus reprimanded them for "marrying and giving in marriage," which means it was an age of tremendous emphasis upon sex.

That's characteristic of this present age. Who could ever doubt that? Movie actresses in scanty clothing are shown on the front pages of our daily newspapers all across America. Worse than that—they hardly have on any clothing at all. And these are lauded as the idols of the nation! Nudity and sex are the order of the day. Loose morals, disrespect for marriage and its vows, divorce and sex—all characteristic of these last days.

We hear a lot these days about the racial problem. I hardly know exactly what to say about it. I love all colors of people. It would be mockery, hypocritical and a farce not to love the colored people of America and seek to win them to Christ and to educate and train them, then send missionaries to Africa and Ethiopia.

In the next few years, if Jesus tarries, the racial barriers in America will be almost completely broken down. But the Word of God teaches that every time one nation has intermarried with another, it has never in the history of the world produced a strong race, but it has always produced a weaker race, a mongrel race, and has brought about the destruction of that nation, and brought the judgment of God upon it.

This is the age of sexual emphasis, and God's wrath is upon such emphasis.

Here's something else about Noah's day. They were eating and drinking, marrying and giving in marriage, right up to the time Noah entered the ark, "and knew not until the flood came, and took them all away." Why didn't they know? Was there no preaching? The Bible teaches us that for 120 years Noah had preached in that land. Every time his hammer hit the side of that boat, it was a message from God that judgment was coming and the people must prepare.

For 120 years he thundered forth his message, yet people did not know the Flood was coming. It wasn't because they hadn't heard but because they would not believe. They had heard but had refused to believe that what God had said to Noah was going to come to pass.

Now notice: "By faith Noah...." If these days are like the days in which Noah lived, then Christians need the same kind of faith today. We need what Noah needed.

Let's see what kind of faith he had.

THE KIND OF FAITH WE NEED TODAY

I. NOAH'S FAITH WAS PROVEN BY HIS WORKS

"By faith Noah, being warned of God of things not seen as yet, moved with fear, prepared an ark to the saving of his house; by the which he condemned the world, and became heir of the righteousness which is by faith."

Noah evidenced his faith. James said, "Faith without works is dead." Faith without works is a corpse. Faith without works is like a body without spirit. Faith without works is like a dead body that the spirit has gone out of. And faith on the part of God's people, that is not proven by zealous work for God, is dead.

We urge people to work because the Bible teaches that faith must be shown by our works. We are justified in God's sight by our faith; we are justified in men's sight by our works. Noah showed his faith by his works.

I wish fundamental, Bible-believing Baptist people could see that every time in the New Testament the grace of God is spoken of, in that same connection the works of a Christian are referred to. We talk about being "saved by his grace." But those who are saved by God's grace and Spirit-filled will work for Jesus.

"For by grace are ye saved through faith; and that not of yourselves: it is the gift of God: Not of works, lest any man should boast. For we are his workmanship, created in Christ Jesus unto good works [Watch this:], *which God hath before ordained that we should walk in them."*—Eph. 2:8-10.

You speak about being ordained, predestinated, chosen beforehand. What for? The Bible says believers are foreordained and predestinated that they should walk in "good works."

The great hindrance, the great obstacle, the great blockade in the church today is the fact that it is made up of people who do not serve God.

Noah said, 'I believe in God, and I'll show it by my works.' And for 120 years he served the Lord.

Titus 2:11 says, "For the grace of God that bringeth salvation hath appeared to all men." Notice verse 14 in that connection: "Who gave himself for us, that he might redeem us from all iniquity, and purify unto himself a peculiar people, ZEALOUS OF GOOD WORKS."

The grace of God is always mentioned in connection with the works of a believer. God has ordained and commanded that every Christian not only be saved, but be serving.

Years ago in the stormy history of England, a criminal by the name of Charles Peace was condemned to die. He became a national figure because of his crime and rebellion against the government of England. As he was being led to his execution, a clergyman dressed in a long, flowing robe walked alongside him and read him the Scriptures. He read, "For God so loved the world...." He read, "The wicked and all nations that forget God shall be turned into hell...."

All of a sudden Charles Peace stopped that procession, turned to the clergyman and said, "Listen! Do you really believe what you are saying?"

"Why," this clergyman said, "sure, Charles, I believe what I'm saying."

"Do you believe that Christ died for people like me? Do you believe that every unsaved person will be turned into Hell someday? Do you believe that?"

The clergyman answered, "Sure, I believe it. It's in the Book, and I'm reading to you God's Word."

Charles Peace looked at that clergyman and said, "If you believe that the unsaved are going to Hell, that Jesus died for all men, then why in God's name are you waiting until we are led to the gallows before telling us about it?"

I ask you this morning, if you have faith in this Book, faith in God's Son, faith in God's church and faith in the truth of this Book,

THE KIND OF FAITH WE NEED TODAY

then why in God's name don't you tell folks about it before they die?

Noah said, 'People are going to die, so I had better warn them.' He proved his faith by his works.

Listen! If you're not serving Jesus this morning, seeking to win people to Him, I hope you go home with this ringing in your ears: "FAITH WITHOUT WORKS IS DEAD!" You are like a corpse, like a dead man. God said so.

We need a faith today that will prove itself by working for Jesus. The only hope of this age is a working church. The only salvation of the world is through a church that will go out and tell individuals about the Lord and His power to save.

II. NOAH'S FAITH WAS PATIENT IN WAITING

Noah's faith was patient in waiting: proven by his works, patient by his waiting.

One day God said, "Noah, it's going to rain." Noah had never seen rain, for it had never before rained on the earth. The Bible tells us in Genesis 2 that the earth was watered with a mist: "...there went up a mist from the earth, and watered the whole face of the ground."

God told him, "Noah, it's going to rain. The fountains of the deep are going to be broken up, and the heavens are going to open up with a deluge. You build an ark, and everyone that enters into that ark will be saved. Those who will not hear you and will not enter into the ark, will be lost."

Think how long Noah had to wait before God fulfilled His Word. He was laughed at for 120 years. Some of you will go to the plant or store or shop tomorrow; and if you are laughed at for 120 seconds, it will shake your faith and make you wonder about being a Christian. People said, "I told you so," when it hadn't rained for 120 years. They said to their children for all this time, "Look at that old long-bearded man! Look at that old fanatic! There comes that old fool!" But for 120 years Noah waited for God to honor his faith.

How many times Christians—when it looked as if God was about to do something for them, was about to save their loved ones, was about to answer their prayers—have given up. Their faith grew weak, and they let loose of the promises of God.

Read the life of George Mueller, perhaps the most faithful, wonderful warrior of prayer since the days of the Apostle Paul. Books are written about how he prayed, how he believed God, and how God sent through his hands millions of dollars to build orphanages. A mighty man of prayer was he. And a great soul winner.

But there's something about George Mueller that a lot of people don't know. He stood up in Chicago one time and said, "I have never missed a day in twenty-seven years praying for two men. For twenty-seven years there has never been a day when I have failed to mention these two men to God by name and ask Him to save their souls. These two are my own brothers."

After he made that statement, George Mueller lived for thirty-five more years. So for sixty-two years he prayed for two of his own brothers who were lost and on their way to Hell. And both were saved after George Mueller died. It took sixty-two years of believing God to bring them into the family of God.

Noah's faith was patient in waiting!

Some of you sitting here in this building—your faith has been tried. You're praying for loved ones. You're asking God to save them in this revival meeting. You've asked God to do something for you. God tries the faith of His people.

I don't know when He will honor your faith, but I know that, if you will believe God, He will someday honor your faith. It might be sixty-two years or 60 seconds, but God will keep His Word and honor your faith.

He has honored the faith of the people of this church for twelve years.

Before I came to this pulpit to teach my Sunday school class, I was thinking about those we want God to save, and a thought came to me. Here is a work that takes hundreds and hundreds of dollars every week to operate, in the neighborhood of $2,000 every week to keep this work of God operating. I thought: *Not one human being has ever signed a contract. Not one human being has ever signed a pledge. Not one human being is obligated to give one nickel.* Where is the money coming from? People believe God. You can't see it, but you know it's there because this is God's work.

Noah's faith was patient in waiting. I urge you this morning to strengthen your faith in God and keep on waiting until the answer comes.

III. NOAH'S FAITH PREVAILED IN THE MIDST OF UNBELIEF

Someone asked a young lady in a store the other day, "Why do you smoke now? You used not to. I'm disappointed that you do now." The lady answered her: "Well, everybody else is doing it."

Isn't that a good reason! Isn't that a wonderful reason for debauching your body! That's the same reason unsaved people give for their unwillingness to face their responsibility to Christ and for loving the world and the things of the world. Isn't that a wonderful reason for going to Hell! Isn't that a marvelous reason for committing spiritual suicide! Isn't that a wonderful reason for damning your soul! "Everybody else is doing it"—the theme of the day. "What's the crowd doing? Which way are most of the people going? That's the way I want to go. I want to go with the crowd. I want to be like the world. I want to do like most of the others are doing."

Not Noah. Have you ever tried walking against everybody else? Have you ever tried to get up the steps over here when all the departments have been turned loose and everybody's going down, and you're trying to go up? Did you ever try to go down the street when there's a parade on and everybody's going the other way, but you're going that way? People will knock you down, look at you like you're a fool and say, "What's wrong with that maniac? Why doesn't he go the way the rest of us are going?"

That's the way they acted toward Noah—"There's old Noah, going in one direction. Here's his wife and his three little boys, and later his three grown boys and their three wives—eight people going one way, and all the rest going another." People thought, *We must be right, there's so many of us. They must be wrong, they're so few.* But God showed them who was right. Noah's faith prevailed in the midst of unbelief.

Don't let it bother you that thousands in Pontiac don't believe in God and don't believe the Bible. Jesus said:

"Enter ye in at the strait gate: for wide is the gate, and broad is the way, that leadeth to destruction, and many there be which go in thereat: Because strait is the gate, and narrow is the way, which leadeth unto life, and few there be that find it."—Matt. 7:13,14.

Just thank God that you are in the narrow road with the little group this morning!

IV. NOAH'S FAITH WAS PROVOKED BY FEAR

Noah got scared. Notice what it says. He was "moved by fear." When God said, "Noah, I'm going to destroy this world," Noah's knees began to shake. When God said, "Noah, I'm going to bring judgment. I'm going to destroy these people because they won't get saved," Noah began to tremble. He was "moved by fear."

I've heard preachers say, "I don't want to scare anybody." I

THE KIND OF FAITH WE NEED TODAY 93

do. I want people to be scared of Hell. I want them to be afraid of judgment, to be afraid to meet God unprepared. I want people to be afraid to stand before Jesus with His blood on their hands.

The other day after I had preached a 76-year-old man's funeral, I thought of a man 74 whose name and address I had been carrying around, waiting to call on him. The thought gripped my heart that a man 74 is not long for this world. The Bible says a man's life is threescore years and ten, and anything over that is the grace and mercy of God.

So I got in my car and drove immediately to his house. I sat down and talked with him about half an hour, showing him one verse after another, how he could be saved, how Jesus died for his sins, and how people who have rejected Christ are lost and on their way to Hell.

It seemed as though he wouldn't be saved that day. But all of a sudden I became most frightened. I thought, *I may walk out that door and in a week or two they'll call me and say, "Brother Tom, can you preach Mr. So-and-so's funeral?"* I thought, *When that news comes, my heart will be gripped with the awful reality that I left a man before he was saved.*

I knew right then I couldn't go; everything else must wait. Here was a man 74 years old without God and on his way to Hell. My heart was gripped with a holy fear.

I stayed, prayed and talked. After awhile he looked at me and said, "Brother Tom, I'd like to pray and ask God to forgive me of my sins." He bowed his head and prayed, "God be merciful to me, a sinner, and save me for Jesus' sake."

Then I took the Bible and showed him some verses that proved to him that God would keep His Word and that because he believed in God's Son, his sins were forever gone. Then I asked, "How do you know you're saved?"

With tears on his cheeks and a smile on his lips, the 74-year-old man said, "Why, Brother Tom, because God said so. I know because I believe what God says." He took God at His Word, and God saved his soul from sin.

Friend, Noah believed God, and God saved Noah from judgment and from wrath and destruction.

Will you too put your faith in Him? Will you too look to God this morning and lay hold on Him as your personal Saviour? Will you too trust Him?

V. NOAH'S FAITH WAS DEMONSTRATED BY OBEDIENCE

Noah obeyed the plain command of God. God asked Noah to do something that, as far as we know, no one had ever done before. He asked him to build a boat. He asked him to believe about something he had never seen before. He had never seen rain. Noah could have said, "I believe God will do what He said He would do," and stopped there. But Noah's faith did not stop by saying, "I believe." He demonstrated his faith by complete obedience to the command of God. "Thus did Noah; according to all that God commanded him, so did he" (Gen. 6:22).

If Noah's family had not seen the demonstration of his faith, they might not have believed. Noah saw the world before the Flood, during the Flood, after the Flood. His faith was clearly demonstrated in that he believed that infinite power could accomplish what infinite truth had predicted. By faith he saw what only the eyes of omniscience had already seen.

He demonstrated his faith by building the ark and building it according to God's blueprint. God knew about weight, balance and displacement. Noah knew nothing of these things but demonstrated his faith by building.

God warned Noah, and he demonstrated his faith by warning others. If we believe that Jesus is coming again and the age of

THE KIND OF FAITH WE NEED TODAY

grace is going to end, then we are to warn others that they might be saved and escape the coming judgment of God.

Noah demonstrated his faith by accepting God's invitation to come into the ark. When God said, "Noah, come thou and all thy house into the ark; for thee have I seen righteous before me in this generation," we read that "Noah went in, and his sons, and his wife, and his son's wives with him, into the ark, because of the waters of the flood" (Gen. 7:1,7).

It is not enough to say, "I believe the Gospel is true." One must demonstrate that faith by entering into Christ, as Noah entered the ark, which in some ways is a type of Christ. Noah was not saved by works. No one ever has been nor ever will be saved by works. Noah was saved by faith and faith alone, but he demonstrated the reality and sincerity of his faith. When the floods came, the scoffers climbed the highest trees and scaled the most lofty mountains, but the judgment waters of God climbed higher than the scoffers and unbelievers could climb. But Noah and his family were safe in the ark. The unbelievers demonstrated their unbelief by waiting too late, while Noah demonstrated his faith by obeying God before the judgment came.

"By faith Noah, being warned of God of things not seen as yet, moved with fear, prepared an ark to the saving of his house; by the which he condemned the world, and became heir of the righteousness which is by faith."—Heb. 11:7.

Chapter VII

Faith Abiding

(Preached in the Emmanuel Baptist Church on Sunday morning, September 14, 1975)

>   READ: I Corinthians 13

"And now abideth faith, hope, charity [love], *these three; but the greatest of these is charity* [love].*"*—I Cor. 13:13.

Faith, hope and love are grouped together at least ten times in the New Testament. It is impossible to realize fully how much emphasis is given in the Word of God to these three tremendous themes. In a sense, the whole Bible is devoted to these three tremendous things: faith, hope and love.

Someone has said that, if you were to build a great spiritual superstructure, a temple of God, you would begin with a very solid foundation: The foundation is faith; the walls are hope; the roof is love. Then from within the temple of God would come the melodic sounds of praise.

That is what is emphasized in the great superstructure in the New Testament: faith, hope and love. Faith is the foundation. Hope is the outward and visible result of it all. Love is the demonstration of our Christian faith to the world.

God does three things in His Word. First, He shows how firm a foundation we have for our faith and hope. He shows what this firm foundation is that He has laid for our faith. In fact, you can talk about faith, preach about it, think about it; but in only one place is *faith* defined, explained and set forth, and this is in the Word of God.

Then He shows what a glorious hope is set forth in the Gospel. What a glorious hope the Christian has! Let me say quickly that some people think the Christian life only means that a Christian is saved from Hell. But it means a lot more than that. I am enjoying myself on my way to Heaven. I am going to Heaven, but I am rich while I am on my way there. My possessions in Christ defy description. It is great and glorious to have hope in the Gospel.

Third, this Bible demonstrates and explains how supremely blessed is the life ruled by love.

We have these three things. I will spend most of my time today talking about the first of these—faith. Then I will bring them together again: faith, hope and love.

There are three great apostles, the ones whom the Lord used to do the most writing in the New Testament. The Apostle Paul wrote fourteen books. The Apostle Peter wrote two tremendous epistles. The Apostle John wrote five of the New Testament books.

God led each to emphasize each of these three graces. In fact, the Apostle Paul is the apostle of faith. The Apostle Peter is the apostle of hope. The Apostle John is the apostle of love. I want you to see a beautiful design by the Holy Spirit leading men to write God's holy Word and give the great emphasis to faith, hope and love.

You need but read his great book of Romans, that God inspired him to write, to come to the definite conclusion that Paul is the apostle of faith. In fact, he talks about our being justified by faith. Only one way can a person be declared holy and righteous in the sight of God, as righteous as if he had never sinned; and that is by faith in the Lord Jesus Christ: "Therefore being justified by faith, we have peace with God through our Lord Jesus Christ" (Rom. 5:1).

FAITH ABIDING

Not only are we justified by faith, but we live by faith. Paul said in Galatians 2:20, "I am crucified with Christ: nevertheless I live; yet not I, but Christ liveth in me: and the life which I now live in the flesh I live by the faith of the Son of God...." We are not only saved by faith; we live by faith. I want all to see how important faith is in our lives.

Not only are we saved by faith and live by faith, but we walk by faith. In II Corinthians 5:7 Paul declared, "For we walk by faith, not by sight." A Christian doesn't need to see what is ahead, doesn't need to know what is around the corner, nor necessarily see the future. In his life is the One who holds his future. He walks by faith and not by sight.

Not only are we justified by faith, living by faith and walking by faith, but we also please God by faith, declares Hebrews 11:6: "But without faith it is impossible to please him...." The Word of God places tremendous importance upon our faith.

Paul was the apostle of faith.

Peter, the apostle of hope, says in I Peter 1:3, while praising the Lord, "Blessed be the God and Father of our Lord Jesus Christ, which according to his abundant mercy hath begotten us again unto a lively hope...."

Peter's two epistles set forth the hope of a Christian. Thank God for hope! Thank God this morning, like Paul wrote to the Thessalonians, "...that ye sorrow not, even as others which have no hope." The Christian has hope which gives him peace in this world of chaos and trouble.

John is the apostle of love. Paul, the apostle of faith, emphasizes the tremendous importance of faith. Peter describes the glorious hope of a believer. John is the apostle of love. We see it in John 13 when Jesus is teaching the disciples the institution of the Lord's Supper. He is to go into the Garden of Gethsemane that night. He now sits at the table with His own. "Now there was leaning on Jesus' bosom one of his disciples, whom Jesus loved" (vs. 23). John is demonstrating love when he leans his head upon the shoulder of Jesus. If you don't have love, you are worthless. There is no substitute for love. God said in His Word, "And now abideth faith, hope, charity [love], these three; but the greatest of these is charity [love]."

What I am about to say may startle you. But most of you have never reached the place that God wants a Christian to reach in demonstration and exhibition of love. Most Christians live a selfish life, just the opposite of demonstrating the love described in the Word of God. Think about it. Observe Christians. Observe what goes on in churches. Then see whether or not you agree with me. God said love is the greatest thing in all the world.

John is the apostle of love. He is the one who wrote, "For God so loved the world...." He is the one who wrote, "Behold, what manner of love the Father hath bestowed upon us...." He is the one who wrote, "Herein is love, not that we loved God, but that he loved us, and sent his Son to be the propitiation for our sins."

Faith, hope and love embrace every phase of Christian character. All point to Christ. All determine the extent of our enjoyment of the Christian life. I will talk about the three this morning.

I. WHAT IS FAITH?

You say, "Faith is believing and trusting." It is more than that. Faith is a most common thing. You see faith demonstrated every day. When you see a man working for wages, that man is demonstrating faith. He has faith to believe that, when the weekend comes or the day of remuneration, he will be paid. A man working demonstrates faith.

When one buys a ticket on a train or bus or plane, he is demonstrating faith in that vehicle to transport him from where he is to his desired destination. You see faith demonstrated every day.

We see faith when a man reads a compass. He believes it points to the right direction, shows him the direction in which he must go. We see faith in everyday life.

Faith is the only vehicle God could use to make salvation available to all men. I will demonstrate.

Suppose God used the vehicle of money or material possessions to make salvation available to people. It is a ridiculous thought, for God does not do that. But if He did, some would be excluded. Some could not be saved if it had to be bought.

Suppose God used wisdom—that is, wisdom as the vehicle by which people came into possession of eternal life. If He did, the unwise could not be saved. Those who are mentally incapable could never know the Lord.

So we can see that God could never use any vehicle except faith.

Faith is one of the most common things in all the world. Listen to this. Lots of people from time to time say, "I don't know whether I'm saved or not!" People say, "I don't know how one can know he is saved." It comes right back to this basic and foundational principle of faith.

Faith involves at least three things.

1. It involves **knowledge**. Romans 10:17 reads, "So then faith cometh by hearing, and hearing by the word of God." Faith comes from a knowledge of the Word of God. That doesn't mean you have to know all the Bible. It means faith comes by hearing, and hearing by the Word of God. A person cannot have saving, keeping, living faith apart from the Word of God. That is why no one can be saved apart from the truth of the Word of God. Faith involves knowledge.

2. Faith involves **confidence**. There must be some sort of confidence in someone or something. I will illustrate.

Some came to Jesus who wanted to be healed. Jesus told them, "If you believe...." They replied, 'Lord, we believe that You are able to heal us.' These had heart-confidence.

The other day I was reading about the days of the great and godly king, Hezekiah. An ungodly, wretched, miserable, heathen king from Assyria, Sennacherib, mocked God's people, mocked every virtue of Christianity. He sent word to the people of God and Hezekiah, and he asked this question in Isaiah 36:4, "What confidence is this wherein thou trustest." In other words, "In what do you put your trust? What is your confidence? If you trust other nations, we've already defeated them. If you trust in God, we've already seen many nations with their gods defeated. In what do you put your confidence and your trust?"

Hezekiah, as you read on, said, "We trust in the Lord our God" (vs. 7). Hezekiah said, 'He is different from gods of stone, wood and silver. He is a living God.'

Faith involves knowledge, then confidence.

I read a story which is very often quoted by reliable people. Some scientists discovered a particular plant over the edge of a cliff. They wanted to get it and examine it, but someone must go over this cliff and secure that plant. So they asked a little boy, "Son, if we put a rope around you and let you down over the cliff, will you get that plant for us?"

The little fellow said, "Sure, on one condition."

"What is it?"

"On the condition that my father holds the rope."

Faith is knowing that God holds the rope, and at the other end is not human resources but a living God.

Faith involves confidence.

3. Faith involves **committal**. Turn to John 2:24: "But Jesus did not commit himself unto them, because he knew all men." Now look at John 3:16: "For God so loved the world, that he gave his only begotten Son, that whosoever believeth in him should not perish, but have everlasting life." The word *commit* in John

2:24 and the word *believe* in John 3:16 are the same in the original language of the Bible. Jesus did not commit Himself unto them because He knew all men, knew their fickleness. In John 3:16 we read that whosoever committeth himself unto God is going to be saved.

When Dr. John Paton went to the New Hebrides, there was no Bible translated in the native language. He set out to translate the entire Bible, starting with the New Testament, with the Gospel of John. Ninety-nine times in the Gospel of John a synonym of faith is used—that is, the word *believe, believed* or *believing*. Dr. Paton said, "If I am to reach these people and get them out of darkness and heathenism and superstition, into faith in Jesus Christ, I must know the right word." Though he prayed and prayed, yet he could not find the right word.

One day he was sitting in a chair with his feet on the floor when a native of the New Hebrides came in. They exchanged greetings. In his language this native said, "I see you are sitting in the chair."

A thought gripped Dr. Paton's mind. He leaned back, put his feet upon the rung of the chair so that his body touched nothing but the chair, then said to the native, "Now what am I doing?"

The native, in his language, said, "You have lifted yourself from every other support and committed your weight to the chair."

Dr. Paton struck his hands together and said, "Thank the Lord! That's what I want. I lifted myself from every other means of support and committed my weight unto this object."

That leads me to say that many are not really saved who profess to be because they still believe in their good works; they still hold on and are praying through.

Faith is putting the weight of your soul's salvation upon Jesus Christ. Faith leans upon no other support but God and His unchanging Word.

I am not calling the matter of being saved a "committal" but am saying that faith commits the matter of being saved and forgiven to the sole responsibility of Jesus. Faith is not in Jesus—plus something else; faith is in Him alone.

II. WHAT DOES FAITH INVOLVE?

Faith involves every faculty that one possesses.

When Isaiah 45:22 says, "Look unto me, and be ye saved, all the ends of the earth...," that involves the eyes.

When the Lord says in John 6:37, "All that the Father giveth me shall come to me; and him that cometh to me I will in no wise cast out," that involves the feet.

When God invites us in Revelation 22:17 to "take the water of life freely," that involves the hands.

When the psalmist says in 34:8, "O taste and see that the Lord is good," that involves the lips.

When Isaiah 39:5 says, "Hear ye the word of the Lord," that involves man's ears.

When God says in Joshua 24:15, "Choose you this day whom ye will serve," that involves man's will.

When God commanded in Psalm 37:3, "Trust in the Lord," that involves man's heart to trust in God.

"Be still and know that I am God" (Ps. 46:10) involves man's mind to trust in God.

Faith involves every faculty of the human being in order to believe and trust God.

"And now abideth faith, hope, charity [love], *these three; but the greatest of these is charity* [love].*"*

III. HOW DOES FAITH COME?

You ask, "Preacher, if that is faith, how does faith come about? How can I know and have that faith?"

Go back to Romans 10:17: "So then faith cometh by hearing,

and hearing by the word of God." Faith comes by listening, by hearing the Word of God.

Dwight L. Moody gave a tremendous illustration of this.

One time on a train he was praying for the support of his ministries in Chicago—praying for faith: "O Lord, increase my faith. O Lord, make my faith living and powerful, to lay hold on all that I need." Then this verse came to his mind: "... faith cometh by hearing, and hearing by the word of God." He stopped praying, opened his Bible and began to read. He thought, *If faith comes by the Word of God, then I must read it in order to have my faith strengthened.*

Faith is based upon the Bible.

A wonderful verse is John 3:33: "He that hath received his testimony hath set to his seal that God is true." A person hears the Word of God, sets his own human seal to it, then says, "That Bible is true. Faith in Jesus makes me a child of God."

Faith comes by the Word of God, by listening to God's Word.

Its value is determined by its object. This is not difficult. The things of God are to be put out simply. Nothing grieves me more than for somebody, who thinks he is a scholar or profound, to get up and try to be what he really is not. There are very few scholars in the world.

Faith is a simple thing. It comes from listening to the Word of God. Listen! The value of your faith is determined by its object. I will illustrate.

Here are two men who want to go into business. They both have a lot of money and want to invest that money. One looks at a business opportunity and believes with all of his heart that business is sound and valid and that, by the investment of his money, it will be a sound business investment. He believes in that enterprise and has faith in it to the extent that he is going to put his money in it.

The other, who has the same experience, the same reaction, sees a different business. He believes it is a sound investment, so he puts his money in it.

One invests his fortune and finds that this business is not good and loses all his money. This one invests, and he finds it is good and makes much more money.

What is the problem? This first man had as much faith as this second one. The first man's faith resulted in nothing. This second fellow's faith got good results. What is the difference? The object of their faith. It is not their faith, but the object of their faith!

My friend, faith is only as valuable as the object of faith. The object of a Christian's faith is the Word of God and the Lord Jesus Christ.

Thank God, the object of our faith measures up! Our faith is capable of endless development. Our faith can just grow and grow, says II Peter 3:18: "But grow in grace, and in the knowledge of our Lord and Saviour Jesus Christ." Grow in it.

I wonder if your faith is stronger today than it was a year ago. How is your faith getting along? How is your faith doing? How is your faith growing?

IV. WHAT DOES FAITH DO?

First, what is faith? How does it come? What does it do?

Faith makes all things possible, we read in Mark 9:23: "...all things are possible to him that believeth." Did you know that by faith a Christian can literally tap the resources of Heaven? John 14:13,14 promises, "And whatsoever ye shall ask in my name, that will I do, that the Father may be glorified in the Son. If ye shall ask any thing in my name, I will do it."

I am afraid that, to many Christians, God is not real. Think about the people you know. Think about the people of your church. Do they live, act and pray as if God were real?

FAITH ABIDING

Lady Sommerset faced this problem: "Lord, I believe and I'm saved, but I want to know that God is real!" One day it seemed that a still, small voice silently spoke to her heart, saying, "My child, act as if I were real, and you shall know that I am."

God must be real to a child of God. And faith makes God real. It links us with omnipotence. Faith says, "I can do all things through Christ which strengtheneth me." "...this is the victory that overcometh the world, even our faith."

The three Hebrew children lived down in Babylon. They lived in the world, but they were not of the world. One day Nebuchadnezzar the king told them, "We are going to put you in this fiery furnace unless you denounce the name of God."

The three answered, "Our God whom we serve is able to deliver us from the burning fiery furnace. But if not, be it known unto thee, O king, we will not serve thy gods, nor worship the golden image." They were not going to denounce their faith in their God, their hope, their trust. "We believe God is able."

So the three Hebrews were put in the fiery furnace while God up in Heaven was looking down. God must have said, "Amen! Praise God for Shadrach, Meshach and Abednego!" The Lord said, 'I believe I'll just go down and get in there with them.' They had heated it "seven times more than it was wont to be heated...and cast them into the burning fiery furnace." It burned, "slew" those men that threw them in. Forgive me, but I like that! It burned them up!

After awhile they thought, *They ought to be well done. Let's see how the cooking goes.* When the furnace door was opened, they saw, not three, but four men walking in the midst of the fire unharmed. The only thing burned was the bindings put on them. Not a hair of their head was singed. "How many did we throw in there?"

"Three."

"How many are now in there?"

"Four."

"You're crazy! You can't see straight. Somebody else count them."

"One, two, three, four—there's four!"

"You're nuts, too. Let me count them! One, two, three, four. Yes, you're right. Who's the fourth One? How'd He get in there?"

The Bible says, "...the form of the fourth is like the Son of God."

Nebuchadnezzar now knew "no other God can deliver after this sort." Then he promoted Shadrach, Meshach and Abednego in the province of Babylon.

In order to find out sometimes what something is, we need to know what it is not. There are three great contrasts with faith set forth in the Bible: faith in feeling, faith in works and faith in sight.

1. **Faith or feelings.** Many think they are saved only when they feel saved. Some of you sitting here are thinking right now, *I know I'm saved because I feel saved.*

Dr. McKay Hall was noted for his happiness, his radiant countenance. Dr. Hall was a joyful Christian. One day a lady said to him, "Dr. Hall, do you always feel saved?"

He answered her, "Why, my dear lady, I never feel saved."

"What? That sounds hypocritical. You look so happy, yet you never feel saved?"

"I am supremely happy, not because I feel saved but because I know I'm saved! Feeling has nothing to do with it."

I know a lot of you would say what a lot of others say: "Preacher, I believe you ought to feel saved." Yes, and someday you will feel lost. Faith is not feeling.

The Bible gives a demonstration of this. Blind Isaac had two boys. Esau was hairy, while Jacob was smooth and cunning. Jacob wanted the birthright, so he deceived his brother, who was easily deceived and didn't want it anyway.

Esau was a great and cunning hunter. Jacob pretended he was Esau. He put some goatskins on his arms and got his mother, who loved him, to cook some venison. He brought it, with the goatskins on his arms, and gave it to his old blind father, Isaac, who loved Esau. Jacob said, "I'm Esau." Isaac thought the voice sounded like Jacob's voice, so he said to Jacob, "Let me feel of you." So Isaac felt his arms and the goat hair, then said, "Yes, that's Esau." Blind Isaac should have gone by what he had heard, not by what he felt.

If you are to have securing in the Lord and peace of heart, it will be by what you hear, not what you feel. The search for feeling has sent thousands to Hell. There is great contrast between faith and feeling.

2. **Faith or works.** How many people have said to me since I have been in the ministry, "Preacher, you know we're all working for the same place." No, we're not! I am not working—pardon the ungrammatical expression—for nowhere, for anywhere. I am working because I am going there. "Not by works of righteousness which we have done, but according to his mercy he saved us, by the washing of regeneration, and renewing of the Holy Ghost" (Titus 3:5). Faith in works. Make the distinction: faith or feeling, faith or works.

3. **Faith or sight.** Declares II Corinthians 5:7, "(For we walk by faith, not by sight...)." People say, "If I can see it, I'll believe it." Some say, "I'm not going to believe anything I can't understand." You say, "I won't accept anything that I can't understand."

Let me tell you what to do. You come after the service and explain these lights to me. You say, "Preacher, that's electricity!" I know it, but what is electricity? Something that runs through a little wire as big as a pencil lead that lights up this whole room? Explain it to me! The fellow that knows how to do it does not even understand it.

You go home and listen to your radio. We can hear a man in California talking! I can hear him just as plain as if he were sitting here in my room. Explain it! Is there anybody here who can explain how you can sit in your room and listen to somebody in California? Explain how this is done by radio. You do not understand it. Some people say, "If I can't understand it, if I can't rationalize it, I'm not going to believe it."

I do not understand automobiles. If I get in and start it and it does not fire up, I get out and look for another one. The most hypocritical thing I could ever do is to go around in front of my car and lift up the hood. Good night! That is the most jumbled up mess I have ever seen! I do not understand the workings of a car, but I drove over here this morning in one.

Listen! You are never going to understand faith. It is a belief based upon the knowledge and confidence in the sweet Word of God. We do not walk by sight; we walk by faith.

You say, "Preacher, I want to see where I'm going." Faith has to do with the unseen, not the seen. The Bible makes this very clear in II Corinthians 4:18: "...we look not at the things which are seen, but at the things which are not seen; for the things which are seen are temporal; but the things which are not seen are eternal."

I have never understood how a brown cow could eat green grass and give white milk from which we get yellow butter. But pass me the butter and let me enjoy it whether I understand it or not.

Faith has to do with eternal things, and eternal things cannot be seen with the physical eye. They must be seen with the eye of faith.

Moses demonstrated a faith that sees the unseen—Hebrews 11:27: "By faith he forsook Egypt, not fearing the wrath of the king: for he endured, as seeing him who is invisible." By faith he saw the invisible God, forsook Egypt and started for the promised land.

Make a clear distinction between faith and feeling, faith and works, and faith and sight.

"And now abideth faith, hope, charity [love], *these three; but the greatest of these is charity* [love]."

Chapter VIII

Faith for Slaying Giants

(Preached in Emmanuel Baptist Church on January 27, 1980)

READ: Deuteronomy 1:19-46

"Yet in this thing ye did not believe the Lord your God."—Deut. 1:32.

I would far more enjoy talking about the grapes of Canaan than the giants of Canaan. The grapes speak of the wonderful fruit of the pleasant land, while the giants speak of the ferocious foes of that land.

Before we can enjoy the spiritual fruits, we must fight our spiritual foes. The giants of the land frightened away many of God's people from the grapes of the land. We will deal more in this message with the lack of faith than with faith itself.

God said, "In this thing ye did not believe."

Some of our old songs have made Canaan a picture of Heaven, but that is not true. There was war in Canaan, but there is no war in Heaven. There were giants to be killed in Canaan, but there is no death nor killing in Heaven. There was failure and sin in Canaan, but there will be no sin in the land that is fairer than day.

Joshua in the Old Testament corresponds with the book of Ephesians in the New Testament. Canaan speaks of the possessions of a Christian here and now in Christ. Evil giants would keep us from laying hold of our great blessings in Christ. These giants must be slain, but they cannot be slain with doubt and unbelief; they must be conquered by faith in God and His immutable promises.

Such faith was by no means demonstrated by God's people. "Yea, they despised the pleasant land, they believed not his word" (Ps. 106:24). Caleb and Joshua believed that the giants could be slain: "for we are well able to overcome it." Forty years later they marched triumphantly in. All the rest twenty years of age and older died in the wilderness because of their lack of faith.

I move on to the giants of unbelief.

These twelve spies were sent out into the land. The majority report was, "It is a land like God said. The cities are well walled; it is a great land flowing with milk and honey. But there are giants in the land. The people are 'greater and taller than we.' " When these spies saw the giants, the giants of unbelief, they turned back and were punished for forty years.

I must say, there still stands many a giant to keep the child of God from possessing all the spiritual blessing of victory that he should have. Who are these giants? We will look at seven of them.

I. A GIANT OF DIFFICULTY

"This does not look easy," was the report. "The villages are walled and fortified. The people are of a vast multitude."

When God said long before to Abraham, "I will give you this land of Canaan," He said, "There are already seven nations in the land, but I am going to give it to you anyway. You shall drive them out and fear not the face of man, for no one can stand before you."

When these men saw the giants in the land, they said, "We be not able to go up against the people; for they are stronger than we."

Genesis 18:14: "Is any thing too hard for the Lord?" The occasion for that question was when the angel of God appeared to

Abraham—Abraham is one hundred years old; Sarah, ninety—and announced, "Sarah thy wife shall have a son through whom the whole world will be blessed."

Here is a man one hundred years of age and a woman ninety; yet God is saying, "I will still make My promise good." An angel of God asks, "Is any thing too hard for the Lord?"

Many a Christian expects the Christian life to be easy when it is not. It is beautiful, it is happy, it is glorious, it is victorious; but there are giants in the land.

Many times I have read chapter 17 of the book of Matthew. It records when our Lord, Peter, James and John went on the Mount of Transfiguration. When they came down, they saw a multitude gathered around a distraught father with a demon-possessed boy wallowing in the gravel and foaming at the mouth. The father turned to Jesus and said, "I brought him to thy disciples, but they could not cure him."

Jesus spoke to the young man, restored him to health and gave him to his father.

Here is what I am saying. The disciples then asked Jesus, "Why could not we cast him out?" Jesus answered, "If ye have faith as a grain of mustard seed, ye shall say unto this mountain, Remove hence to yonder place; and it shall remove; and nothing shall be impossible unto you." Then He said, "Howbeit this kind goeth not out but by prayer and fasting." Jesus was telling them, "This kind is hard, and it takes fasting and praying to get the demon out, but you could have gotten him out."

There is never a difficulty that God cannot overcome. We say it to our students, but we ought to say it also to our churches: Christians are quitters! They quit when it takes the power of God. They quit when a miracle is needed.

Sure there are giants in the land. No one has ever said it is easy to be a good Christian. It is not easy to build a Christian home and family. It is not easy to live a separated life and win souls. It is not easy to build a soul-winning church family with a world vision. It is not easy to stand for something. There are giants of difficulty who must be overcome. It was not easy for Joshua and Caleb, but they knew that what God ordered, He would empower them to do.

There is no mountain God cannot remove, no river God cannot cross. No giant of difficulty stands between us and our blessings in Christ that cannot be overcome by faith.

"Yet in this thing ye did not believe the Lord your God."

II. THE GIANT OF DOUBT

Satan is the master of skepticism. He works on the mind of a Christian to get him to doubt. If he can, he will have him doubt about his salvation. But the Word of God takes care of that. "Verily, verily, I say unto you, He that heareth my word, and believeth on him that sent me, hath everlasting life, and shall not come into condemnation, but is passed from death unto life."

When the Devil comes to you and says, "How do you know you are saved? Look what thoughts are in your mind, what things are in your heart. Look how you have failed, how weak you are," quote him the Word of God which says, if one has Christ, he has life—life forevermore. The Lord gave us the first epistle of John to dispel any doubts about our salvation, especially I John 5:13: "These things have I written unto you that believe on the name of the Son of God; that ye may know that ye have eternal life, and that ye may believe on the name of the Son of God."

There will always be times of doubt. When I was first saved, I thought I needed to feel saved all the time. It was a tremendous problem for me. It was a wonderful day in my life when I could say that I knew I was a Christian, not because of feeling, even though I do feel it, but because the Bible told me so.

FAITH FOR SLAYING GIANTS

I feel sorry for those people who never feel anything. I think of a fellow in a play. Someone was to fire a blank gun, and he was to say, "I'm shot." He did, but the director said, "No good. You have to say, 'I'm shot!' with a lot of emotion!"

One day they put some ketchup in the bullet and fired it. It hit him. When the ketchup oozed down his coat, he said, "My Lord, I'm shot!" The director said, "That is exactly the way we want it said."

I don't depend on feeling to make me know I'm a Christian, but I do feel something. Don't you? I feel like I'm a child of the King. I feel like I'm riding in the chariots of the King. I feel like the royal blood of the Son of God flows in my veins. I know that I am saved because the blessed Word of God tells me that I am.

Oh, but when you get into this land, this land of spiritual plenty, you will find the giants of doubt.

Perhaps Satan's great device is that of deception. He causes millions of unsaved people to think they are saved. He also deceives many who are saved into doubting their salvation.

Paul described the condition of the unsaved when he described the blinded condition of his own people, the Jews:

"For I bear them record that they have a zeal of God, but not according to knowledge. For they being ignorant of God's righteousness, and going about to establish their own righteousness, have not submitted themselves unto the righteousness of God."—Rom. 10:2,3.

Many lost people think they are saved. Satan has made some saved people fear they are lost. Anytime someone has asked me, "How do you know you are saved?" my answer has been, "Because the Bible says I am." God's Word says I "shall never thirst" (John 4:14); "shall never perish" (John 10:28); "shall never die" (John 11:26); that He will "never leave [me], nor forsake [me]"

(Heb. 13:5), and that I "shall never fall" (II Pet. 1:10). What more do we need!

God's Word is David's sword that slew the giant of unbelief. We need no other resting place for the security of our souls than God's own Word, which is settled in Heaven and as immutable as God Himself.

III. THE GIANT OF DEPRESSION

Hundreds, maybe thousands, of Christians have said to me since I have been in the Lord's work, "Preacher, I just feel depressed." How many have asked me, "Brother Tom, do you ever get down? Do you ever feel depressed?"

Oh, yes—and I take great comfort in the fact that some of the greatest men of God have gone through the same experience. If I were to ask you, "How many here have had a time when you felt that you were in the valley or in the storm, when you were overcome with melancholy, when you were despondent and depressed and you needed to be lifted up?" every one of you would lift your hand. Why? In this spiritual land a giant of depression stands before the child of God to keep him from having what God wants him to have.

I fell in love with Elijah a long time ago. One reason was that he was so great in his life and in his Homegoing. He went to Heaven without dying.

But one day Elijah did a strange thing. He ran into the woods, lay down under a juniper tree and had a nervous breakdown. He came apart at the seams. He said, "I might as well die. I have had it! It's enough. I don't want any more."

For three and a half years, during the drought, he stood like a giant for God. Then Jezebel sent him this message: "So let the gods do to me, and more also, if I make not thy life as the life of one of them [the prophets Elijah had slain with the sword] by

FAITH FOR SLAYING GIANTS

to morrow about this time" (I Kings 19:2). "I am going to cut off your head before tomorrow night."

Elijah ran into the woods, got down under a juniper tree and literally requested to die. Why? Because the giant of depression had set in. Jezebel had said, "Oh, you mighty man of God, I am going to get you down"—and she did.

Here is a beautiful thing. In I Kings 19:5 we read that, when he sat under that juniper tree, "behold, then an angel touched him, and said unto him, Arise and eat."

How would you like to be awakened by an angel? This angel came and awakened Elijah. He looked and saw food to eat and water to drink. He ate and drank and went back to sleep. Verse 7 says an angel came and awoke him the second time and said, "Arise and eat; because the journey is too great for thee." God gave him strength to go on for forty days and nights.

When a Christian is depressed, God is able to dispatch an angel to say, "Wake up. Get up and go. I will give you strength."

God is the answer to depression. There is always this giant in this spiritual land.

As pilgrims in this barren wilderness world, your journey and mine is "too great for us." We need the help of God to stay on top of the circumstances of life. The same Devil who brought Elijah to a place of discouragement can bring you to the same place.

Depression or discouragement is a great enemy of the soul. When we are depressed, we are defeated. Great visions of service and holy burning aspirations for godliness suffer at the hands of depression. Depression is often the fear of failure. Victory over depression comes from faith in God and His blessed Word.

I was recently reading and meditating on Isaiah 43:2:

"When thou passest through the waters, I will be with thee; and through the rivers, they shall not overflow thee: when thou walkest through the fire, thou shalt not be burned; neither shall the flame kindle upon thee."

The Lord promised, "I will be with thee." Through raging rivers and scorching flames, He is always near.

Praise and faith will overcome depression. Thank Him for His blessings and believe His precious promises; then depression will give way to peace and confidence.

IV. THE GIANT OF DELAY

Many a soul is lost because of procrastination. Many a Christian loses the blessings because he delays.

Just this afternoon a preacher from another state called me at my home. He said that a young man, twenty some years of age, had been called of God. "He has fifteen thousand dollars at his disposal to go to school. His parents want to be sure that he goes to a state school with great accreditation and great recognition. But this young man said, 'God has called me to be a preacher. I want to go to Midwestern Baptist College.'"

The preacher told him that he had already delayed his decision a week. He also told him that sometimes delay was the Devil's tool.

What that preacher told him is right. If God has put it on your heart to do something for Jesus, then do it now because the giant of delay is dangerous. In Hebrews 3:7,8 we read:

"Wherefore (as the Holy Ghost saith, To day if ye will hear his voice, Harden not your hearts, as in the provocation, in the day of temptation in the wilderness....)"

God was saying, "This day listen to Me, not to the giant of delay."

How many souls have been lost because of delay! Jesus must have had this in mind when He spoke the words of John 4:35: "Say not ye, There are yet four months, and then cometh harvest? behold, I say unto you, Lift up your eyes, and look on the fields; for they are white already to harvest."

Procrastination is not only the thief of time; it is also the thief of souls. How often have I had Christians say they waited too late to win their loved ones. How many blessings and opportunities for service have been lost because of the giant of delay.

Someone has written these solemn words:

> The clock of life is wound but once,
> And no man has the power
> To tell just when the hands will stop,
> At late or early hour.
>
> To lose one's wealth is sad indeed,
> To lose one's health is more.
> To lose one's soul is such a loss
> That no man can restore.

"Yet in this thing ye did not believe the Lord your God."

V. GIANT OF DELUSION

I need to spend some time on this giant. Lots of people are living in an unreal world. I know what the Bible says:

"While we look not at the things which are seen, but at the things which are not seen: for the things which are seen are temporal; but the things which are not seen are eternal."—II Cor. 4:18.

I am not talking about the unseen world in which a Christian lives victoriously but about a Christian that just does not see things as they are. They are like the blind man at Bethsaida. When the Lord came, He put His fingers to his lips and laid them upon his eyes. Jesus asked him, "Do you see?" The man said, "I see men as trees, walking." Now, men don't look like trees. Trees don't walk. The Lord knew that He was not through with him, so He touched him again and made him look up. He then said he saw every man clearly.

Many Christians need a touch from God to see life as it really is. Life is real. Many a person has encountered the giant of delusion. They see life out of focus, but life is real. Here is this giant of delusion.

Don't ever be afraid because giants are nine feet tall. We have a God who reaches from earth to Heaven and fills the universe, and that God says, "Dread not, neither be afraid of them" (Deut. 1:29).

Moses "endured as seeing him who is invisible" (Heb. 11:27). However, he saw the real and visible things of this world also. He saw the cruelty and ungodliness of men and their disregard for the souls of men. He saw things as they were. He saw life as it really is. He saw no Utopia on this earth but saw men as they really were. He was no dreamer who sat and waited for things to change. He learned that faith in the blood of the Lamb was the only hope.

Sin is real. Broken hearts are real. Hell is real. May God give us faith to see things as they are, faith to believe that lives can be changed by the power of God.

VI. GIANT OF DEFEAT

Now notice: If you do not have faith to look at the grapes of Canaan, you will be tempted to look at the giants of Anakim. And the results of this misappropriation of your vision lead to what happened in Numbers 13. Why, these people said, "We were like grasshoppers in their sight." They got a grasshopper complex. I don't want to be cocky, egotistical or arrogant. God does not use those who are conceited about themselves. But neither does God mean for us to be grasshoppers, which in the Bible are called many times locusts. We read of them in Exodus 10:15: "For they covered the face of the whole earth, so that the land was darkened." That means there were so many millions of them that they blotted out the sun in Egypt. They came between the earth and sun until darkness covered the land.

That says to me that this grasshopper complex can come between you and the S-O-N of God if you do not see yourself as

FAITH FOR SLAYING GIANTS 123

you really are. Proverbs says, "The locusts have no king" (30:27). They acknowledge no leadership; they are grasshoppers. They do not know their way through the dark. I don't want that. I want to be able to walk by night, with a light of the fire in Heaven.

Oh, this grasshopper complex! I have heard people say all sorts of stupid things from the pulpit. I am a good judge of that because I have heard so many stupid things from my own lips. I have heard people say, "Now, folks, don't look at me. I am nothing." I am not going to say that.

A fellow said one time, "I wish I had a sheet so I could stand behind it and the people could not see me but just hear my voice." Now that was silly. He didn't want to stand behind a bed sheet. If he had wanted to, he could have brought one from home.

Folks go around with this false humility: "I am nothing but a worm." I'm not a worm! That is not spirituality. Nothing makes me any sicker than false humility: "Oh, I'm nothing." You are a child of the King! That is something. You are washed in the blood. That is something. Your body is the temple of the Holy Ghost. That is something. You are a citizen of the land of Glory. That is something.

A young man came into my office, and he looked at the floor the whole time. I could relate to him because I was that way. I went to Bob Jones College in 1935 when it was in Cleveland, Tennessee. I thought, "I can't look people in the face. I'm not even fit to talk to people." There were eight people at the dining table at the college. A host was at one end and a hostess at the other. They sat me at the corner of a table. A young lady came to deliver the food. She stubbed her toe. A bowl of hot gravy landed on the side of my head, and that hot gravy was running down everywhere. Here is this country boy from down in Alabama, who never looked up one time. They were busy taking the napkins and wiping the gravy off me, but I never looked up once. That was my life.

Listen! May God deliver us from looking at the ground. "I will lift up mine eyes unto the hills, from whence cometh my help" (Ps. 121:1). You and I are somebody.

Back to this young man who came to my office, who just kept looking at the floor. I said, "Son, look up, look me in the face and speak out so you can be heard. You are as good as anybody on this earth." I am no better than the next person, but I am somebody. So are you. Don't ever get that grasshopper complex. It is a spiritual problem, I mean a real spiritual problem. It is not humility, not virtue; it is a problem.

I mentioned Elijah a moment ago, who said, "Lord, I am the only one." He got a persecution complex.

A lot of preachers have one. Some preachers look behind every bush thinking nine communists are about to jump out. They are all the time putting up straw men and knocking them down. I don't want that. My God is going to take me up and out, and I'll be sitting on high during the Tribulation, and I'm coming back with Him riding a white horse and putting the Devil in his place.

God said to Elijah when he had said, "I, even I only, am left," "Yet I have left me seven thousand in Israel, all the knees which have not bowed unto Baal."

There were seven thousand, yet Elijah thought he was the only one. A grasshopper complex. Things are not seen in their right image when you get this way. If you do not see yourself as somebody, in the Lord, no one else is going to see you that way. If you don't have a good self-concept, self-esteem, then no one else will see it in you. They'll see you as a grasshopper. And you will not see other people as you ought to.

Folks criticize other Christians because they have a grasshopper complex: "He is taller than I," or, "She is prettier than I," or, "She has a nicer car than I can afford"—a grasshopper complex. God says, "What difference does it make when you have a mighty God?"

I was reading about the time the Lord had arisen from the grave and Simon Peter met the disciples at the Sea of Galilee. Jesus came there. He said to Simon Peter:

"When thou wast young, thou girdedst thyself, and walkedst whither thou wouldest: but when thou shalt be old, thou shalt stretch forth thy hands, and another shall gird thee, and carry thee whither thou wouldest not."—John 21:18.

Then the Bible says, "This spake he, signifying by what death he [Peter] should glorify God."

Peter listens to the Lord; then he says, with John standing by him, "Lord, and what shall this man do?"—'What about John?'

Simon Peter did not have the right image of himself. When Pentecost came, he did have the right image and could say, "I am somebody! Even the Lord prophesied about the way I will die." But he looked over at somebody else and asked, 'Well, what about John?' Jesus said, "What is that to thee? follow thou me."

You are not a grasshopper; you are somebody. An ineffective Christian has a grasshopper complex. It will render you totally useless in the work of God.

I am not criticizing Elijah because James said that he was a "man of like passions as we are"—same human nature, same temptations. Finally the Lord said to Elijah when he got down in the mouth, "Anoint someone else to be prophet because you are going Home." God does not take this grasshopper business too kindly. An ineffective Christian can no longer be used.

We must have faith to overcome the giant of defeat.

VII. THE GIANT OF DEFICIENCY

God said:

"Behold, I have set the land before you: go in and possess the land which the Lord sware unto your fathers, Abraham, Isaac,

and Jacob, to give unto them and to their seed after them."—Deut. 1:8.

God said, "There it is—go get it." If you read this account in Deuteronomy 1 and the account in Numbers 13, you come up with this conclusion: God showed them the land from Kadesh-barnea and said, "There it is. It is yours. I gave it to your fathers and to you. There it is—go get it." But they said, "We had better go and search it out first." So the Lord said, "All right, go search it out." It was the permissive will of God to send the spies but not His directive will. As a result, they wandered forty years in the wilderness, and hundreds of thousands died. God was displeased. He had said, "There it is. It is for you. I have told you what it would be like. Go get it."

God is to be believed.

I think of a man in Russia. It is said that years ago he was persecuted and was being tried because of his faith in Jesus Christ.

They asked, "Do you believe the Bible?"

He replied, "Every word of it."

"Do you believe Mark chapter 16?"

He answered, "I do."

"Do you believe the part where it is said that, if you drink any poison, it will not harm you?"

"God said it, and I believe it," was his answer.

He was given a bottle.

He turned it up and drank it. A few minutes later, when he was supposed to be dead, the doctor came and examined his pulse, his blood pressure, shook his head and said, "This man is perfectly normal."

Here is a man who actually believed God! God said that, if you drink any deadly poison, it will not harm you. Now don't you go around drinking poison! There is a good deal more to be said about this. God closed the mouth of lions for Daniel. And Hebrews

FAITH FOR SLAYING GIANTS

11 said some people even stopped the mouths of lions. Believe God, whether you can see the results or not, whether circumstances seem to substantiate it or not. The God who is enough wants us just to believe Him.

God is to be reckoned with. Deuteronomy 1:42 says, "Go not up, neither fight; for I am not among you." You had better reckon with God. God always honors His Word. "God is not a man, that he should lie; neither the son of man, that he should repent: hath he said, and shall he not do it? or hath he spoken, and shall he not make it good?" (Num. 23:19). God is not a man to lie, but what He has spoken, He will make good. God is enough.

"Yet in this thing ye did not believe the Lord your God."—Deut. 1:32.

Chapter IX

A Faith That Wins

"...there is no restraint to the Lord to save by many or by few."—I Sam. 14:6.

This text has a most unusual and wonderful setting. I suggest you read I Samuel 14:1-15.

Saul had been chosen and anointed as the first king over Israel. These were perilous times in Israel because the Philistines had completely overthrown and defeated these chosen people of God. We read this astounding thing in the previous chapter: The people of Israel had no means of sharpening their weapons of war.

"Now there was no smith found throughout all the land of Israel: for the Philistines said, Lest the Hebrews make them swords or spears: But all the Israelites went down to the Philistines, to sharpen every man his share, and his coulter, and his axe, and his mattock."—I Sam. 13:19,20.

Since there was no blacksmith in Israel, the only way they could get a weapon sharpened was when they became friendly with a Philistine who had the means of sharpening instruments.

King Saul, with a pitiful army of 600 men, had retired to a far-off place. He was completely out of contact with the Philistines and had no plan of battle. God's chosen nation was in total disarray. It was truly a dark day in the kingdom, and the people had no hope.

Jonathan, the king's son, was not of those who had no hope. He evidently believed that, if one had a strong faith in God, there was always hope of victory. Jonathan and his armorbearer were a long ways away from Saul's pitiful army, and these two were alone.

Jonathan, with a divine impulse from the Lord, said to his armorbearer, "There is no restraint to the Lord to save by many or by few." He said to his companion, 'Follow me. We are going down to the garrison of the Philistines. It may be that the Lord will work for us in overcoming these enemies of God, the Philistines.' Jonathan did not say that they would put out a fleece, as Gideon did; but he did determine that they would "discover" themselves to the enemy, then wait upon God to see what happened. He knew that, when the Philistines saw them, they would either threaten them to come on down to them or dare them to come up to them and to battle.

I mention this because I want you to see that Jonathan did not plan all the details himself. He gave God room to work. He had faith to trust God for victory, no matter how the battle was ordered. He was willing to let the enemy make his move; then he and his armorbearer would wait upon God. He knew he was outnumbered many times over, but he believed that with God there was no hindrance to win by many or by few.

What we are seeing here is one of the greatest demonstrations of faith to be found in the Bible. Jonathan is not mentioned by name in the great faith chapter, Hebrews 11. However, I do believe that he at least was on the mind of God when the great faith chapter was written. Notice the words of Hebrews 11:34 about those who "...escaped the edge of the sword, out of weakness were made strong, waxed valiant in fight, turned to flight the armies of the aliens"—an accurate description of what happened to Jonathan and his companion. They escaped the edge of the sword, they were brave in the day of battle, they put the Philistines to flight.

Jonathan believed God could "work for him" regardless of the extreme circumstance.

I believe there is a divine principle set forth in the Bible to the effect that God delights to do a great work with few people. That doesn't mean that He doesn't want many to be saved, but God often does a tremendous work with only a few to work with. It is true that many times in the Bible God did a great work with few workers. This was certainly true in the case of Gideon, whom God used to overcome the great host of the Midianites.

"And the Lord said unto Gideon, The people that are with thee are too many for me to give the Midianites into their hands, lest Israel vaunt themselves against me, saying, Mine own hand hath saved me. Now therefore go to, proclaim in the ears of the people, saying, Whosoever is fearful and afraid, let him return and depart early from mount Gilead. And there returned of the people twenty and two thousand; and there remained ten thousand. And the Lord said unto Gideon, The people are yet too many; bring them down unto the water, and I will try them for thee there: and it shall be, that of whom I say unto thee, This shall go with thee, the same shall go with thee; and of whomsoever I say unto thee, This shall not go with thee, the same shall not go."—Judges 7:2-4.

Notice in verse 2 and again in verse 4 that God Himself uses the expression "too many." When Gideon issued the call for soldiers, 32,000 responded. God said "too many." Gideon made an announcement: "Whosoever is fearful and afraid, let him return" home. Twenty-two thousand soldiers said, "Well, 'fearful and afraid' describes my case. I am going home."

Now Gideon had 10,000 soldiers. And can you believe it! God said "too many." The Lord told Gideon to take the 10,000 down to the water to drink. Nine thousand seven hundred got down on their knees and leisurely drank of the water. Three hundred were so anxious to get on with the war that they threw the water into their mouths with their hands and kept on going. God said to Gideon, "Here's your army, these 300 men."

Had I been Gideon and had God said "too many" one more time, I would have said, "God is trying to disband this army, and I'll help Him. I too will go home."

God did not say "too many" this time, but I am sure a lot of people said "too few." God wanted to teach Gideon that "there is no restraint to the Lord to save by many or by few."

If, as we sometimes say, "one plus God is a majority," then two plus God is a landslide! God said to Gideon that He wanted a small army, "lest Israel vaunt themselves against me, saying, Mine own hand hath saved me."

Surely something happened in Jonathan's heart. He had a divine impulse to do something unselfish for God and His cause, and he knew it would take faith to get it done.

The outcome of the battle was thrilling. Jonathan and his companion slew many Philistines. The Bible says that the "first" slaughter was about twenty men. We do not know how many there were after that. The earth quaked and trembled, and the Philistines started killing each other. God won a great victory because He had a man who had a faith that wins. It may have been that Jonathan knew of Deuteronomy 32:30, "How should one chase a thousand, and two put ten thousand to flight, except their Rock had sold them, and the Lord had shut them up?"

It may have been that 10,000 Philistines were overcome because Jonathan believed that, if he was on "the Rock," two could put 10,000 to flight. Jonathan was not as interested in the rocks of I Samuel 14:4—Bozez and Seneh—as he was interested in the Rock of Ages. Jonathan might have heard of the promise of God in

Joshua 23:10, "One man of you shall chase a thousand: for the Lord your God, he it is that fighteth for you, as he hath promised you."

No man could do what Jonathan did without believing in and standing on the promises of God. He had great reason to believe that "there is no restraint to the Lord to save by many or by few."

I. WHERE FAITH IS FOUND, GOD'S STRENGTH IS DISPLAYED

"Thy shoes shall be iron and brass; and as thy days, so shall thy strength be."—Deut. 33:25.

What a wonderful promise: ". . . as thy days, so shall thy strength be"! God has promised us strength for every day. He will not give tomorrow's strength today, but He will give us strength for today. It matters not what the day may bring forth, God has promised strength for it. One ring of the telephone or one letter in the mail or one knock on the door may call for God's strength. Where faith is found, God's strength is found. "He giveth power to the faint; and to them that have no might he increaseth strength" (Isa. 40:29). The whole 40th chapter is on the certainty of God's eternal Word and the availability of His strong and mighty arm.

He "increaseth strength" to equal your need of strength. He who measured the oceans in His hand and spread the heavens with a gesture of His hand and weighed the dust of the earth in a balance—it is He who has promised power to the faint.

Recently I was very tired in a long preaching journey across several states. I thought I didn't have strength to travel another mile or carry a briefcase another step; then I thought of the promise of God: ". . . to them that have no might he increaseth strength." I not only went on, but I enjoyed the journey because He gave power to the faint and He increased my strength to meet the demand.

Where faith is found, God's strength is displayed.

"Fear thou not; for I am with thee: be not dismayed; for I am thy God: I will strengthen thee; yea, I will help thee; yea, I will uphold thee with the right hand of my righteousness."—Isa. 41:10.

Five times in this wonderful promise God uses the personal pronoun "I" in reference to Himself:

"I am with thee";

"I am thy God";

"I will strengthen thee";

"I will help thee";

"I will uphold thee with the right hand of my righteousness."

Though this promise is directed to Israel, it is for every child of God. It is a great reservoir of strength upon which we can draw. Faith is the instrument to make all His strength and power available. God is always ready to display this strength and power whenever He finds one with faith to believe that He is ready and willing.

Jonathan had that kind of faith, the faith that wins.

"There is no restraint to the Lord to save by many or by few."

II. FAITH NULLIFIES CIRCUMSTANCES

The Israelites were hid in caves and in the dens of the woods. The pitiful little army of Saul gave no comfort. The cowardice of Saul and his reluctance to engage the enemy lent no support for their weakness and fear. They were greatly outnumbered, and they had no sharp weapons and virtually no leader, for Saul was in hiding.

Jonathan rose to the occasion with faith to believe that God could overcome circumstances. It looked as though Jonathan literally laughed in the face of circumstances. His faith was contagious, for his armorbearer said unto him, "Do all that is in thy heart: turn thee; behold, I am with thee according to thy heart" (I Sam. 14:7).

Circumstances do not dictate the course of a Christian with faith in God. Circumstances usually dictate a certain course of action for one who knows nothing of the miracle-working power of God.

The prevailing circumstances said to Jonathan and his companion, "Go join your companions in defeat and in hiding. The enemy is too great for you." Jonathan's faith led him to believe that God could use him to win the battle, to believe that "there was no restraint to the Lord to save by many or by few."

Almost fifty years ago I read of a dear old saint of God who had great need in her life. Her food supply was very scarce, and each day she prayed for her need to be met.

One day she felt impressed to pray that God would send her a hen egg for her breakfast. Satan seemed to say to her, "But you have no chickens, and there is not a hen in your neighborhood. Besides, you have no money." However, she prayed. She trusted God and expected the next morning to receive a hen egg. Believe it or not, when she arose she heard a cackle and looked up. At the top of the attic stairs stood a hen in her house! She climbed up the stairs and found on an old rug a beautiful white hen egg.

This dear praying saint never questioned how that hen got in her house, but she thanked the Lord for supplying her an egg, for which she had prayed. He had always supplied her needs, and she knew He always would.

That kind of faith gets not only the attention of God but changes and nullifies the prevailing circumstances.

No Christian need get too concerned with circumstances. I am not a pessimist; but if I were, the circumstances of this age would be most discouraging. Whatever sin or crime some religious person commits, it is all laid to the charge of fundamentalists. If some cultist or false religionist falls into sin—"That's fundamentalism for you."

This world is no friend of grace; and from the human standpoint, the circumstances have never been worse. The truly born-again, blood-washed, Spirit-indwelt child of God is laughed at and taunted in many circles today. That doesn't bother me. I am laughing all the way to Heaven! Victory is ours through our Lord Jesus Christ!

"There is no restraint to the Lord to save by many or by few."

III. FAITH BUILDS UPON DIVINE PROMISES

I have mentioned before that Jonathan probably knew some truth of the Word of God, such as, "One shall chase a thousand, and two shall put ten thousand to flight." I do know that faith builds upon the promises of the Word of God. "So then faith cometh by hearing, and hearing by the word of God" (Rom. 10:17).

The Word of God is the only sure foundation for faith. Peter said to the Lord, "...at thy word I will let down the net" (Luke 5:5). The Word of the Lord gave Peter faith to let down his fishing net in places where he had fished all night without success.

The centurion whose servant was sick said to the Lord, "...speak the word only, and my servant shall be healed" (Matt. 8:8). The faith of the centurion to believe that his servant would be healed was founded upon the Word of the Lord. All faith rests upon the truth and promises of God. All thoughts and planning, all schemes and human devisings, are as dirt compared to the Word of God. The psalmist tells us, "It is better to trust in the Lord than to put confidence in man" (118:8).

Faith built on the Word of God is often illustrated in the Bible. "By faith Noah, being warned of God of things not seen as yet, moved with fear, prepared an ark to the saving of his house; by the which he condemned the world, and became heir of the righteousness which is by faith" (Heb. 11:7).

Notice the expression in this verse, "...being warned of God." God spoke to him. He heard God's words, and what he did and believed about the impending Flood of judgment was based upon the Word of God. Noah's faith was founded in the Word of God. He had never before seen rain, but what did that matter? He had the Word of God for it.

People sometimes say, "Seeing is believing"; but with God, hearing is believing. We believe a message because it came from God. Faith finds its nesting place and foundation upon the Word of God.

"There is no restraint to the Lord to save by many or by few."

IV. FAITH IS NOT FOOLISHNESS

Many times foolish plans, which later do not work out, have at first been called an adventure of faith. Faith is daring and venturesome, but it is never foolish. Jonathan left room for God to lead and direct even after he was impressed to go against the Philistine garrison. He was not arrogant, not self-willed as to how it was to work out. He was not presumptuous nor demanding. Jonathan just firmly believed that God could give him the victory, though all odds were against him. His faith might have looked foolish to the Philistines, but they soon changed their minds. Faith is not foolishness.

I heard years ago of a church which was in a great building fund drive. People were pledging what they would give toward the new building. A man about sixty pledged $10,000. When asked how he was going to pay the amount, he replied, "I will give $2.00 a week until the $10,000 is paid." The building fund committee quickly concluded that it would take him ninety-six years to pay his pledge. The man would have been in Heaven long before that. And likely the building would not be there that long. His pledge was not faith but foolishness.

Faith is always confined to the Word and wisdom of God.

A man said to me years ago, "I will never wash my car again

because I strongly believe the Lord is coming any day." His was not a faith built upon the Word of God. The Bible tells us that we cannot know the date of His coming but that we are to be ready in every sense of the word. It would have been a better testimony to the Lord and to the world to have a clean car while waiting for the Lord to come.

There were no car washes in those days; and the truth was, he was too lazy to wash his own car. His attitude toward life was not one of faith but of foolishness.

If anything about our faith violates one single word of God's revelation, then it ceases to be faith. Faith is never foolishness because it is wise and prudent to trust God to do something that His Word says He will do.

"There is no restraint to the Lord to save by many or by few."

V. FAITH CONFERS NOT WITH FLESH AND BLOOD

We read in I Samuel 14:1, "But he told not his father." Why? Jonathan knew his father would try to talk him out of it. Saul was not of mind and heart to engage the Philistines at this time. Jonathan was a grown man and great soldier. He was not disobedient to his father Saul, but he felt he was not obligated to discuss this divine impulse from God with any counselor.

Jonathan conferred not with flesh and blood. He asked no one if it were wise to trust God and exercise faith in His Word. He gave direction to his armorbearer but asked no direction from him.

Faith waits upon God, and faith walks with God. When God's directions are clear, the directions of men seem insignificant. Faith depends not upon flesh and blood for direction. Men might either try to talk one out of a venture of faith or suggest a better, more logical and reasonable way of accomplishing the venture.

"But when it pleased God, who separated me from my mother's womb, and called me by his grace, To reveal his Son in me, that

I might preach him among the heathen; immediately I conferred not with flesh and blood."—Gal. 1:15,16.

When Paul knew that the Lord had saved him and called him, he didn't need to ask one soul if this was a good idea. He had faith to believe that having heard the voice of God was all the assurance he needed. He had good counsel from Barnabas and others, but not about his call. This rested purely upon the Word of God which spoke to his soul.

Forty-six years ago when Mrs. Malone said, "Let's go home some other way," it determined where Emmanuel Baptist Church would be started. We had prayed for days for God's leadership. As we left the drive-in restaurant where we had eaten, sitting in the car, we had spent our last penny. As we started back to our apartment, she said, "Let's go home some other way."

We went another way and saw a "For Sale" sign on a deserted tavern building. We stopped, looked and prayed. In less than an hour I signed an agreement to buy.

Thousands have been saved here and have taken the Gospel all over the world. There is $20 million in land and buildings and a Bible college, where hundreds of preachers and missionaries have been trained who now labor for Christ all over America and many parts of the globe.

Faith needs no conference with flesh and blood when God has clearly made known His plans.

"There is no restraint to the Lord to save by many or by few."

Chapter X

The Measure of Your Faith

(Preached in the Emmanuel Baptist Church, Wednesday evening, January 18, 1967)

READ: Romans 12:1-21

"For I say, through the grace given unto me, to every man that is among you, not to think of himself more highly than he ought to think; but to think soberly, according as God hath dealt to every man the measure of faith."—Rom. 12:3.

Literally scores of verses in the Bible deal with the Christian's faith. This text came to mind which has in it this expression: "...the measure of faith."

Tonight I will take the holy Book of God and ask you to use it as a rule to measure your faith, to see what kind of faith you have, to see how strong your faith is, to see where your faith is and to see how much your faith means to you.

It's unbelievable how much emphasis God puts in His Word on the faith of His people. For instance, in the great love chapter, in I Corinthians 13:13, God says, "And now abideth faith, hope, charity, these three; but the greatest of these is charity." God is saying here that the three greatest things in the life of a Christian are faith, hope and love. Your faith, your hope, your love are most essential.

God keeps on in His Word, both in the Old and New Testaments, putting emphasis on the faith of a Christian.

When I was a young Christian, one day I read where Jesus was talking to Simon Peter. I was so arrested, so gripped with what Jesus said to him: "Peter, Satan hath desired to have you, that he may sift you as wheat."

Now Peter was saved—as saved as he ever will be; yet Jesus said to him in Luke 22:31,32:

"Simon, Simon, behold, Satan hath desired to have you, that he may sift you as wheat: But I have prayed for thee, that thy faith fail not...."

Jesus is talking to a Christian: "I have prayed for you that your faith may not waver, may not fail; that your faith may be strong." Jesus thought faith important enough that He made it a matter of prayer for one of His children.

So many wonderful things Jesus said about faith. In Mark 11:22 one day He said, "Have faith in God." Oh, what a challenge these four words are in this old world of uncertainty, turmoil and compromise.

One time He asked His disciples a question. I'll ask the same of you tonight: "Where is your faith?" (Luke 8:25). When it seemed they didn't know what trust meant, didn't know what reliance meant and didn't seem to know how to lay hold on the precious promises of God and bring the things of God into reality, He asked them, "Where is your faith?"

In Matthew, chapter 9, two blind men said to Jesus, "Thou son of David, have mercy on us." In other words, "We want You to do something for us." Jesus asked, 'What would you have Me do?' They answered, 'Open our eyes that we may see.' This involves a miracle. It will take the power of God. No human being can do it. But they knew Jesus could: "We want You to open our eyes, to give us back our eyesight." What did Jesus say to them? These plain, simple, wonderful words: "According to your faith be it unto you." Jesus was saying, "Whatever your faith demands, whatever your faith claims, whatever your faith wants, whatever your faith lays hold of, that is what I will do for you." They believed He could open their eyes, and He did.

You will never be any stronger Christian than your faith will let you be. Your faith is tremendously important.

One day His disciples made a great request of Jesus. Jesus saw a man with his son and the disciples standing around. Here was the father in consternation. Defeat was evident, everywhere. The father said to Jesus, "I brought him [my demon-possessed son] to thy disciples, and they could not cure him," could not cast out the demons. When Jesus rebuked the Devil and cast the demon out of him, the disciples said to Him, "Why could not we cast him out?" Notice the answer Jesus gave: "Because of your unbelief: for verily I say unto you, If ye have faith as a grain of mustard seed...nothing shall be impossible unto you."

On another occasion the disciples requested of Jesus, "Increase our faith" (Luke 17:5).

WHAT FAITH DOES

Charles Haddon Spurgeon said, "Little faith will bring your soul to Heaven. Great faith will bring Heaven to your soul." That's what I'm talking about tonight, about a faith that claims and makes the things of God a living reality in our lives. That's the kind of faith the Bible describes.

I was so interested to see in the Bible what faith does for us that I made a list of seven things.

1. Faith Justifies

Romans 5:1 promises, "Therefore being justified by faith, we have peace with God through our Lord Jesus Christ." Justification before God means to be declared righteous and holy in His sight, as clean as if we had never sinned. And God's holy Book says that only comes about by faith. "Therefore being justified by faith, we have peace with God...."

2. Faith Guides the Christian's Life

Faith guides the Christian. You don't know what you're doing nor where you are going until you learn to trust and walk with God. Paul said, "For we walk by faith, not by sight" (II Cor. 5:7).

Have you students, have you housewives, have you business people, have you Christian workers, have you schoolteachers learned to walk by faith? Not by sight, not by touch, not by feel, but by trust?

3. Faith Protects

When Paul described in Ephesians chapter 6 the armor of a Christian, he started at the head and wound up at the feet; then he urged, "Above all, [take] the shield of faith, wherewith ye shall be able to quench all the fiery darts of the wicked."

You may not think your faith is important. You may think you can drift along and not give any thought to it, put any emphasis on it; but if you want to bring Heaven into your soul, you must have the kind of faith the Bible describes.

4. Faith Pleases God

Paul, in Hebrews 11:6, tells us who are saved, "But without faith it is impossible to please him...." This is talking to a believer, a Christian. Without faith, trust, complete reliance or abandonment to God, it is impossible to please Him.

5. Faith Overcomes

On and on and on in the Bible we read what faith does. First John 5:4: "...this is the victory that overcometh the world, even our faith." To overcome the world, to be a victorious Christian, one must have this kind of Bible faith I am talking about tonight.

6. We Live and Are Kept by Faith

A verse dealing with faith is found three times in the Bible, in Habakkuk, in Romans, in Galatians—one of the great classic verses to be found on the subject in all the Word of God: "The just shall live by faith." Not only does faith save, but faith in Christ gives the believer his eternal security, because faith brings God's righteousness upon us.

7. Faith Works

Galatians 5:6 tells us that "faith...worketh by love." Those who have a strong faith in God know how to get things done in the service of the Lord.

THREE DIFFERENT KINDS OF FAITH

Thinking about this the other day while reading in the book of Matthew, I was amazed to find how the first New Testament book is literally filled with teaching from the lips of Jesus Himself on the subject of faith. Three different kinds of faith are described in this book.

1. People With Great Faith

Jesus said there were people who had "great faith." Then He spoke of those who had "no faith." Then He spoke of people with "little faith."

In two instances Jesus spoke of people with great faith. One is in Matthew 8:10: "Verily I say unto you, I have not found so great faith, no, not in Israel."

Here's a man, a Roman, an outsider, you might say, since he was not a Jew, not one of the elect, not one of the chosen ones at the time. One day he comes to Jesus. He has heard of the miracles. He has listened to Jesus teach. This Roman said to Jesus, "Lord, my servant lieth at home sick of the palsy, grievously tormented." When Jesus said, "I will come and heal him," this man said to Jesus, "Lord, I am not worthy that thou shouldest come under my roof: but speak the word only, and my servant shall be healed."

Those words meant something to Jesus—'Jesus, at *Your word* I believe. Whatever You say will surely come to pass. Just say the word, and my servant shall be made whole.' Then it was that Jesus answered him, "I have not found so great faith, no, not in Israel." And the Bible says that "servant was healed in the self-same hour."

Measure your faith tonight. Is it a great faith? Or is it a little faith? Or could it be no faith? The "measure of your faith," says Paul.

Jesus spoke of a great faith again. It is also in Matthew, chapter 15, verse 28. Jesus said to a woman, "O woman, great is thy faith...."

This is a Syrophenician woman. Neither is she one of the elect. She is not a Jew, not one of the chosen ones. She comes to Jesus about a very important matter to any mother: "My daughter is grievously vexed with a devil." She is telling Jesus that her precious daughter is lost and needs help.

Many things were against this woman's faith, against all she wanted.

First, she was a Gentile. Until then the Gospel had not gone officially to any but the Jews. Second, when she spoke to Jesus, "he answered her not a word."

That's all it takes to shake the faith of many a Christian. Just pray about a thing a time or two, and if you don't get an immediate answer, you give up the ship and quit praying. I've seen it happen in this church many times.

Though Jesus answered her not a word, yet she kept on believing.

Then the disciples came to Jesus, asking Him to send her away. They wanted to get rid of her, but her faith overcame.

Her faith overcame the silence of Jesus and the opposition of the disciples. She kept trusting.

Finally Jesus said, "It's not meet to take the children's bread, and cast it to dogs." ("Children" are the Jews. "Dogs" are a symbol of the Gentiles.) When Jesus said to the begging Syrophenician, 'It is not meet to take what belongs to the Jew and give it to a Gentile,' she just kept on believing. Even what Jesus said could not discourage her faith. All she said was, "Truth, Lord: yet the dogs eat of the crumbs which fall from their masters' table."

This time Jesus looked at her and declared, "O woman, GREAT IS THY FAITH: be it unto thee even as thou wilt. And her daughter was made whole from that very hour."

While I'm preaching, some of you need to have God work a miracle in your life. Some of you have wrestled with the opposition of the Devil in your mind, body and spirit. Tonight by faith you could have victory over it. "Great faith."

2. Some People Have No Faith

Then Jesus spoke to the people, and He said unto them, in Mark 4:40, "Why are ye so fearful? how is it that ye have no faith?"

There are three accounts of this incident given in the Gospels. In Matthew 8:26 Jesus said, "O ye of little faith." In Luke 8:25 He asked the disciples, "Where is your faith?" However, in Mark 4:40 it is recorded that Jesus asked them, "Why are ye so fearful? how is it that ye have no faith?"

Remember that Jesus is speaking to His disciples, saved men. When He uses the expression, "no faith," He is not saying they did not have faith to be saved but is relating their faith to the problem at hand. The problem was the stormy Sea of Galilee which threatened their lives. He had put them in that boat. He had said, 'We are going to the other side.' Jesus is in that boat with them! Could the sea drown the One who created it? And would He destroy His own? He is saying to them, "Have ye no faith?" that is, faith to believe that He can take care of them in this storm.

It doesn't take much faith to sail the calm seas of life, but it takes a lot of faith to sail through the dark storms of life.

3. Some People Have Little Faith

But I move on in order to go over with you these five things. Five times Jesus said, not to lost people but to saved people, active people in the service of the Lord, "O ye of little faith." And each time He said these words, the Scripture will show that He spoke it to overcome a certain problem these Christians faced.

He spoke to overcome CARE. In Matthew 6:30 Jesus said, "Wherefore, if God so clothe the grass of the field, which to day is, and to morrow is cast into the oven, shall he not much more clothe you, O ye of little faith?"

Jesus is here speaking to His disciples. He gives them two great illustrations.

First, He talks about something mighty hard for a Christian to get settled:

"Lay not up for yourselves treasures upon earth, where moth and rust doth corrupt, and where thieves break through and steal: But lay up for yourselves treasures in heaven, where neither moth nor rust doth corrupt, and where thieves do not break through nor steal: For where your treasure is, there will your heart be also."—Matt. 6:19,20.

He continued to talk, saying, "Consider the lilies of the field, how they grow; they toil not, neither do they spin...even Solomon in all his glory was not arrayed [clothed] like one of these."

Then Jesus said, "Behold the fowls of the air: for they sow not,

THE MEASURE OF YOUR FAITH

neither do they reap, nor gather into barns; yet your heavenly Father feedeth them.''

And using these illustrations, Jesus said, 'If God can take care of these, shall He not much more take care of us, O YE OF LITTLE FAITH?'

Some, I'm afraid, do not believe God is big enough to take care of them. A God who can dress up a flower in many beautiful colors, feed a little bird that's not eternal like you and me, can take care of His own children. If the believer has the faith to claim it, God can meet any of his needs.

As a freshman in college, I went to school on just the prayers of a good mother. No money, no backing, no promises, no jobs—nothing! Everything that I owned I could have held in my two hands.

When I got to school, I began looking for a promise. I read, I wept, I prayed, I looked to God and told Him I wanted a promise that would help me get an education, help me get training for the ministry. The Lord laid on my heart Philippians 4:19, "But my God shall supply all your need according to his riches in glory by Christ Jesus." I underscored that in my Bible, and not a day went by that I did not turn to Philippians 4:19 and read, "My God shall supply all your need according to his riches in glory by Christ Jesus."

I still had trouble about money to pay tuition and money to take care of other needs. Many a time I wouldn't know where my next clean shirt was coming from. Then one roommate would say, "Here, wear mine. It'll just about fit you." Sometimes it would choke my neck, while another offered by another would be three inches too big! But the Lord always met my need.

One day while reading Philippians 4:19, I learned something I'd never seen before. This is a prison epistle, and Paul is writing to a group of Christians, "Your care of me hath flourished again";

then he said to them again, "No church communicated with me...but ye only." After complimenting these Christians for giving to the Gospel and sending out the Word, he said to them, "But my God shall supply all your need according to his riches in glory by Christ Jesus."

To whom is that promise addressed? Not to just any Christian. It is given to Christians who shoot straight with God.

If you love God, then don't quote Philippians 4:19 and think God won't supply your need. When I saw that, I went down in the poor slums of Cleveland, Tennessee, and found little children with no shoes, no clothes on their backs, and hungry. I went back to the dormitory, called the boys together, took an offering and went back to the slums to buy food and clothes for little children.

I can say to you, since God made that promise a reality in my life, I've seen Him work miracles to take care of the needs of my own life.

"My God shall supply all your need."

The same thing is taught in Matthew 6 where Jesus said, in verse 30, "O ye of little faith." He said in verse 33, "But seek ye first the kingdom of God, and his righteousness; and all *these things* ..."—what things? Something to eat, something to wear, a car to ride in, a house to live in—"all *these things* shall be added unto you."

God does not owe to us to meet our need if we cheat and rob Him of that which belongs to Him. I say it kindly, tenderly: If you want God to give to you, if you want these promises fulfilled, then you must meet God's requirement. You must put God first. You must seek first the kingdom of God. When a Christian shoots straight with God in this, he can plan on God's meeting his needs.

People have said to me, "I couldn't tithe, Preacher; you don't know how far in debt I am."

THE MEASURE OF YOUR FAITH

The best way in the world to get out of debt is to start shooting straight with God.

I've had people tell me, "Well, I can't live on what I've got now; so how could I live if I gave God a tenth?" You could do it because God would get involved. He would put His hand on you and bless you.

O ye of little faith! If God can clothe the lilies of the field and feed the birds that never lay up in store for themselves, then be sure God will take care of you.

I read a wonderful story of Hudson Taylor, father and founder of the China Inland Mission. In 1875 he got on a train somewhere in England and headed back to London. A fine looking gentleman came along and asked him, "May I ride with you?"

Hudson Taylor, the missionary, said, "I'm riding third class. Maybe you are not that poor."

The gentleman said, "My ticket will allow me to ride anywhere on the train that I wish."

Then the missionary said, "I would be glad to have you sit with me."

This fine gentleman sat with Hudson Taylor. He said, "I've been listening to you speak and hearing you tell about the needs of the mission work in China and the teeming millions who are lost and need the Gospel. Mr. Taylor, I'm going to give you a little gift to help meet those needs."

The stranger handed him a bill. Hudson Taylor looked and saw it was a 50-pound English note. Amazed, he said, "Sir, I'm wondering if you made a mistake. Did you think that perhaps you had given me 5 pounds? This is a 50-pound note, a very large sum." This was in 1875, and Hudson Taylor said, "Perhaps you didn't mean to give me that."

This gentleman replied, "To be perfectly honest with you, I can't take it back, but I did think I was giving you a 5-pound note rather than a 50-pound note."

Hudson Taylor said, "Don't be embarrassed. Take it back and give me the 5 pounds. Do take it back."

The gentleman said, "God must have meant it that way."

Hudson Taylor then took it.

Hours later, when he arrived at London, Hudson Taylor went straight from the train to the offices of the China Inland Mission. When he walked in, a little band of Christians were down on their knees praying, "Lord, You know how to meet the needs of the missionaries on the field. You know we need 49 pounds more and so many shillings—nearly 50 pounds. God, send it to us."

Hudson Taylor interrupted: "Here it is, dear Christians," and laid what had been given him on the table.

Happy is the church, blessed is the church, where God puts the members where they have to pray to see their needs met. Happy is the Christian who learns that God takes care of His own.

Jesus spoke to overcome our cares, "O ye of little faith!"

He spoke to overcome FEAR. In Matthew 8:26 He saith unto them, "Why are ye fearful, O ye of little faith? Then he arose, and rebuked the winds and the sea...."

You already know this beautiful story. Jesus, on the little boat, on the little tempestuous Sea of Galilee, fell asleep. His body was subject to fatigue like ours. A storm came, and the disciples awakened Jesus and said, "Lord, save us: we perish." He arose, rebuked the wind and the sea and said to them, "O ye of little faith." In other words He is saying, "You don't need to be afraid." Why? Because of the presence of Christ. How can a boat sink with Jesus on it? How can a ship go down with the One asleep on its deck who made the sea and sent the storm? To overcome their fears, He said, "Why are ye fearful, O ye of little faith?" A gentle rebuke. He isn't condemning them but trying to help them by saying, "You need not be afraid."

Oh, the fears that some of the Lord's people wrestle with, when the answer is believing God!

THE MEASURE OF YOUR FAITH

I read a story of a native woman on a mission field who was won to the Lord by the missionary. One day the little girl of that native Christian, that former heathen, took deathly sick. Neighbors and others that gathered said, "What that little baby needs is an ice pack." This was a tropical land, hot weather, no modern conveniences and no such thing as ice anywhere around. The native Christian said to the missionary, "I'll pray for God to give me some ice. If my baby needs ice, that's what I'll ask for."

Even the missionary lady said, "Listen! This is tropical country, with no refrigerators. God won't give ice here."

The native new Christian said, "If that's what it takes for my little baby to get well, that's what God will do. I'm going to pray He will send some ice to my home in the next few moments and save my little baby."

A woman saved out of heathenism and with faith in a mighty God dropped on her knees and from her weeping soul cried, "My God, You are big enough to send ice to a hot tropical country."

In a moment the thunder began to roll, the lightning flashed, and the rain began to fall. Hail half as big as your fist fell all over the yard. When the storm subsided somewhat, she went out and picked it up by the handful and said to the astounded missionary, "See what my God can do!"

Yes, He can send ice to a hot country. Listen! God can do what needs to be done anytime, anyplace, anywhere!

What are your fears? Isaiah 41:10 is one of those scores of great promises telling us that God wants to alleviate the fears of His own:

"Fear thou not; for I am with thee"—that ought to be enough. Just knowing the Lord is with us ought to keep us from being afraid—*"be not dismayed; for I am thy God: I will strengthen thee; yea, I will help thee; yea, I will uphold thee with the right hand of my righteousness."*

Oh, if we could see the picture tonight! God upholds every one of us with the right hand of His power. What are your fears? Commit them to God, O ye of little faith!

He spoke to overcome DOUBTS. The first time to overcome cares; the second, to overcome fears; the third time, to overcome doubts. Matthew 14:31:

"And immediately Jesus stretched forth his hand, and caught him, and said unto him, O thou of little faith, wherefore didst thou doubt?"—Matt. 14:31.

I love this man Simon Peter who is involved with Jesus here. This is another instance when Jesus put them in the boat—a sweet, beautiful story and a great symbolical picture, too. While they were in the boat on the sea, Jesus was alone on the mountaintop. (That's the way it is tonight. You are in the midst of this world; Jesus is on the mountaintop.) He was on the mountain praying for them. The storm came; and in the midst of the storm, the fourth watch of the night, the darkest hour of all the night, Jesus had His disciples on His heart. About three o'clock in the morning, as they looked out across the tempestuous waves, heard the whistling wind and felt the tossing of the boat, they saw the form of Someone coming across the water. Simon Peter stood out on the edge of the vessel and said, "Lord, if it be thou, bid me come unto thee on the water." Jesus said, "Come."

You know, John could have walked on the water had he wanted to get to Jesus badly enough. Thomas could have, James could have, Bartholomew could have. None of them wanted to, but Simon Peter did, and said, 'Jesus, if it's You, just tell me to come to You. No matter if there is a storm, a tempestuous sea, high waves, high winds; if it's You, tell me to come.' Jesus said, 'Come on, Peter.'

I love this! Peter jumped off that boat and became the only living man who ever walked on water. He has been criticized for backsliding and for failing the Lord more than anybody else, but

THE MEASURE OF YOUR FAITH

he was the only person who had faith to walk on water.

In the midst of it all, Peter took his eyes off Jesus—just what we do sometimes. Instead of looking at the Master, he looked at the situation. When he looked at the stormy waves, the high winds, the tempestuous sea, he started to go down. A simple little prayer saved him, though: "Lord, save me." Immediately Jesus got him by the hand and said, "O thou of little faith, wherefore didst thou doubt?" Jesus was saying, 'Peter, had you kept on believing, you and I would have walked back on this water and into the boat together. And down through the history of the world, no one would have ever said, "Peter's faith failed him in the midst of the storm." '

"O thou of little faith." The reason you and I don't get more from God is because of doubt and unbelief, the opposite of faith.

"O ye of little faith." We doubt. We doubt God's ability. We doubt God's power.

He spoke to overcome POOR REASONING. That's just exactly what the Scripture talks about in Matthew 16:8: "O ye of little faith, why reason ye among yourselves...?"

I'll not go into it, but Jesus had said to them, "Beware of the leaven of the Pharisees and of the Sadducees." They got it all mixed up, like we do sometimes when we don't know what the Lord is trying to tell us. They began to reason among themselves: 'When He said, "Beware of the leaven of the Pharisees," it must be He was saying we have come over here on this side of the sea and brought no bread and we are going to starve to death.'

Jesus, listening to that conversation, said:

"Do you not yet understand, neither remember the five loaves of the five thousand, and how many baskets ye took up? Neither the seven loaves of the four thousand, and how many baskets ye took up? How is it that ye do not understand that I spake it not to you concerning bread, that ye should beware of the leaven

of the Pharisees and of the Sadducees?"—Vss. 9-11.

They didn't understand because they didn't take God at His Word.

Oh, God help us tonight! God give us a faith just to believe God!

I think of the time when someone tried to make fun of a dear believer. It was like this.

"Do you believe God can do anything?"

"Yes, anything."

"Suppose God told you to jump through that brick wall."

The believer thought for a minute, blinked his eyes a time or two, then said, "Be my responsibility to jump and God's responsibility to open a hole in it."

That's the way a Christian should feel: "If I do what God tells me to do, it is up to God to take care of the rest."

Get your eyes open to behold and believe what God is saying!

Dwight L. Moody told a sweet story of three little girls at Christmastime. They were all looking in a window. The girl in the middle was blind. The two on either side were trying to describe a pretty little doll, little stuffed animals and pretty Christmas toys. One was saying, "Can't you see? Can't you see the little blue-eyed doll with blond curly hair, pink dress and white shoes? Can't you see?" The sightless one stood listening.

Dwight L. Moody had heard that story and in a meeting was telling it.

A man came to him afterwards weeping. He said, "Mr. Moody, I'm a newspaper reporter and the man who saw with my own eyes and heard with my own ears the conversation of two little girls trying to describe the beauty of Christmas to a little blind girl. And as I listened to you tell it tonight, I thought, *Oh, how blind I've been not to trust God, not to believe the promises, not to rest upon the Lord!* Mr. Moody, I've learned what faith is. I shall not try to reason it out for myself, but I shall believe God and His Word."

God, help us to believe! "O ye of little faith."

> **Oh, blissful lack of wisdom,**
> **'Tis blessed not to know;**
> **He holds me with His own right hand**
> **And will not let me go;**
> **And lulls my troubled soul to rest,**
> **In Him who loves me so.**
> **So on I go—not knowing,**
> **I would not if I might;**
> **I'd rather walk in the dark with God**
> **Than go alone in the light;**
> **I'd rather walk by faith with Him**
> **Than go alone by sight.**

"O ye of little faith, why reason ye among yourselves?"

He spoke to overcome CONCERN ABOUT OUR FUTURE. The fifth time the statement, "O ye of little faith," is recorded is in Luke 12:28:

"If then God so clothe the grass, which is to day in the field, and to morrow is cast into the oven; how much more will he clothe you, O ye of little faith?"

Jesus had just related the parable of the rich fool. This was the man who had everything he wanted except one thing—more barns and more bins to store more fruits and grain. He had all that this world could offer; still his heart was not happy.

The rich fool made the mistake that many make. He thought he could feed his soul on material things.

Jesus told how the rich fool died and went out to meet God unprepared. The real reason Jesus told the parable of the rich fool is given in Luke 12:13-15. A man came to Jesus concerned about an inheritance which was to be his. Jesus said to him: "Take heed, and beware of covetousness: for a man's life consisteth not in the abundance of the things which he possesseth." Then Jesus told the parable of the rich fool, who laid up all his treasures on earth, then died and left them and went to Hell. Jesus warned, "So is he that layeth up treasure for himself, and is not rich toward God."

No Christian should feel that he is losing out when he tithes his income, when he wins souls to Christ and when he lays up treasures in Heaven. God will take care of the Christian's future. The child of God should be more concerned about his treasures in Heaven than his barns on earth. The emphasis must be on the rewards yet to come rather than the things which he now possesses.

The psalmist knew the secret of happiness now and security for the future: "Trust in the Lord, and do good; so shalt thou dwell in the land, and verily thou shalt be fed" (Ps. 37:3).

May God give us faith to trust Him for all things and at all times.

"O ye of little faith, why reason ye among yourselves?"—Matt. 16:8.

Chapter XI

The Expansion of Faith

(Preached in Emmanuel Baptist Church on Sunday morning, March 23, 1975.)

READ: Luke 17:1-11

"And the apostles said unto the Lord, Increase our faith."—Luke 17:5.

I have chosen to call our message today "The Expansion of Faith." Our text says, "Increase [expand] our faith." Remember, these are saved people requesting this, people who already knew something about faith. Faith had brought these people into a vital, saving, redeeming contact with the Lord. These disciples are asking the Lord, "Increase our faith."

There are three great requests the disciples made of the Lord found in the Gospels. Once they came as He was praying and said, "Lord, teach us to pray, as John also taught his disciples" (Luke 11:1). They wanted to learn how to pray as the Lord Jesus prayed and as John prayed and his disciples.

They asked the Lord for another request on another occasion in Matthew 17. When Jesus and the three disciples came down from the mountaintop where the transfiguration had taken place, they saw a man with a bedeviled son who needed a miracle from God. The disciples, amazed as the son was miraculously cured, asked Jesus, "Why could not we cast him out?" In other words,

'Why did we not have the power?' They were requesting power from the Lord to do the work of God. Jesus said, "Howbeit this kind goeth not out but by prayer and fasting."

So they asked the Lord that they might learn to pray. They asked the Lord that they might have power. Now here in Luke they are asking for a third thing: 'Lord, increase our faith.'

One of the most profound questions one could ask is this: "What is faith?" The Bible gives a clear-cut definition of what many things are, but there is only one attempt to define *faith,* and that is found in Hebrews 11:1: "Now faith is the substance of things hoped for, the evidence of things not seen." Faith is the confidence or the substance of things hoped for.

I do not know if that is really always true or not, but faith deals with the unseen and the future. It certainly doesn't deal with the seen. When you see something, have something, it takes no faith to believe it. You believe it because of sight, not because of faith. You know the presence of something as it relates to you, and it takes no faith; you can walk by sight. But the future is another thing. No one knows but God.

Faith brings into substance that which is unseen and may be unreal at the moment. Faith is the confidence that the unreal and the unseen can be brought into substance, into reality.

There are many, many Bible examples of faith. In Hebrews 11 we find one after another of these tremendous examples.

When we think of faith as dealing with the unseen and with the future, we think of the faith of Noah. One day God said a very strange thing to Noah. Remember, it had never rained on the earth. The earth had been watered by a mist. Noah had never seen lightning, nor heard thunder, nor seen water come from the sky.

Then there came a day when God said, "The end of all flesh is come before me: for the earth is filled with violence through them; and, behold, I will destroy them with the earth" (Gen. 6:13).

THE EXPANSION OF FAITH

God said He would bring a flood of waters to destroy all flesh. It would rain forty days and forty nights. The water would be on the whole earth fifteen cubits deep, on all the earth under the canopy of Heaven.

This was something that dealt with the future. Something man had never seen was to take place in the future. Noah believed God that it would be as He said. His faith laid hold upon the unseen and upon the future.

When Noah went out to get in that ark, I doubt that he looked in the sky and wondered, *Is it really going to rain?* A hundred and twenty years he had believed God and worked in building a boat and waited for the promise to come to pass. I don't think he said to any of his family, "Have you heard any thunder? Have you seen any lightning? Have you seen any dark clouds?"

Here is a man whose faith laid hold upon the unseen and that which had not yet come to pass!

What is faith? "...the substance of things hoped for, the evidence of things not seen."

I. FAITH IS ALWAYS ON TRIAL

There is never a time when your faith is not on trial. I can well understand the disciples' saying to the Lord, "Increase our faith." The Lord had said some strange things here—that if a person offends another or injures another to the extent that it becomes to them a stumbling block over which they go into Hell, "It were better for him that a millstone were hanged about his neck, and he cast into the sea." This punishment seemed almost unreasonable.

If you have ever seen a millstone, like the Lord is speaking of here, you would not want one around your neck even on dry land, much less on water. They are as big as this pulpit and weigh hundreds and hundreds of pounds, maybe several tons. It was not an unheard-of punishment for someone to have one of these huge stones tied around his neck, taken out and cast into the sea—removed from the face of the earth forever.

When the Lord said that, He followed it with a very difficult thing: "Take heed to yourselves: If thy brother trespass against thee, rebuke him; and if he repent, forgive him. And if he trespass against thee seven times in a day, and seven times in a day turn again to thee, saying, I repent; thou shalt forgive him." In other words, He said to the disciples, "If someone trespass against thee and if he repents, forgive him." And, "If he trespass against thee seven times in a day...."

Let me use an illustration.

Suppose a person comes up and slaps you in the face. He comes back a bit later and says, "I'm sorry I did that. I want you to forgive me." You say, "Yes, I forgive you."

A little later here is another slap from the same person. A little later back he comes. "I'm awful sorry I hit you. Will you please forgive me?" It is a little more difficult this time, but you say, "Well, yes, I will."

In a few more days, here is a third slap, then a fourth slap, then a fifth slap, then a sixth slap. Now the Lord says, "Every time that happens, if that man repents, you are to forgive him."

Do you blame the disciples for saying, '...Lord, increase our faith'? I don't blame them one bit. Anybody in the world would have asked for the same thing—more faith.

You are in the presence of the Lord Jesus; you dare not tell Him what you think you would do in such a case. He has made it plain what your attitude is to be in this matter of forgiveness. Now the disciples ask the Lord, "Increase our faith." They needed power over themselves in such a predicament.

There are two great sins mentioned here: the sin of offense or injury or being a stumbling block, and the sin of overpiety. Do you know what the Lord is talking about when He says forgive these people when they do something and repent, do it again and repent, then they do it again and again? Listen! Not only one day does it happen, but the next day it starts all over again. The next morning—SLAP. Then he comes back and says, "Forgive me." A little while goes by, then—SLAP! This could go on forever and forever, until you had no face to slap!

The disciples said, 'Lord, increase our faith.' They needed faith to believe that whatever God said was true, that whatever God said was best, that whatever God said, we are to do. They prayed God would give them power over themselves so that they would have the right attitude toward others and not judge others wrongly. Overpiety is judging others in the wrong way, setting one's self over others.

I used to hear Dr. Bob Jones, Sr., say, "Overpiety is the most wicked sin in the world." I didn't know much about it then, and I used to think, *That surely is not true. A person overly pious— that is the worst sin he can commit?* But I believe it now. I do not know a more grievous sin than the sin of overpiety or piously judging the other fellow.

Styles change. Fashions change. Fashion is not necessarily wrong unless it is something that violates the principles of a Christian and the teaching of the Word of God.

I remember a few years ago when people wore—I think they were called—zoot suits. The trousers were pistol-legged. Man, you had to have your shoes off and your legs greased to get them on! I remember preachers preaching about pistol-legged trousers on men. The style changed. Now they wear what is called "flares." Preachers are now preaching that it is wicked for a Christian to wear "flares."

Do you know what that is called? Overpiety. Every time you find overpiety in a Christian, you find one not right with God. You find one who comes out at the seams somewhere else.

A young lady took me and my wife to task years ago. She said,

"You claim to be Christians, and the women at your church wear make-up." (You can overdo anything.) "I don't see how a Christian can wear make-up."

I said, "We do believe that the Bible speaks of being modest, and we try to adhere to that."

Not many days after that, we were trying to win a man to the Lord. This young lady and her husband got that person and said, "Don't believe what they say. They're not separated. They're worldly. They're not really saved." Certainly that ruined the possibility of leading a young man to Jesus Christ.

Some days later that same woman called me sobbing. "Preacher, my husband and I need your help. We have two children. We have lived together all these years, but we have never had a wedding. Preacher, can you tell us what to do?"

I said, "Yes, I can tell you what to do—get married." I went to their home and performed a marriage ceremony.

I could not get out of my mind that a few days before they were talking about a woman's make-up! That is judging, criticism, overpiety! And God hates it! He hates it as much as on that morning way back yonder when an archangel said, "I will be like God. I will lift up my throne above the stars of God." His name was Lucifer, and he is the Devil. He started out in overpiety.

No wonder these disciples said, 'Lord, increase our faith.'

Give me the fellow who isn't always boasting about what he is, what his stand is. I will trust him. First Corinthians 10:13 says, "Wherefore let him that thinketh he standeth take heed lest he fall."

"And the apostles said unto the Lord, Increase our faith." They needed power over themselves.

II. FAITH IS DEFENSE AGAINST THE DEVIL

There is another need for it. They wanted the Lord to increase their faith because they needed a defense against the Devil. And there is not another defense against him. You may think you may have one, but there is no other. Ephesians 6 describes the armor of a child of God. There is the helmet of salvation, the breastplate of righteousness, loins gird about with truth, the sword of the Spirit and prayer, and feet shod with the preparation of the Gospel of peace. Then it says, "Above all, taking the shield of faith, wherewith ye shall be able to quench all the fiery darts of the wicked [or wicked one]."

My friend, there is only one defense against the Devil, his subtlety, his wisdom, his schemes and his power, and that is faith to believe God. First John 4:4 reads, "...greater is he that is in you, than he that is in the world." I must have faith to believe that He that is within me—the Holy Spirit of God—is more powerful than he that is in the world—the Devil. The Devil is powerful, but God is all-powerful.

When I think of how we need a defense against the Devil, I think of Romans 8:31: "What shall we then say to these things? If God be for us, who can be against us?" No one, if we have faith as our defense.

There are many illustrations in the Bible. There is David and Goliath. Some think David killed the giant because he was accurate with the slingshot. That is not the reason. There is no human reasoning that could explain how a little shepherd boy could have killed a great big giant and made a fool out of him, a dead fool at that, like David did.

David came to the camp of the Israelites to bring a lunch to his brothers, some home cooking. He heard this big giant come down into the valley every day and challenge the people and say to the Israelites, "Send a man to fight with me!" No one would go. Many of them stood head and shoulders above David, including King Saul. David said, "Is there not a cause?" He said, "Isn't God on our side? I'll fight him."

Saul armed David with his armor. You couldn't find David in

that armor. David said, "I cannot go with these; for I have not proved them." So he took it all off and picked up five little stones and his slingshot. In his shepherd's garb, he runs toward the giant. As he runs, he swings and "smote the Philistine in his forehead," right between the eyes. Listen! Don't tell me that a man, running as fast as he can go, can put a slingshot around his head, turn loose a stone and hit a guy right between the eyes because he is such a good marksman. He is running at top speed, "hasted"; the giant is dressed in full armor. There is only a place or two that a stone would hurt anyway. There it goes, with faith guiding it. And faith brings it home! God's man wins!

We need faith for a defense against the fiery darts of the Wicked One.

When the Lord talked about what the Devil could do and his power was demonstrated in so many ways, the concerned disciples said, '...Lord, increase our faith.'

III. FAITH IS PLEASING GOD

The disciples knew that what pleased God more than anything was faith in the heart of a man or woman. They had seen it demonstrated. They had seen how the Lord's people had come to Him and He had said, "If you can believe, all things are possible."

One said to Him, "Lord, I believe; help thou mine unbelief"; and a miracle took place.

They remembered that a woman which had an issue of blood for twelve years, passed through a crowd and just touched the hem of His garment. Immediately a miracle took place. "The fountain of her blood was dried up...and she was healed." The Lord said, "...thy faith hath made thee whole..." (Mark 5:34).

The disciples knew that faith pleased the Lord. And when the Lord mentioned these things, saying that without faith one could not do them, they said, 'Lord, increase our faith.'

THE EXPANSION OF FAITH

Hebrews 11:6 tells us: "But without faith it is impossible to please him: for he that cometh to God must believe that he is, and that he is a rewarder of them that diligently seek him."

Now think of that. Without faith it is impossible to please God. If you want to please God, then have faith.

"...he that cometh to God must believe that he is...." He must believe that God is alive. Many folks today think, though they won't come out and tell you this, *I wonder if God is alive.* A lot of folks are wondering if the Lord has passed off the scene or if He ever was. You can look at people and tell that many of them do not really believe that God is alive. They look like a funeral has taken place.

Listen! God is alive. How do I know? It has been only an hour or so since my family and I read the Word of God and went to the throne of grace. I felt His love, was conscious that He was listening to me. He is at the throne, and He is alive and well!

Faith pleasing to God was wonderfully illustrated in the life of Enoch. "And Enoch walked with God: and he was not; for God took him" (Gen. 5:24). Let us see what God says about Enoch's faith and how it pleased Him.

"By faith Enoch was translated that he should not see death; and was not found, because God had translated him: for before his translation he had this testimony, that he pleased God. But without faith it is impossible to please him: for he that cometh to God must believe that he is, and that he is a rewarder of them that diligently seek him."—Heb. 11:5,6.

Notice these expressions: "...he had this testimony that he pleased God"; "...without faith it is impossible to please him." Faith pleases God!

We must believe that He is, and that He is a rewarder of those who diligently seek Him. God honors the person who lives the right kind of life. Yes, God rewards righteous living.

IV. FAITH IS FOR GETTING ANSWERS TO PRAYER

"And all things, whatsoever ye shall ask in prayer, believing, ye shall receive."—Matt. 21:22.

"If ye abide in me, and my words abide in you, ye shall ask what ye will, and it shall be done unto you."—John 15:7.

God today answers prayer just as much as He has ever answered prayer. He can and will answer mine and yours just as He did Elijah's. We read in Psalm 65:2, "O thou that hearest prayer, unto thee shall all flesh come." It is typical of God to answer prayer.

I pray about even simple little things, things you might think were foolish.

The other day I lost my glasses. I couldn't find them anywhere. I looked all over this church. I asked people in the offices. I looked all over my office. No glasses. I prayed, "Lord, I need my glasses. You know where they are, and You're not telling me. I need to know where they are. Lord, help me find my glasses."

There is a little case up in my office that I rarely ever carry with me. The day I prayed, I went over, lifted up the lid on that case, reached in, picked up my glasses and put them on. I might have been looking for them yet had I not prayed.

You say, "Well, that was a little thing." But He is not a little God! God can also answer prayers that take a miracle. In the supernatural and unusual, God will answer prayer!

When the doctor told me I would never be able to preach again, the only thing I could do was pray. I had had two operations on my throat; now I was told that I would never be able to preach again. I was advised to seek some other way to serve the Lord.

My heart was broken. Preaching was my life. My wife and I fell prostrate on our faces before God. I couldn't even pray aloud, but my wife cried out to God to work a miracle, heal my throat and restore my voice. We both claimed Matthew 18:19, "...if two of you shall agree on earth as touching any thing that they shall ask, it shall be done for them of my Father which is in heaven.''

God heard that prayer years ago, and I have been preaching several times a week ever since.

God answers prayers! 'Lord, increase our faith' in getting answers to prayer.

Every sincere Christian, unless he has an ax to grind or there is something wrong with him somewhere else, should be praying for the Lord to bless the work of God. Every member of this church and every friend of Jesus should every day pray, "O Lord, bless this work where thousands have been saved, and keep it going for the glory of God.''

He answers prayer!

V. FAITH OVERCOMES THE WORLD

The last reason they said, "Increase our faith,'' is that they wanted to overcome the world. The world is brought into focus by the words of the Lord Jesus in I John 5:4: ''. . . and this is the victory that overcometh the world, even our faith.'' Jesus asked, ''For what shall it profit a man, if he shall gain the whole world, and lose his own soul?'' (Mark 8:36). The one victory over the world is faith.

> **Encamped along the hills of light,**
> **Ye Christian soldiers, rise,**
> **And press the battle ere the night**
> **Shall veil the glowing skies.**
> **Against the foe in vales below**
> **Let all our strength be hurled;**
> **Faith is the victory, we know,**
> **That overcomes the world.**

R. A. Torrey told of a man who had lived in Europe and had made his fortune. He wanted to come back and live in the United States. He pondered how he could best take his entire fortune back with him to this country. In those days the only means across the ocean was by boat, and it took a long time. He finally decided to put all his earnings in one precious little jewel and bring his fortune back in that jewel.

This daring and adventuresome sort of fellow would stand on the deck of the vessel and flip the jewel up, then catch it in his hand.

Someone said to him, "What is that that you flip in the air and catch with your hand?"

He said, "All I own in this world is summed up in this little stone."

"Well, sir, you're on the deck of a vessel; there are waves and winds; the boat rolls and tosses as it plows through the sea. Don't you think there is danger that you might lose your treasure?"

He replied, "No, I've done it hundreds of times, and I've never failed to catch it."

One day the boat reeled to and fro across the waves as it plowed across the ocean. People on deck saw him standing near the edge flipping the precious jewel in the air and catching it as it fell. Almost in horror one said, "Man, don't do that! That's everything you own! You may lose it." As the onlooker spoke to him, he flipped it higher, higher in the air. But then this time it fell just beyond his reach. He watched in horror as his fortune hit the water, never to be seen again.

I say to you, all you own that is worthwhile is within your body. Your soul, your spirit are as eternal as God Himself! The greatest treasure a man can ever have is his soul. Do not gamble with it! The only way to save that soul from this world is by faith in the Lord Jesus Christ.

"And the apostles said unto the Lord, Increase our faith."—Luke 17:5.

Chapter XII

Faith Defeating Our Fears

(Preached in Emmanuel Baptist Church, Sunday, February 3, 1974)

"And he saith unto them, Why are ye fearful, O ye of little faith?"—Matt. 8:26.

This question, or statement, was provoked from the Lord when the storm came. He was asleep on the deck of the vessel on the little Sea of Galilee. When the tempest came, the disciples woke Him and said, "Lord, save us: we perish." Jesus said, "Why are ye fearful, O ye of little faith?"

I want to speak to you today on "Faith Defeating Our Fears." I am not a psychiatrist, nor do I claim to be able to analyze people's lives, their emotions and feelings. I do know that the Bible speaks about fears that people face, and gives the answer to those fears.

A great man said to me some years ago, "Tom, people have two kinds of courage. There is such a thing as physical courage. Some folks are not afraid of anything physical—anybody, anytime, anywhere. And there is another kind of courage, moral courage, the courage always to do right." This wise old preacher said, "You rarely find one who has both types—physical and moral courage."

Fear is common to all kinds of people.

There is a good kind of fear: "The fear of the Lord is the beginning of knowledge" (Prov. 1:7). And the fear of the Lord is the beginning of wisdom. The only fear that ought to ever be in any man or woman, boy or girl, is the fear of the Lord; not that shuddering fear but a reverential trust and respect for God. When one fears God, he has no reason to fear man.

Everyone has some kind of fear. People fear failure. People fear loneliness. Though some go through life with their family all around them and friends by the score, yet deep down in their hearts they fear loneliness.

People fear old age. I am not enjoying it myself! If I had my choice, I would rather be young than old. I might say, though, that I doubt that I would want to go back through some things I went through in my youth and middle age. A lot of folks go through life fearing old age, not remembering that many of the Bible promises are given to people in old age.

Some feel rejection. Most doctors will tell you that those in institutions are there because they were gripped with the fear of rejection. This literally drove them from their mental health.

Everyone has fear of some kind.

Job went through an experience that I guess no other human has ever gone through. "Upon earth there is not his like, who is made without fear" (Job 41:33). Great people have had and do have fear. When he wrote his first letter to the church at Corinth, Paul said, "I was with you in weakness, and in fear, and in much trembling" (I Cor. 2:3). That was Paul speaking, the greatest Christian that ever lived. Paul was probably closer to God and knew God in His person better than any other Christian has ever known Him. He knew more of God's revelation and God's truth than any other Christian has known.

One verse of Scripture I almost hesitate to mention. Hebrews 5 speaks of Jesus, "who in the days of his flesh, when he had offered up prayers and supplications with strong crying and tears unto him that was able to save him from death, and was heard

FAITH DEFEATING OUR FEARS

in that he feared." I do not know how to explain that. The divine Son of God, who knew no imperfection, had an hour in His life when fear was His enemy.

The disciples had fear rooted in a weak faith. Jesus was on the deck of that vessel. The Son of God, who made the Sea of Galilee, the mountains that surrounded it, the sky that covered it, lay asleep on that vessel. When the storm came and the waves tossed high and the heavens became black, even with God on that boat they became fearful and began to cry, "Lord, save us: we perish." Jesus asked, 'Why are ye fearful, O ye of little faith? I am on this boat. It cannot go down unless I will it so, yet ye are frightened.'

That is the way with human life. People have fear.

Many folks fear impending judgment. I have never heard folks talk as much before about what will happen if this country goes the way it is going. I am not a diagnostician of times, not astute in history; but I can predict this: This country cannot continue the way it is going and survive some sort of catastrophic judgment from God.

We read in our family devotions this morning Proverbs 14:34, where the Bible says, "Righteousness exalteth a nation: but sin is a reproach to any people." People are fearful about what is going to happen in this country.

What is going to happen? Just like what happened when God took Israel out of Egypt: "Fear and dread shall fall upon them; by the greatness of thine arm they shall be as still as a stone..." (Exod. 15:16). God said that Israel has lived in darkness. Egypt has been without God. Egypt has oppressed the truth. Egypt has afflicted the people of God. So fear and dread shall come upon this nation as a result of it.

God only knows what will happen in this country unless there comes an old-fashioned revival from Heaven or unless the Lord soon returns and raptures His church.

The politicians, the leaders, the brilliant minds of America, do not come forth with a solution. On television comes one man who says, "Here is the solution to the problems that face the people of America." Two nights later comes a man to rebuke that solution. Nobody knows the solution but God. Old people are having it hard. Children are almost destitute of a sound education. Economics are out of control. Some politicians are crooked. People all over this nation are fearful, like Luke 21:26 says, "Men's hearts failing them for fear, and for looking after those things which are coming on the earth: for the powers of heaven shall be shaken." The Bible says fear is typical of times like these. Men's hearts are failing them for fear, for looking after those things which are coming on the earth.

I talk to you today about fear in the lives, emotions, hearts and souls of people. I would also like to give you the most thrilling remedy for it all, which is an unshakable faith in God and His Word.

I. THE FEAR OF DEATH

There are eight basic fears. From the cradle to the grave, people fear death. From the time we are old enough to think that one day this heart may stop beating, these lungs may stop breathing, these ears may stop hearing, these eyes may stop seeing, the fear of death grips us.

The Bible says people are going to die. "...it is appointed unto men once to die, but after this the judgment" (Heb. 9:27); "Wherefore, as by one man sin entered into the world, and death by sin; and so death passed upon all men, for that all have sinned" (Rom. 5:12).

As far as physical death is concerned, everyone in this room one day will lie cold and lifeless in his casket, unless the Lord comes before our time.

FAITH DEFEATING OUR FEARS

One day God said to a man, Hananiah, "Behold, I will cast thee from off the face of the earth: this year thou shalt die, because thou hast taught rebellion against the Lord" (Jer. 28:16). That year he died.

All will die if the Lord tarries. Today, if we only knew to how many people the voice of God is saying, "This year thou shalt die," what a day of reckoning it would be in our hearts and lives!

Death is a common lot. We see our loved ones precede us in death. With a broken heart we follow them to the grave, and with empty arms we go back to an empty chair. From the first family, when a man went out and slew his brother, men have been dying. Nearly ten times we read in chapter 5 of Genesis, "And he died."

Men fear death. But there is a remedy for that. For a Christian, it is in being right with God. When Stephen died, he was right with the Lord.

"But he, being full of the Holy Ghost, looked up stedfastly into heaven, and saw the glory of God, and Jesus standing on the right hand of God, And said, Behold, I see the heavens opened, and the Son of man standing on the right hand of God."—Acts 7:55,56.

When they gnashed on him with their teeth, stopped their ears, ran upon him with one accord, cast him out of their city and stoned him, Stephen did one of the most wonderful things a person could do in the hour of death or at any other time: he prayed, "Lord, lay not this sin to their charge."

Stephen was so right with God, so ready to die, that he did not even have to search his own heart when the time came. He could pray for people around him.

Being right with God subdues, covers and overcomes the fear of death.

Then for the Christian, there is the glorious hope of the resurrection from the grave.

"For the Lord himself shall descend from heaven with a shout,

with the voice of the archangel, and with the trump of God: and the dead in Christ shall rise first: Then we which are alive and remain shall be caught up together with them in the clouds, to meet the Lord in the air: and so shall we ever be with the Lord."
—I Thess. 4:16,17.

The Christian knows that, if he passes off the scene of this earth before the Lord comes, Jesus will call him from the grave at the second coming. There will be the glorious resurrection. And the hope of the resurrection calms the fear of death.

The hope and knowledge of Heaven also calms the fear of death. In His last night on earth, while thinking about this, Jesus said:

"Let not your heart be troubled: ye believe in God, believe also in me. In my Father's house are many mansions: if it were not so, I would have told you. I go to prepare a place for you. And if I go and prepare a place for you, I will come again, and receive you unto myself; that where I am, there ye may be also."—John 14:1-3.

When a Christian ponders death, he thinks of a City in the sky, a City which knows no pain nor sorrow, no regrets, no sin—a City where the sun never sets and the lights never go out. Not only that, but he will be in the presence of Jesus Christ forever.

When a Christian thinks of death and being absent from the body and present with the Lord in Heaven, he thinks also of the reunion with loved ones.

You may not believe it nor think much about it now, especially you young ones, but you will one day. One day you will stand on this side of the river where you have lived life and feared death, and you will look on the other side and say, "Most of my family are over There. Over There are people whom I long to see. I would give anything to hear their voices once again, see their faces and know once again their sweet and tender love." You will one day say, "I have more on the other side than on this side."

When I would think of my dear old grandfather, it used to break my heart. I loved him so much. He was saved after I was—in his seventies. He raised me and taught me. The character I have, he built into me.

Nearing ninety, he still had a beautiful head of gray hair, and not a false tooth in his mouth.

I would go to his bedside when no one else was in the room, and he would say, "Tom, I want us to pray."

"All right, Grandpa. I will pray for you."

"But Tom, here is what I want you to pray for. Pray the Lord will take me Home. I'm no good to Ada [his wife of seventy years]. It is breaking the health of your mother to care for me. Pray the Lord will take me Home."

He never talked about this to others.

One night the phone rang. Across the miles the trembling voice of my mother said, "Your grandfather just went to be with the Lord." In my heart I said, "He went in answer to prayer."

Be right with God, think of the resurrection, think of the hope and knowledge of Heaven, think of the presence of the Lord, and it will take care of the fear of death.

"Why are ye fearful, O ye of little faith?"

II. THE FEAR OF THE UNKNOWN

There is in life the fear of the unknown. Talk to people about something mysterious, and they get frightened.

There is a damnable movie called "The Exorcist." Any Christian who would go to see something put out by the Devil ought to have his head examined. "Well, the Catholic church approved it," you say. I don't care who approved it: it is all about the mysterious, unknown power of the Devil.

I was told that in Texas a few days ago a young lady went to see it and it "blew her mind," according to the expression they used. She has been in a psychiatric ward ever since.

There is in the heart of people a fear of the unknown. What they cannot understand, they are afraid of.

When somebody passed away in the country where I was raised, it was altogether different than now. The folks at home laid the body out. Sometimes men got together and built the casket, a pine box. The dead were laid out on the bed for awhile. People used to put money on the dead person's eyes to be sure they would not open. (As a boy, I sure was hoping they would not open, once they were declared dead!)

Folks would sit up with the corpse. When one died, he was usually buried the next day. I am not being irreverent, but it was just so different back then. Loved ones would take the casket out to the country graveyard and bury it. The country folks would pass around a few songbooks and sing old songs about Heaven, home and being with the Lord.

Perhaps you have heard this one. Loved ones and friends were sitting up one night with a man that had died. A lady mourning his passing said as she looked toward him, "Speak to me! Speak to me!"

One of those old country boys turned to another and said, "Now if he does, I'm going out that door over there!"

There is something fearful about the unknown, what you cannot know. It is like the time Jesus came walking on the sea in the midst of a storm. When the disciples saw Him walking on the water, they were troubled, saying, "It is a spirit; and they cried out for fear." They could not discern what it was, and it terrified them. They wanted to know what evil power lurked in the atmosphere. In fact, when these disciples saw this figure walking on water, it frightened them because they could not discern it. Jesus said, "It is I. Be not afraid. I am here."

FAITH DEFEATING OUR FEARS

Whatever lurks in the atmosphere, whether it be UFO's, whether little green, froglike men come from Mars or somewhere else and say, "We want you," it makes no difference to me. **The Lord is where I am!**

People wonder what lies beyond the door of death. It is Jesus!

A member of our church died. Her husband called me and my wife and said, "My wife just passed away." Before anyone else got there, we were there.

There she lay in that room. The husband said, "Brother Tom, this experience has been one of the sweetest I have ever had. She was lying right there when she died. That window there was open. Then all of a sudden she lifted her hand toward that window and said, 'He is here!' Her hand fell across her chest, and her eyes closed. That is the way she went."

Sometimes a Christian will wonder what lies just beyond that door. When you step across that threshold, out of life into death, over there is Jesus! He who conquered death, arose from the grave and said, "I am alive for evermore," is just beyond the door of death for a Christian.

Some wonder what awful disease may lurk within their bodies. I guess all of us have been guilty of this at one time or another. With a body as healthy as any body could be, we worry ourselves to death, wondering if there is something wrong with us. "What awful disease may be lurking within my body? What terrible thing may happen to me today?"

I know some who cannot sleep because they are afraid something is going to fall on them, afraid someone is going to hit them or their car is suddenly going to explode. The fear of the unknown worries people.

I mentioned my grandfather. I remember a lesson that I learned from him.

In order to get to the little church where I was saved, I had to walk about a mile and a half down a railroad track. An old graveyard was alongside that railroad track. The shortest way home was to walk right through that graveyard. Most of the time I took the long way home! A few times I went through that graveyard. It was unkempt. Some of the graves had sunk in. Some of the tombstones had fallen. It was not a very pleasant experience to walk through there and see the moonlight on the old-fashioned tombstones. One had to be careful where he walked. Some of the graves had fallen in, and he might fall into one of them.

One night as I came home I heard a noise. My mind got to playing tricks on me. I went on into the house and awoke my grandfather. "Granddaddy, someone is in the hallway of the barn." An old 1928 car, which has long since died, was there and had not been used for a long time. I said, "Granddaddy, somebody is up on that car, and they are taking corn out of that crib. They are stealing our corn."

I was never a hunter, nor did I know anything about the double-barrel shotgun with a 32-inch barrel. One side was choke bored, and the other side was open bored. It has big hammers on it. It lay up on the wall above my grandfather's bed. When I said, "Somebody is stealing corn down there," Grandfather never got out of bed, never lifted a hand, just said, "Take the gun and go down there and shoot them."

I took the gun. I have never been so scared in all my life. When I got where I could see right through the hallway of the barn, I saw a man—I mean, in my mind there was a man. Here was this gun shaking in my hands. If I had shot, I wouldn't have hit him. I probably wouldn't have even hit the barn!

Finally when I laid that gun down and walked into that hallway, I want to tell you what I found. Remember what I thought I saw? I thought I saw a man on top of that car with the crib door open and a sack over his shoulders loading it with corn. I saw it! But when I got in there, a calf was standing in some shucks and itching and scratching himself on the old car!

I went back to the house and, with great embarrassment, told my grandfather what it was. He said, "Everything has an explanation. Don't always get excited. Look into it and see what it is."

God never wants a Christian to be going around scared to death. "Something is going to fall on me out of the sky." "I am going to have an accident." You may, for life is that way; but God is with you. No Christian should live in fear. There is no unknown to the child of God. We have in us the Son of all wisdom. He knows everything. When your life is in His hands, what matters if there is something you don't understand?

"And he saith unto them, Why are ye fearful, O ye of little faith?"

III. THE FEAR OF MAN

The Bible has a lot to say about the fear of man. "The fear of man bringeth a snare: but whoso putteth his trust in the Lord shall be safe" (Prov. 29:25). Man fears man. The Bible has much to say about how a person ought not fear man. Said the psalmist, "The Lord is on my side; I will not fear: what can man do unto me?" (118:6). The real you cannot be hurt if you belong to God.

You remember when we studied the great lesson on blood redemption a couple of weeks ago and saw how the Lord delivered the children of Israel out of the bondage of Egypt. For over 400 years they had been slaves in that land; then God wrought a mighty miracle to bring them out.

They are ready to cross the Red Sea. But there is no way to cross it unless God works a miracle. God did. He parted the waters. With the chariots of Pharaoh rumbling behind them, the people were afraid. Moses said to them, "Fear ye not, stand still, and see the salvation of the Lord, which he will shew you to day: for the Egyptians whom ye have seen to day, ye shall see them again no more for ever" (Exod. 14:13).

No Christian ought ever fear man. "...we may boldly say, The Lord is my helper, and I will not fear what man shall do unto me" (Heb. 13:6).

People fear man, saying, "Man may take what is mine." Even some lose their mental health with the fear that somebody will get what is theirs.

Then there is the fear, "Someone will turn others against me"; the fear, "Somebody will cause me to do wrong"; the fear, "Somebody will keep me from success"; the fear, "Somebody will do me bodily injury"; the fear, "Someone may ruin my reputation." And the fear of man has kept many a person from being saved: "I wonder what So-and-so would think if I became a Christian and trusted the Lord?"

A letter from one of our missionaries the other day told of the many dozens of visits made and the many who were saved. "But only a few have come out and professed the Lord publicly because they are afraid of their families," he added. Afraid of man.

My friend, you are not to fear man. You are to fear God, in whose hands your soul is today. If you are not a Christian, God help you to trust Him and not be afraid of the outcome. Be afraid if your life is not in His hands. No person ought to fear to trust, believe and surrender to the Lord Jesus Christ.

Fear: is it in your life today? God can take it away.

Look at I John 4:18: "There is no fear in love; but perfect love casteth out fear: because fear hath torment. He that feareth is not made perfect in love."

An elderly lady called me about three o'clock one morning. She said, "I am not a member of your church, but I need help. I am gripped with a horrible fear. I am a Christian, I know the Lord, Brother Malone, and I know that I am saved; but I do not want my own pastor to know how fear has gripped my heart and seems to be destroying my life."

I said to her, "Dear sister, do you know what you are afraid of?"

"No, I have no idea," she answered.

Then I talked to her about fear.

Many people have that same experience she had somewhere along the journey of life. God diagnoses this thing. The Lord tells us what men fear, then gives us the answer to it. When you go to a doctor, he has two responsibilities. First, of diagnosing you, finding out what is wrong before he knows how to help you.

There are jokes about doctors like there are about preachers. A fellow went to see a doctor once. The doctor said, "Have you ever had this before?" The patient said, "Yes, I have." The doctor said, "Well, you have it again." This was his diagnosis.

The doctor's second responsibility is to prescribe for your illness the remedy he believes will cure it.

God is the greatest diagnostician of the human heart and emotions. He not only diagnoses our fears but has the remedy for them.

I had a case worker come to see me one time. She was talking to me about a member of our church. This member needed to be subjected to a certain very drastic type of emotional treatment but didn't know whether she ought to submit herself to it or not. She said, "I have asked my pastor to pray whether I should have this drastic treatment for my emotions, fears and problems. My pastor is praying about it."

The case worker then came to see me, her pastor.

She asked, "Do you think this person ought to be submitted to this treatment?"

I said, "First, I am not a doctor, and I am not a psychiatrist. I don't really know."

The case worker explained: "Preacher, one thing you may not understand: In the treatment of this sort of thing in one's life, we who have studied it and who deal with it regularly, put one emotion against another in order to solve a certain problem."

After she left my office, I thought on that statement.

That is what God is talking about in this verse—about the two extremes, the two opposites, about perfect love without human fear.

God's love for us; our love for God; our love for each other makes up the whole system, the whole doctrine, the whole teaching of love as found in the Bible.

The Bible says, "Perfect love casteth out fear." Love implies an attraction; fear implies repulsion. These cannot co-exist in the same life, heart, mind, soul. A perfect love and human fear will not dwell together.

God's remedy for fear is perfection or maturity in those three avenues of love: the full enjoyment, the full understanding, the full belief in God's immeasurable, unchanging love for His children. Our love for our Heavenly Father depends on those three things.

There are two tremendous loves: the love for people, our brothers and sisters in Christ; and an evangelistic love for all those outside the body of Christ. God says so; and where God speaks, we speak. What God says, we believe. What God prescribes, we take as the cure. And God said the cure for fear is a perfect love.

"And he saith unto them, Why are ye fearful, O ye of little faith?"

IV. THE FEAR OF BEING FORSAKEN

I am sure that is true of many here tonight. The fear of loneliness, the fear of being forsaken, is one of the most common fears known to the human family. Let me give you a Bible illustration.

In the days of the Prophet Samuel, God's great plan of government was a theocracy—that is, God ruling people through prophets who then told the people, through priests who interceded to God for the people.

The heathen nations who knew not God had kings. One day, to God's Prophet Samuel they clamored for a king and said, "Give us a king like the other nations have." It was not the directive will of God; but in the permissive will of God, He granted the wishes of the people to have a king. It was King Saul.

One day it was determined in the sovereign purpose of God that the kingdom must be wrested from his hands. He no longer could reign. The thing the people wanted was not working out.

One day Samuel talked to the people (read it in I Samuel 12) and said, 'I want to give you a sign today that God is talking to you and that God is here. It is wheat harvest time, not the time for thunderstorms and torrential rains, but one will come.' It did. That proved that God was listening to the Prophet Samuel. There came the torrential rain and the peal of thunder. The people greatly feared the Lord and Samuel. They said, 'We have added unto all of our sins this evil, to ask us a king. He has failed, and so have we.' Samuel said, "Fear not... for the Lord will not forsake his people for his great name's sake: because it hath pleased the Lord to make you his people." Samuel told them, 'Yes, you have sinned. Yes, you have failed. Yes, you fear that you will be forsaken because of it. But fear not. God hath made you His people, and He will not forsake you for His name's sake.'

If God ever forsook one of His own, it would not be any compliment to God, to His name's sake, nor His testimony. God will never forsake one of His own.

We find in the Bible many people who suffered and went through and endured the fear of rejection. I think of a man who was born blind. When Jesus was asked by His disciples, "Master, who did sin, this man, or his parents, that he was born blind?" He answered, "Neither hath this man sinned, nor his parents: but that the works of God should be made manifest in him" (John 9:2,3).

The Lord healed this man and made him to see, leaving no doubt that a miracle had been performed. A man who had been blind from his birth could now see. His parents knew he was blind, his neighbors knew he was blind; now God wrought a miracle, and he could see. They came to the once blind man. They wanted to get theological. "How were thine eyes opened?" In other words, "Who was this Man who came, touched your eyes and made you see?"

The answer they got was, 'I know not who He is, but one thing I do know is, whereas I was blind, now I see.'

You know what they did to that man? If this were not so tragic, it would be funny. They cast him out. 'You have been blind, and you have no right to see. Get out!' And they literally cast him out. He became an outcast.

I am thrilled with this mighty miracle. This man expresses my testimony and yours when he says, "One thing I know, that, whereas I was blind, now I see."

My heart about broke when I read in John 9:24 where they cast him out. I read on, and I got on shouting grounds when I read verse 35 where it says that Jesus sought him and found him and said to him, 'Son, you may be cast out of some human circle, and out of this unbelieving synagogue, but you are not ever out of My presence.' They repelled him, but Jesus drew him.

In this world man suffers the fear of being forsaken and of being lonely. If you are a Christian and doing the will of God and walking with God, sometimes emotion will flood in. It was so with the Apostle Paul. One night, down in that prison on that cold, stone, dungeon floor, with a little light coming through the crevice of the rock, he wrote his last words: "Demas hath forsaken me, having loved this present world....Only Luke is with me" (II Tim. 4:10,11). Humanly speaking, Paul said, "In this great imperial city of Rome, I have been forsaken of all those who professed to know the Lord except one man—Luke." Paul knew what it was to go through a period of loneliness, of feeling rejection and of being forsaken.

FAITH DEFEATING OUR FEARS

If fear of being forsaken or loneliness ever grips your heart, remember, first, that according to the Word of the living God, the Lord has promised that the Holy Spirit will never leave you.

Before He left this world one day, Jesus said to His own, "I will pray the Father, and he shall give you another Comforter, that he may abide with you for ever" (John 14:16). No Christian can ever say, "I am forsaken, rejected, alone." The Holy Spirit of God lives with you forever.

Then you should remember that the Lord has so ordered your life, has placed you in a wonderful place. I am not just talking to you that are here, but to any Christian. The Lord has so ordered the steps of a Christian that he who follows the Lord will find himself in a New Testament, Bible-believing church. He who follows the Lord and is yielded to Him will find himself in fellowship with others who are saved, just like he is. That is God's will for a Christian.

When those back in Bible times got saved, they continued stedfastly, breaking bread, in prayer from house to house, and in fellowship. The Lord has so ordered a Christian's life that he can never, if he is in the will of God, say, "I am suffering rejection and loneliness." The last thing the Lord Jesus said before leaving this earth was, "Lo, I am with you alway, even unto the end of the world."

There is the indwelling of the Holy Spirit, the fellowship of the people of God and the constant companionship of the Lord Jesus Christ.

A Christian goes through testing times. I don't think there is anybody who is saved for any length of time but somewhere along the way does not meet testing. As your vessel sails along the sunny seas and the soft winds fill your sails, all of a sudden the waves become boisterous and the wind becomes rowdy. God sends a storm in your life. It comes from a direction you never thought it would come from. Your little boat rocks and reels upon that stormy sea until you cry almost like the disciples, "Lord, save me or I perish."

Paul had that experience. When he said, "I must see Rome," I think he knew he was going to his death. He boarded the ship down there in Caesarea along the Mediterranean coast. He set out and sailed with smooth waters and sunny skies by the isle of Crete. After awhile God revealed to him that a storm would assail that ship until it would break every board into splinters.

Paul admonished them, "Sirs, I perceive that this voyage will be with hurt and much damage." Paul was saying, "If we leave this port, we do it to our peril."

They said, 'Preachers know nothing about sailing. Let loose of the tackle and raise the sail. We are headed for Rome.' They launched out, and the storm came. Paul is talking about that when he said, "A day and a night I was in the deep." One day Paul disappeared. That storm was so bad they saw neither sun, moon nor stars for many days (Acts 27:20).

"And now I exhort you to be of good cheer: for there shall be no loss of any man's life among you, but of the ship. For there stood by me this night the angel of God, whose I am, and whom I serve."—Acts 27:22,23.

Down in the hold of this ship there stood by him God's angel, saying, 'Fear not, Paul, you are not alone' (vs. 24).

God will never leave one of His children alone.

I led a 79-year-old lady to Christ a good many years ago. She lived in a humble little home up here on the Northwest side of the city of Pontiac. With tears streaming down her wrinkled face, she said, "Preacher, my husband died when I was 50. For 29 years I have lived alone in this house. I'm the most lonely person in the world."

I replied, "I can tell you Someone who will take up His abode not only in your home but in your heart so that you need never feel rejected again.''

I led her to Christ.

God has a remedy for the feeling of rejection and loneliness, a common fear to all.

"And he saith unto them, Why are ye fearful, O ye of little faith?"

V. THE FEAR OF PAST FAILURES

Another fear that is an enemy to many people, maybe everybody, is the fear of past failures.

People say to themselves, *I have failed once; I could easily fail again.* Many people in the Bible failed, and the Lord describes their failures, not covering any of them up. He paints no pretty picture. He shows the failure, then how, through the grace and power of God, to rise again.

To Joshua (8:1) the Lord said, "Fear not, neither be thou dismayed: take all the people of war with thee, and arise, go up to Ai: see, I have given into thy hand the king of Ai, and his people, and his city, and his land...."

There is a wonderful story in back of that. The Lord had to say unto Joshua, a brave man, 'Do not be afraid. Go up against that city. It is not a big city. I said I would give it to you. Go take it.' God had to say to Joshua, "Fear not; do not be afraid." There is a reason for His saying that. A few days before, the children of Israel had said, 'It is not a big city. It will not take many people. We are strong now.' They had overcome Jericho; now they said, 'We can take Ai. Nothing to it.'

But there was Achan, who had, against the command of God, taken the Babylonian garment and hidden the wedge of gold and silver. The Lord's army had been defeated. Some of God's people had been killed. Here is God's mighty leader, Joshua. In his trembling heart he, no doubt, was thinking: *We failed to take it.*

They sent us running back to our camp in utter defeat and shame. Now God said, 'Fear not, Joshua. Take all the people of war and go against that city. I am with thee. Arise and go. I have given them into thy hands.'

If the Devil can get a Christian who has failed to put his lip down on the ground, live in the slough of despond, in the valley of melancholy and whine for the rest of his life, *I am nothing but a worm in the dust,* he has you where he wants you.

Let me tell you, I'm no worm; I'm a prince of God, a child of God. I have in me royal blood.

I get so sick of these folks who go around and do nothing, say nothing, feel nothing—"I'm just a poor worm in the dust." You need a strong dose of medicine if you are all that wormy. God never means for a Christian to live like that. He said to Joshua, 'I know you failed. But do not be afraid. I am with you.'

A preacher in Detroit once said a most brilliant thing: "I hate to see folks defeated and sitting around doing nothing. Do something if you do nothing but fall down." Wouldn't you rather see a man try to do something and fall down than to just sit his life out?

James and John's mother came to Jesus and made a request: "Grant that these my two sons may sit...." In other words, 'We pray that, when You come into the kingdom, we may sit.' A lot of people are doing that. This is their prayer: "Lord, I pray that I may sit."

That is not God's will.

If you fail once, remember that Peter failed, too. Oh, the shame and embarrassment that night when Peter denied his Lord with an oath! He spoke profanity. He dipped his tongue to the cesspool of corruption and swore.

When one said, 'You talk like a Galilean from up near Capernaum. You were with Jesus of Galilee,' three times he denied it.

After awhile he caught those magnetic eyes that see everything. When Jesus looked at him, it broke Peter's heart.

I imagine the world said, "The chief of the twelve has fallen, and he will never rise again." Wait a minute! Forty days after Jesus went back to Heaven, He appeared again. One time it was to Peter alone. Again He appeared to Peter with several others. Ten days after He went back to Heaven, the Holy Spirit of God came. A preacher stands up to preach. He preaches with such wonderful power that thousands are saved. The church is literally born into existence. Who was that preacher? That fellow who warmed his hands at the Devil's fire that night and denied even being a Christian.

Don't ever let the Devil cause you to fear because of past failures.

John Mark failed. When they came to the mountainous country of Perga, John Mark said, 'I'm going home,' and returned to Jerusalem. On his first missionary journey, he turned a coward and went back.

Years passed. One day while in jail Paul wrote a letter: 'Bring John Mark, for I have need of him in the ministry.' He had been restored.

The Devil defeats a Christian when he gets you to fear because of some past failure.

David failed, but he so lived that God one day said, "He is a man after My own heart."

Perhaps that is what Paul is talking about in Philippians 3:13: "...forgetting those things which are behind, and reaching forth unto those things which are before."

No Christian ought ever live in the past; forget those things which are behind. Let them go. They are under the blood. Don't let the Devil bring them up before you as a failure in your life.

A lady, once a member of this church, came one day and said she wanted to talk to me. Then she told me of one sin which had happened 3,000 miles away and fourteen years before.

I said, "But dear sister, you are saved, and all your sins are under the blood."

"Yes, I know," she said, "but the failures of my life are literally driving me to destruction." (The Devil uses fear to torment a Christian's mind and trouble his/her soul. Fear is your enemy.)

I said, "I don't know all the answers, but my thinking is, God has forgiven you, but you have never forgiven yourself."

She paused for a moment before saying, "I believe you're right."

She walked out of the office a little straighter, and her face showed she was a lot happier. She served God here for many years before she and her husband moved away.

The fear of past failures.

"And he saith unto them, Why are ye fearful, O ye of little faith?"

VI. THE FEAR OF BEING IN THE MINORITY

Some have fear of being in the minority, in the smaller group. This is a fear that is inherent in the human heart and mind. All humanity would rather be on the winning side. It has always been that way with the Lord's people.

It was so with people in the Old Testament. Deuteronomy 20:1 admonishes:

"When thou goest out to battle against thine enemies, and seest horses, and chariots, and a people more than thou, be not afraid of them: for the Lord thy God is with thee, which brought thee up out of the land of Egypt."

The people said, "But Lord, there are chariots and horses and many people—thousands of them and few of us." "That makes no difference. God is with you," was the assurance.

Don't be afraid just because you are in the minority.

How many Christians don't grow much in the Lord because they

FAITH DEFEATING OUR FEARS

are afraid of losing something by being in the little group! The vast millions on this earth go about their sinful ways without God or even a thought of Him. People fear being in the minority.

In Deuteronomy 20:3,4 the Lord says:

"...let not your hearts faint, fear not, and do not tremble, neither be ye terrified because of them; For the Lord your God is he that goeth with you, to fight for you against your enemies, to save you."

Don't be afraid because you are in the minority.

This happened to Elisha's servant, the wonderful story in II Kings 6. It is a funny story.

Here is this baldheaded preacher. They want to arrest him. Instead of saying to one squad car or maybe two policemen, "Go get that little baldheaded preacher," they sent a whole army! I can't help but laugh—sending a whole army for one little preacher! The servant of Elisha got up early the next morning, looked out the window and saw the hills filled with chariots, horses, soldiers—a whole army to get one little preacher! Seeing that almost scared the servant to death.

He ran, woke up Elisha and said, 'Elisha, come here! Look out this window!'

Elisha looked, and just as calm as he could be, said, "Fear not: for they that be with us are more than they that be with them."

If you have any "tickle" in you, you'll get tickled right there. Here are this baldheaded preacher and his minister, who pours water on his hands, standing in that little home seeing an army fill the hills; and the preacher is saying, "They that be with us are more than they that be with them"!

The angels of God camp round about those who love Him. I don't know how many angels I have, but I know I have some. I can imagine that my angels get sick of me sometimes, but the Lord has assigned them to you and me nevertheless. The angels of God encamp round about those who love Him. Listen! More are with you tonight than there are in all the power in the earth. So don't fear being in the minority.

Jesus said to His disciples, "Fear not, little flock; for it is your Father's good pleasure to give you the kingdom" (Luke 12:32).

God said to His people in Joshua 23:10, "One man of you shall chase a thousand: for the Lord your God, he it is that fighteth for you, as he hath promised you." One man of God can chase a thousand who do not know God.

Twelve spies were sent to spy out the land. If you want to mess something up, just appoint a big committee. That is what happened here. A committee was chosen to spy out the land to see what it was like.

They came back with a majority report and a minority report. Like people always do, they took the majority report. Ten, the majority, reported, "It is just like God said it was, a land of fruit, milk and honey—a wonderful land. A land of hills, valleys and water—a tremendous land. But we can't take it. The cities are walled, and there are giants over there, giants so big that it makes us look like grasshoppers."

(Today many have a grasshopper complex: "I wonder which way I will jump next." God never meant for a Christian to be that way.)

Two men, Joshua and Caleb, the minority, said, 'Yes, it is a land of fruit, milk and honey—a land of water, mountains and valleys. But we can take it. Even though their cities are walled and their men are giants, we are not grasshoppers, for God is with us.'

Many young people's lives have been ruined by fear. In our schools, the vast majority care nothing about the Bible, Christianity nor decency. Sometimes a Christian boy or girl will say, "I'm tired of being in the minority, in the little crowd." In the heart is the fear of being in the minority. Statistically, we are less, but we are more because we have God.

One day the dust will settle, and the war will be over. Who then will be sitting in the catbird seat? Tom Malone will be there. You will be there. We are going to win. The results of the struggle between evil and righteousness are inevitable. But God will win. And we will win with Him. So don't be afraid of being in the minority.

"And he saith unto them, Why are ye fearful, O ye of little faith?"

VII. THE FEAR OF DOING RIGHT

You say, "Preacher, that's a strange thing." But it is here in the Bible.

A magnanimous man did a magnanimous thing in chapter 14 of Genesis. Abraham went and rescued his nephew Lot. Abraham took four hundred men, went against numerous kingdoms, and God gave great victory. These kings and nations had taken possessions from many people, including Lot. Abraham took his four hundred and overcame them. He retrieved all the goods of Sodom and Gomorrah, all the victuals they had taken, all the people held captive.

A man came out to meet him, Melchizedek, who is a type of Christ. He said to Abraham, "Give me the persons, and take the goods to thyself," or, 'Just restore all the people to their homes, but take all the spoil.'

Abraham said, "I will not take any thing that is thine." There were thousands upon thousands of dollars there and fortune upon fortune in all that he had retrieved. But he said, 'I will not take from you even a shoelace. All I will take is what my young men have eaten while they were on their way to get the job done and while coming back home.' Abraham literally turned down the earth's fortune. 'I want nothing of it except the approval of the One who owns both Heaven and earth.'

In chapter 15, in the first verse, is the word *fear*—"Fear not, Abram: I am thy shield, and thy exceeding great reward."

How would you feel turning it all down because it was not yours, turning it all down because you trusted God? That decision Abraham had already made. The Devil says, 'Abraham, what a big fool you are! You could have had it all.' But God says, "Fear not, Abram: I am thy shield, and thy exceeding great reward."

Don't ever be afraid to do the right thing.

Folks have the fear of not being happy. "You cannot do right and be happy," they say. That is the Devil's philosophy. You come to me and say, "Now that I am saved, what will I do about my friends?" I answer, "Nothing except to try to win them." You don't need to make a decision. They will drop you like a hot potato. That is your least problem. If you live for Jesus, your friends will either get saved or drop you.

Some also have the fear of loss of material security. Jesus covered it all when He said:

"Give, and it shall be given unto you; good measure, pressed down, and shaken together, and running over, shall men give into your bosom. For with the same measure that ye mete withal it shall be measured to you again."—Luke 6:38.

The fear of doing right sometimes keeps people from doing right.

"And he saith unto them, Why are ye fearful, O ye of little faith?"

VIII. THE FEAR OF THE FUTURE

Last, there is the fear of the future. Even some Christians fear the future. People have said to me, "I dread for my little children to grow up." In Revelation 2:10 we read, "Fear none of those things which thou shalt suffer. . . ." No Christian need fear the future.

FAITH DEFEATING OUR FEARS

Some fear old age, infirmity or illness, loss of loved ones, loss of security. Why, we have the One in our heart who holds the future in His hand!

Years ago a very good friend who held a meeting in this church told of a fear he had one time when he was a boy and how that fear was met. He said that one day his father said to him, "There are no schools in our community for further education, so you will go to one several miles away. I have arranged for you to board with a family through the week; then Friday afternoon you will walk home."

The father took his son and left him. This teenage boy hardly slept all that week. He knew that to walk home meant going through a place where some folks had been murdered and many robbed. It was a narrow road where tree branches came together at the top to make a canopy, making it dark even in the daytime. The sun would set and darkness would come before he could pass through that place. His heart pounded all week, and he was so afraid. He thought, *I don't believe I can do it.*

But that first Friday he started out after school. He walked as fast as he could. He watched the sun as it went behind the horizon. Suddenly darkness set in. When he came to that one place, he thought, *What if someone is there to do me harm?*

It was pitch dark. As he walked where the trees made a canopy overhead and went through a tunnel of darkness, he heard footsteps. *Sure enough; just as I thought.* With his heart pounding as if it would burst from his bosom, he kept hearing those footsteps coming closer.

Then he heard, "Son."

"Father!"

"Yes, Son. I have come to meet you in the most dangerous place."

That is what God does. No Christian need fear the future because God will always meet you there.

"And he saith unto them, Why are ye fearful, O ye of little faith?"—Matt. 8:26.

Chapter XIII

Faith for Living on High

(Preached in Emmanuel Baptist Church, Sunday morning, July 16, 1978)

READ: Isaiah 57:1-13

"...but he that putteth his trust in me shall possess the land, and shall inherit my holy mountain."—Isa. 57:13.

I call your attention to the above verse, one of the most tremendous texts of encouragement to believing people found in the Bible. For one thing, a tremendous contrast is drawn in this chapter, a contrast between those who believe and trust, and those who do not believe and trust in the living God. In fact, the contrast is drawn in all the Word of God between the godly and ungodly.

Tremendous promises are made to the godly who believe in the Lord. Here the Lord has painted a solemn picture, a picture of judgment upon people who do not believe and do not know God, people who do not truly trust in a living God: "...but he that putteth his trust in me shall possess the land, and shall inherit my holy mountain."

I narrow the subject down just a little more and speak from the expression that God uses in His Word, "...he that putteth his trust in me...shall inherit my holy mountain."

You may read this and not understand, see nor discern that mountains in the Bible speak of tremendous spiritual principles and truths. Here the Lord is saying, "...he that putteth his trust in me...shall inherit my holy mountain."

Many mountains mentioned in the Bible have special significance. Mount Horeb was an important mountain. Moses was with God while the people of Israel went around that mountain again and again. God was so identified with that mountain that Mount Horeb came to be known as "the mountain of God" (Exod. 3:1).

Let's determine the real, actual, primary meaning of our text. Someone has said, "A text taken out of context becomes a pretext." What does this text really mean—"...he that putteth his trust in me...shall inherit my holy mountain"? This appears to be a long-range prophecy to the people of God. No doubt it is speaking prophetically of Mount Zion. If we trace the mentioning of Mount Zion through the Old Testament, we find that Zion is almost synonymous with Jerusalem, the most important and significant city in the world, the city where our Lord died, arose from the dead and to which He will someday return. Mount Zion is an eminence upon which much of Jerusalem was built and upon which it now stands. Several Scriptures identify Mount Zion with Jerusalem and the great spiritual events which took place there.

1. The city where David reigned: "Nevertheless David took the stronghold of Zion: the same is the city of David" (II Sam. 5:7).

2. Called a holy mountain (Isa. 11:9; 27:13; 56:7).

3. God's Word sent forth from there: "...for out of Zion shall go forth the law, and the word of the Lord from Jerusalem" (Isa. 2:3).

4. Speaks of Heaven: "But ye are come unto mount Sion, and unto the city of the living God, the heavenly Jerusalem, and to an innumerable company of angels" (Heb. 12:22).

Your attention is called to these Scriptures to show the significance of this great text. To inherit God's holy mountain is no small thing. It stands for our redemption and justification.

FAITH FOR LIVING ON HIGH

It speaks of our Lord's return, reign and our heavenly Home.

I will talk about living on high, about mountaintop living. I know there is a valley. When the Lord left the Mount of Transfiguration, He taught a tremendous lesson: We cannot always live on mountaintops; it is in the valley where people need our help and ministry.

Caleb was a remarkable man. One day Joshua sent some people over the river into the Promised Land. He appointed twelve people and called them twelve spies because they were to do a secret work. They were to go over into the land and view it, spy it out, then come back and give a report to Joshua if it was exactly like God said it would be.

Two men were appointed by Moses in that committee of twelve, Joshua and Caleb.

When they came back with a report, it was positive. But the majority of the committee, the ten, said, "But there are walled villages, great fortresses; the people are like giants, and there are so many of them that we are as grasshoppers. We cannot take the land." But Caleb said, "Let us go up at once, and possess it; for we are well able to overcome it." 'Yes, we can take the land because God said He would give it to us.'

The place where they went over is called Hebron, Mount Hebron. This is where forty years ago Caleb went over into the promised land and found it exactly like God said it would be. Caleb said, when the land was divided, "Now therefore give me this mountain" (Josh. 14:12)—an echo of the words of a tremendous man who said, "Don't give me valleys; give me mountains, mountains high where the air is pure and where I am closer to Heaven and where God does business with people. Give me that mountain."

God gave Caleb that mountain, Mount Hebron.

Mount Hebron speaks of a number of things. It was a place of fruit bearing. Christian, if you are living anywhere except in the land of fruit bearing, you are living beneath your privilege.

Mount Hebron was a place of fellowship, where people could fellowship together. It was there, sitting under a big oak tree, where heavenly messengers came and talked to Abraham. Mamre was a plain, and Hebron was a mountain. Here an earthly man fellowshiped with heavenly people.

Near there Rachel died, that wonderful woman who cried to Jacob, "Give me children, or else I die." In the shadow of that tremendous mountain Rachel travailed, brought forth a son, died and was buried in the shadow of Hebron.

Here is a man in the Bible who claimed a mountain, claimed the promises of God for fellowship, for fruit bearing, and for a place to leave this world and to meet God.

In talking about mountains, I will confine my mountains to one book of the Bible. I want some mountains, and I believe you do, described in the book of Matthew, mountains all identified with Jesus Christ.

I say, in the words of Caleb, "Give me this mountain." I claim that promise today.

There are seven significant mountains in the book of Matthew, and all are identified with some great part of the redemptive work of our Lord Jesus Christ. By faith I claim each of these mountains. They are so important to me that I must say with Caleb, "Give me this mountain."

I. THE MOUNTAIN OF TEMPTATION

"Again, the devil taketh him up into an exceeding high mountain, and sheweth him all the kingdoms of the world, and the glory of them; And saith unto him, All these things will I give thee, if thou wilt fall down and worship me."—Matt. 4:8,9.

This is an important mountain: the mount where Satan's third great onslaught against the perfection of Christ took place; the mount where Jesus proved His perfection and sinlessness; the mount where we are shown that Satan can be overcome by the Word of God.

Our father Adam was tempted in a garden and failed. Our Saviour, Jesus, was tempted in a wilderness and won the victory. Satan tempted Jesus as the Son of God to turn stones into bread in order to end His forty-day fast. He was tempted as the Son of God to make a display of His power and cast Himself from the high pinnacle of the Temple. He was tempted as the Lamb of God when He was asked to bypass the cross in order to rule over the kingdoms of the world. In all three battles, Jesus showed that one verse from the holy Word of God can defeat the adversary: "It is written," quoting from the Old Testament Scriptures.

Jesus won this victory for us. We, too, can overcome temptation.

"There hath no temptation taken you but such as is common to man: but God is faithful, who will not suffer you to be tempted above that ye are able; but will with the temptation also make a way to escape, that ye may be able to bear it."—I Cor. 10:13.

Jesus knows and cares when we are tempted, for He went before us in this battle.

"For we have not an high priest which cannot be touched with the feeling of our infirmities; but was in all points tempted like as we are, yet without sin."—Heb. 4:15.

Thank God for One who has demonstrated the way for us to overcome temptations. We need not live a life of defeat. On the Mount of Temptation He won the victory.

"Give me this mountain."

II. THE SERMON ON THE MOUNTAIN

I follow the Lord to another mountain. Shortly after the temptation, Jesus began His great earthly ministry with a sermon. The first great sermon, the Sermon on the Mount, was delivered on a mountain near Capernaum, on the Sea of Galilee.

At the close of His ministry, Jesus preached the great prophetical sermon on Mount Olivet, recorded in Matthew, chapters 24 and 25.

His temptation begins His public ministry. The Sermon on the Mount, or The Beatitudes, is recorded in Matthew 5, 6 and 7. I read in Matthew 5:1,2:

"And seeing the multitudes, he went up into a mountain: and when he was set, his disciples came unto him: And he opened his mouth, and taught them...."

The greatest sermon this world has ever heard or read covers three chapters. Oh, the depths, the truths of this tremendous Sermon on the Mount.

It gives me rules for Christian living. It was on that mountaintop when Jesus said, "But seek ye first the kingdom of God, and his righteousness; and all these things shall be added unto you" (6:33). Every person living by that rule will turn out well. Seek first the kingdom of God and His righteousness, and everything else will fall in place.

In the Sermon on the Mount Jesus said many things that develop Christian character. One may be saved and going to Heaven, but if he doesn't have character, he will live a defeated life, with much misery. He will sometimes face deep, dark valleys.

"But thou, when thou prayest, enter into thy closet, and when thou hast shut thy door, pray to thy Father which is in secret; and thy Father which seeth in secret shall reward thee openly" (6:6). The secret things of your spiritual life are most important. It is not how loud you preach, how well you sing, but how well and how much you pray.

In that Sermon on the Mount He gave the very foundation of evangelism: "Let your light so shine before men, that they may see your good works, and glorify your Father which is in heaven" (5:16). It is not what kind of program you have, how many visits you make, how many people come to your church; the very foundation of New Testament evangelism is, "Let your light so shine before men, that they may see your good works." Without the shining light, there is no real Bible evangelism.

In that mountaintop sermon, He gave the model for prayer. Oh, my, how we need to pray for victory in our lives, for prosperity for our church, for blessings on the home and for our own selves. Lord, give me this mountain!

"...but he that putteth his trust in me shall possess the land, and shall inherit my holy mountain."

III. THE MOUNTAIN OF TRANSFIGURATION

How I wish we had time to scale that lofty height, camp there for awhile, and listen to two men who came from Heaven, three who came up from the earth, and the Lord Jesus. These six are on that mountaintop. Two came from Heaven, one had been dead 1500 years, and one had never died—Elijah. As he walked with God one day, a chariot of fire came from Heaven, he stepped into it, and the Lord took him Home. Some 900 years later Elijah comes down out of Glory, and Moses and Elijah meet with Jesus. Peter, James and John come up from the valley to meet with them.

My, what transpired on that mountaintop! I read that "after six days Jesus taketh Peter, James, and John his brother, and bringeth them up into a high mountain apart" (17:1).

I wish we could just camp there awhile. There is Jesus in a human body. Don't ever lose sight of the humanity of Jesus. Oh, I know He is divine, but the humanity of Jesus is important. He climbed that mountain in a human body. While He is on that mountaintop, these five others watch Him—two from Heaven and three from earth. All of a sudden Jesus begins to change. He is surrounded by a heavenly glory. The very garments He wears become white, "... for he is like a refiner's fire, and like fullers' soap" (Mal. 3:2).

Right before their eyes this One in a human body is transfigured, changed; now these five see Him in His glorified body.

Yes—and that wonderful thing is going to happen to every believer. When the Lord comes, "this robe of flesh I'll drop and rise, to seize the everlasting prize." I can shed this old body one day. God will give me a new body, like the transfigured body of our Lord.

"Behold, I shew you a mystery; We shall not all sleep, but we shall all be changed, In a moment, in the twinkling of an eye, at the last trump: for the trumpet shall sound, and the dead shall be raised incorruptible, and we shall be changed. For this corruptible must put on incorruption, and this mortal must put on immortality."—I Cor. 15:51-53.

God, give me that mountain!

On that mountain I see the truth of the immortality of the saints of God. Don't let anyone tell you that, when you die, you die as an animal dies. You just cease to be.

Here are people who have been gone for several hundred years. They are here on the mountaintop. Moses and Elijah still alive. Not only that, but Peter, James and John recognized them.

A lady was talking to her husband. He was one of those fellows who didn't say much, but what he said made sense. She asked him, "Do you think we'll know each other in Heaven?"

The husband, who never said much, replied, "Do you think we'll be bigger fools in Heaven than we are down here?"

She said, "No, I guess not."

He said, "Then we will know each other."

Yes, we will know each other in Heaven. I can hardly wait to shake the hands of some now gone on. I want to take hold of

Brother Campbell, who led me to the Lord, and thank him and thank him and thank him. I can hardly wait to get hold of the hands of my dear grandparents, who loved me and raised me. I can see them this morning in a little country school, their hair white as snow and their shoulders bent and stooped. When I preached, they walked down the aisle arm in arm together, the same way they lived for seventy-two years of married life. Oh, I want to see them! I could preach a whole sermon on those I want to greet on Heaven's shore.

Yes, we will know our loved ones in Heaven. And there are others we'll want to see in Heaven.

We learn in that transfiguration scene about the preeminence of Jesus. "And when they had lifted up their eyes, they saw no man, save Jesus only" (17:8).

That same Jesus, transfigured before them that day and evidently assuming for a time His glorified body, is coming back to give the saints of God a glorified body.

"For our conversation is in heaven; from whence also we look for the Saviour, the Lord Jesus Christ: Who shall change our vile body, that it may be fashioned like unto his glorious body, according to the working whereby he is able even to subdue all things unto himself."—Phil. 3:20,21.

I was preaching in Greenville, South Carolina. A deacon said, "I want to introduce you to one of the most unusual people you will ever meet." He didn't give me the details. I went with him to a rather nice home. A lady in a white nurse's uniform came to the door. When the deacon told her who he was, she opened the door and we went in, walked down a little hall and into a room. In the middle of the room was a hospital bed. There were other things around the room to make this sick and dying man comfortable.

The deacon walked right up to this hospital bed. As I walked up, I saw something lying there that looked like a human. A chest bone stuck up like a tent pole, and the sheet hung over it. There were little hands warped and twisted and fingernails out of place. His eyes, looking like two stone agates, were sunk far deep into his head. His teeth were clenched.

The deacon must have seen the look on my face. He said, "Preacher, this is Brother Jones." I looked around. There hung a college diploma, perhaps more than one, but I remember one from a Christian university. This man's name was on it. The deacon said, "Brother Jones has been sick for a long time. He's a wonderful Christian."

I looked down in those sightless eyes and at that pitiful looking man. Through those clenched teeth he said, "Preacher, don't feel sorry for me. The Lord is coming. Someday I am going to have a new body."

I stood and wept as I thought how wonderful God is. When He comes, every body will be made whole, complete. We will see Him, be made like Him.

God, give me that mountain!

IV. THE MOUNTAIN OF PROPHECY

Another mountain I call the mountain of prophecy. The longest prophetic sermon Jesus ever preached covers two chapters—24 and 25—in the book of Matthew.

"And as he sat upon the mount of Olives, the disciples came unto him privately, saying, Tell us, when shall these things be? and what shall be the sign of thy coming, and of the end of the world?"—24:3.

This is a threefold question. The Lord preached on the Mount of Olives about: the wrath of God being poured out on the world; the wonderful truth of the security for the elect of God, the certainty of His second coming and the tragedy of those left behind.

While sitting on that mountain, with the twelve disciples around Him, and while speaking of things yet to come, He said, "Then shall the kingdom of heaven be likened unto ten virgins, which took their lamps, and went forth to meet the bridegroom" (25:1).

Jesus said that five of those young women were foolish and five were wise. The wise had oil in their lamps; their lights were shining, and they were ready when the bridegroom came and went in with him to the marriage supper. The other five took no oil; their lamps would not burn, and they were shut out and left behind.

Oil speaks of the Holy Spirit who indwells the saved. But five had not the Holy Spirit and were lost. The foolish took their lamps, but took no oil. The foolish said to the wise, "Give us of your oil; for our lamps are gone out." But they refused.

The bridegroom came, and those whose lamps were burning "went in with him to the marriage: and the door was shut" (25:10). Those who pretended to be saved and held lamps that wouldn't burn, said, "Let us in"; but these were told, "The door is shut. The marriage feast is taking place."

Oh, the tragedy of being left behind! Oh, the miracle of the Lord's return!

There is coming a day when airplanes will be without pilots, cars will be without drivers, hospitals will be without nurses and doctors, churches will be without preachers. But a lot of people will be left behind.

Some screaming mother runs to the nursery and discovers her baby is not there. "The covers are like I left them—but where is my child?" The streets will be full of wondering people! The mills will still run, and newspapers will carry headlines:

THOUSANDS MISSING: NO ONE KNOWS WHERE THEY ARE!

You and I know the answer. The Lord has come and taken away His bride.

On that mountaintop Jesus spoke of His sure return and the tragedy of those left behind.

Everyone here has had sad experiences in your childhood. The saddest I ever had was a couple of times when I was left behind. I was in the ninth grade at a country high school called Bell Green High School. Bell Green was a tremendous place. It was near Hall Town and about three miles from Burn Out. Now anybody should know where that is, anybody who knows his geography! To a country boy, going just anywhere was fun!

We used to catch the bus to school. Nowadays you drive the bus up to the front door, toot the horn, get out and help little Johnny in. But I ran a mile and a quarter down the railroad track to catch a bus.

Lots of things were planned the last day of school. My brother and I had to milk six cows each and had lots of other work to do, so we were always rushed.

Turning the curve on the railroad track and running as fast as we could, we saw the back end of the bus pull down the road. We would miss the last day of school. Both of us were in tears. We said, "Another thirty seconds, and we could have caught it!"

Friends, some of you are going to be left behind. If the Lord should come today, some of you would be here when all hell breaks loose, when a holy God turns loose all His thunderbolts of wrath on this wicked world.

How sad to be left behind when the Lord comes! But how blessed to be ready for His return! Can you say, as John said when in exile on the Isle of Patmos, "Even so, come, Lord Jesus"?

"...but he that putteth his trust in me shall possess the land, and shall inherit my holy mountain."

Lord, give me this mountain.

V. MOUNT CALVARY

"And when they were come unto a place called Golgotha, that is to say, a place of a skull, They gave him vinegar to drink mingled with gall: and when he had tasted thereof, he would not drink.

And they crucified him, and parted his garments, casting lots: that it might be fulfilled which was spoken by the prophet, They parted my garments among them, and upon my vesture did they cast lots. And sitting down they watched him there."—Matt. 27:33-36.

This is the little mountain upon which Jesus died for the sins of the world. He died suspended between two thieves. One asked for mercy, was saved and went immediately into Paradise with Jesus. The other wanted Jesus to save him without the cross; this one went to Hell.

Jesus was robed in blood and crowned with thorns as He died for our sins. On that mountain He took our place, died in the sinner's stead.

"And sitting down they watched him there." They sat down to watch Jesus die. What did they see? They saw the depravity of man. They saw men put to death the God who made them. They saw cruel and wicked hands lay hold of the Son of God and nail Him to a cross. They saw the awfulness of sin. They saw how God deals with sin. God put the sins of the world upon His own dear Son.

"Surely he hath borne our griefs, and carried our sorrows: yet we did esteem him stricken, smitten of God, and afflicted. But he was wounded for our transgressions, he was bruised for our iniquities: the chastisement of our peace was upon him; and with his stripes we are healed. All we like sheep have gone astray; we have turned every one to his own way; and the Lord hath laid on him the iniquity of us all."—Isa. 53:4-6.

I once sat in a room talking to an elderly deacon who loved the Lord and was a great student of the Bible. As we talked he said, "Brother Tom, what do you think is the greatest statement in the Bible?" I pondered that question for a few moments before answering. It was a solemn and heart-searching moment. Finally he broke the silence with: "I believe the greatest statement in the Bible is, 'The Lord hath laid on him the iniquity of us all.' "

I don't know if that could be called the greatest statement in the Bible or not, but do you know of a greater one? Christ died for our sins. On the cross the love of God was demonstrated at the highest possible level. A loving God gave His only begotten Son that we might be saved.

What a great mountain is Mount Calvary!

Lord, give me that mountain!

VI. THE MOUNTAIN OF PRAYER

"And when he had sent the multitudes away, he went up into a mountain apart to pray: and when the evening was come, he was there alone."—Matt. 14:23.

Jesus had just fed the 5,000 men besides the women and children. He had ministered to a large multitude. But here He leaves the multitude of human faces for the solitude of the face of His Heavenly Father. Jesus dismissed the disciples to cross the Sea of Galilee in the evening. He met them on the stormy sea at the fourth watch of the night, which means He was alone in prayer for approximately eight hours.

Jesus left the popularity of the crowd for the privacy of prayer. He left the community of hungry people for the communion of a holy Father. He never sought the counsels of men in preference to the calmness of the place of prayer.

Jesus taught that we can do more on our knees than we can do any other way. He wants to show us that there is strength in prayer. He Himself had received this strength from God before. When He prayed and suffered in agony in the Garden of Gethsemane, He received strength from God. "And there appeared an angel from heaven, strengthening him" (Luke 22:43).

Jesus rebuked the ostentatious praying of the Pharisees, but He loved being alone with God. What an example He sets for us! We must not be so dazzled with the crowds that we lose the desire to be alone with God. Prayer not only brings that which is good to us, but prayer brings peace to the starving heart and calmness to the restless mind. No soul can be healthy without prayer. Every Christian needs a prayer mountain where circumstances are nullified, needs are met, fears are overcome, and weakness is exchanged for strength and power.

God, give me that mountain!

VII. THE MOUNTAIN OF EVANGELISM

"Then the eleven disciples went away into Galilee, into a mountain where Jesus had appointed them. And when they saw him, they worshipped him: but some doubted. And Jesus came and spake unto them, saying, All power is given unto me in heaven and in earth. Go ye therefore, and teach all nations, baptizing them in the name of the Father, and of the Son, and of the Holy Ghost: Teaching them to observe all things whatsoever I have commanded you: and, lo, I am with you alway, even unto the end of the world."—Matt. 28:16-20.

This is one of the post-resurrection appearances of Jesus. It is an appointed meeting. On the day of His resurrection He had made an appointment with the disciples to meet them at a later date in Galilee. "Then said Jesus unto them, Be not afraid: go tell my brethren that they go into Galilee, and there shall they see me" (28:10).

Even before He died, He arranged this meeting on a mountain in Galilee. "But after I am risen again, I will go before you into Galilee" (26:32).

On this mountain Jesus established three great things in the hearts of the disciples:

1. His absolute and complete authority and power;

2. His commission to win people to Christ, baptize them and teach them;

3. The guarantee of His presence in the execution of that Great Commission.

It is for these reasons that we call this mountain the mount of evangelism. His parting words were about the winning of souls and great things identified with that task.

God has given us a command to evangelize the world. All will not be saved, but all are to be evangelized. God's Word teaches us that we are to evangelize every creature (Mark 16:15); every house (Acts 5:42); every nation (Luke 24:27). We cannot witness to the wrong person because He said "every creature." We cannot go with the Gospel to the wrong house because He said "every house."

Probably ninety-five percent of all Christians never win a soul to Christ. Not being a soul winner is a sign of disobedience, the sin of not following the Lord Jesus. "Follow me, and I will make you fishers of men" (Matt. 4:19).

A few hours ago I asked a man if anyone had ever shown him from the Bible how to be saved. He answered, "No, no one has ever explained to me how to be saved." I took my Bible and showed him. Today he was baptized and joined the church. It is such a thrill and joy to win souls to Christ!

"Give me this mountain."—Josh. 14:12.

"...but he that putteth his trust in me shall possess the land, and shall inherit my holy mountain."—Isa. 57:13.

Chapter XIV

Rahab's Faith and the Scarlet Cord

(Preached in Emmanuel Baptist Church on Sunday morning, February 19, 1978)

READ: Joshua 2:1-18

"Behold, when we come into the land, thou shalt bind this line of scarlet thread in the window which thou didst let us down by: and thou shalt bring thy father, and thy mother, and thy brethren, and all thy father's household, home unto thee."—Josh. 2:18.

"By faith the harlot Rahab perished not with them that believed not, when she had received the spies with peace."—Heb. 11:31.

Rahab had befriended these two spies and hid them. She was, no doubt, responsible, humanly speaking, for saving their lives. She said, 'Show me a token that you will reciprocate this to me, that when you and your people come to destroy the city of Jericho, my family and I will be saved. I want a sign, a token—visible evidence that, when judgment comes, I and mine shall be spared' (Josh. 2:12). The men whom she let down over the wall with a piece of scarlet red rope said to her, 'Bind this scarlet thread in the window. Let it hang over the wall of Jericho. Then when our armies come across the Jordan to possess the land and destroy this city, we will see that scarlet cord, and your home will be spared, and your family saved' (Josh. 2:18).

It was pointed out to us who visited the ruins and debris of the city of Jericho that the wall where Rahab lived was different, and is even to this day, from the wall of the rest of the city. The Bible said that the wall would fall down flat (Josh. 6:20). Archaeologists have discovered that it did not crumble straight down but fell flat, like a ladder would fall. Not so with the part of the wall where Rahab and her family lived. It was preserved. While the wall was falling, it was preserved so she and her family could be released from the city, which was about to be destroyed.

It is a wonderful story here of Rahab, a harlot, being saved—she and all of her family. There is a wonderful thing God sets forth in His Word that gives us some tremendous teaching about law and grace.

Moses has been God's great leader. God preserved his life by the miraculous little boat his believing mother made. God raised Moses up and made him the mighty leader.

God gave to Moses the Ten Commandments. God literally made him the ruler over these millions of people. To him God gave the Law. Whenever in the Bible we read of Moses, we read of God's law, God's inexorable law, God's unchanging, divine law. Moses represents law.

Moses died. The Lord placed the mantle of Moses, so to speak, upon a young man named Joshua. God said to Joshua, 'Moses my servant is dead. Now you take these people into the promised land.' Even with all of his spirituality, Moses was not allowed to take the children of Israel across the Jordan and into the land of promise. There is a reason for that.

One day God said to Moses, "Smite the rock." He did, and water came out. Another time God said to Moses, "Speak to the rock." But in anger Moses smote the rock. It was like crucifying Jesus twice. God will have no part of that. So God said to Moses, 'Because I said to speak to the rock and you smote it, you are not going into the promised land.' He who represented the Law could lead them in the wilderness, but he could not lead them into the promised land. The Law will never lead anybody into the promised land. Only Jesus can do that.

In the book of John, Jesus speaks of these two great representations—one by Moses and one by Joshua: "For the law was given by Moses, but grace and truth came by Jesus Christ" (John 1:17). You say, "Preacher, we know all that." Some of you know it in your head, but some of you are wondering right now, "Could the Seventh-day Adventists be right in saying you must keep the Law and observe the Sabbath in order to be saved?" No. Jesus said that the Law was given by Moses, but grace and truth came by Jesus Christ. The Law demanded righteousness. Grace provides righteousness. What a difference!

The Law was connected with man's works. The Law said, "Do and live." Grace is connected with man's faith and God's works.

The Law brings blessing to the good. Grace saves the bad and the wicked.

The Law demands; grace gives.

The Law brings death; grace gives life.

Here are two men—Moses, who represents the Law; and Joshua, who represents Jesus, grace and faith.

Like always, the Bible is applicable in this modern day. The Word of God in all of its truth can be applied to the work of God today as it always has.

I learn in this Book that God uses unusual people to accomplish His tasks. Think for a moment. God is going to do a great work. He promised to Abraham that his people were going to have the land of Canaan. When He made the promise, He said, 'There are seven nations in it now, all mightier than Israel; but I am going to give it to Israel, My people.'

Here God is about to perform His oath and make good His Word. He is going to give the land to the people of God. The first city they must overcome is Jericho, one of the oldest cities in the world. Some say that it is the oldest, but it is not because it has not been continuously occupied over the centuries. Here is that city which God is going to overthrow. God is going to make good His Word. God never has broken His Word to anyone. He is going to give this land to the seed of Abraham.

Here are two Jews—two Israelites—two of God's number, who cross the Jordan to spy out the city of Jericho. When I read commentaries by men who are supposed to be scholarly, I find they always raise a lot of questions. "If God said that He was going to give it to them, why did they have to bother to spy it out, risk their lives and delay the taking of it?"

I will tell you why. "...faith without works is dead" (James 2:20). God never saved anybody to sit down and do nothing. You are saved by faith. But the same Bible says, "...faith without works is dead." God's sovereign purpose will never be frustrated. Human responsibility is always there.

God said to Joshua, 'Have these spies go and look at the city of Jericho and see if it can be taken.' Who would have ever believed that the two men sent by General Joshua would meet and be befriended by and have their lives saved by the most dissolute character in all of Jericho!! The first person they met when they stole into the walled city that night, their clothes dripping wet from the waters of Jordan, was this woman Rahab.

Perhaps they asked, "Who are you?"

"My name is Rahab, and I'm a harlot. Men have come to my house by the hundreds over the years."

Rahab became the prominent tool in the hands of God to discharge His purpose and to bring to pass His promise.

Don't ever think that God is confined to using the elite, the moral, the educated, the wealthy. The grace of God makes elite people out of sinful people.

RAHAB'S FAITH AND THE SCARLET CORD

The first person they met was a harlot. God uses unusual people to accomplish His tasks.

I wish I had the time to talk about some unusual people who have had a tremendous part and whose reward awaits them at the coming of Jesus Christ for what they did to establish this work of God, whose message and people have encircled God's earth. They were not educated people, not rich people, not talented people, and not even, sometimes, moral people until God got through with their lives.

The spies met a harlot the first thing.

The Bible teaches me that, when God's workmen die, God's work never dies! The first thing God said to Joshua was "Moses is dead." Is that the end of the world? No. Is that the end of the work of God? No. Is that the end of God's message? No. God's workmen die, but God's work lives on.

A lot of people have said, "I wonder what will happen when So-and-so goes." The work will go on just as usual, just as it always has. They will barely get through patting the dirt on his grave with a spade and mounding it up and making it look nice when the world will have forgotten and somebody else will march in his stead.

God said to Joshua, 'Moses is dead; now you go on with the work.' God wants people to look to God, not to men! God's work is not thwarted and stopped by the passing of His people.

I learn in this Book the importance of the Word of God. I will dwell on this when we talk about how Rahab was saved. This is beautiful. The Lord spoke to Joshua in chapter 1 and said, "Moses my servant is dead...As I was with Moses, so I will be with thee.... Be strong and of a good courage." Then He said, "This book of the law shall not depart out of thy mouth...."

We need the preaching of the Bible instead of entertainers in the pulpit. God is not an enemy to humor, but that is not the message.

We have motivators. I could invite a certain somebody to this pulpit, and you would be so motivated, this church couldn't hold the people. Men of the world motivate. But we are not talking about motivators and comedians. God puts His premium on preachers who preach this Book! "This book of the law shall not depart out of thy mouth...."

I learn in the Bible about God's presence. He is no respecter of persons. God will be with me and you just as He was with Moses or Joshua. The success of God's predetermined, divine plans cannot be stopped by the Devil or any man or woman he may use. The work of God is going to succeed. What is this work? It is not to build the biggest, do the biggest, be the greatest; it is to see a bride brought out of sin into grace, who will be the wife of our Lord Jesus Christ at His coming. That work is going to succeed.

I. RAHAB'S FAITH

In chapter 11 of the book of Hebrews, we read about God's "greats"—about Abel, the first man to offer blood; about Enoch, who walked with God and never died, for the Lord took him; about Abraham, Isaac and Jacob; about Joseph and David—God's "greats" who made God's Honor Roll. Tucked right in there, in verse 31, we read, "By faith the harlot Rahab perished not with them that believed not, when she had received the spies with peace." Here is a harlot who made the Honor Roll of God!

Let us look at three things: Rahab's faith; Joshua's predicament, a predicament that has challenged the minds of Bible scholars throughout the history of man; and Rahab's salvation, her experience in being saved.

1. Faith in a Message

Rahab believed a message. Here in chapter 2 Rahab speaks. It should be marked off in the chapter because she speaks the Word of God. "For we have heard how the Lord dried up the water of the Red Sea for you, when ye came out of Egypt; and what ye did unto the two kings of the Amorites, that were on the other side Jordan...whom ye utterly destroyed." She not only heard it; she believed it. Rahab's faith believed a message.

That is the only way anybody can be saved. You can believe in the existence of God; it will not save you. You can believe that God is the one and only Creator—the Source of all things, animate and inanimate; it will not save you. You have to believe a message about a Person—what God has done through His Son. Rahab's faith led her to believe the message.

In order to be saved, one must hear and believe the message of the Gospel. Paul makes this clear in Romans 1:16,17:

"For I am not ashamed of the gospel of Christ: for it is the power of God unto salvation to every one that believeth; to the Jew first, and also to the Greek. For therein is the righteousness of God revealed from faith to faith: as it is written, The just shall live by faith."

There is the power of God in that message. In that message is the righteousness of God, without which no one will be saved. Rahab heard a message about what God had done for His people and what He was going to do for her and her people (Josh. 2:9-13).

The Lord said, "Go ye into all the world, and preach the gospel to every creature." No one is saved without the Gospel and believing the Gospel, that Christ died for our sins and rose again from the dead according to the Scriptures.

2. Faith That Was Lonely

Someone has referred to her faith as a lonely faith. Think of the multiplied thousands in the ancient, historical, famous city of Jericho. Here comes a message of God to the heathen, a message they had never heard before. Rahab and her family were the only ones that believed that message. Her faith was a lonely faith.

It was like the faith of Noah, to whom God said, 'Build an ark for the saving of your family.' Noah and his family were the only ones who believed that message.

It was like the faith of Joseph who believed in God's providence, plan and program. He trusted God even in a prison dungeon in Egypt; Joseph was the only one of his whole family who really believed it.

Her faith was like the faith of Daniel who said, 'I don't need the king's wine nor the king's meat. Throw me into a lions' den, if you will; my God will preserve me.' In the whole heathen land of Babylon where people mocked God and ridiculed the truth, Daniel believed. His faith was lonely.

Here is a woman who believed God when no one else was believing Him.

3. Faith in the Word

Her faith was in the Word. A lot of people are saved who do not know it. I am not God, nor am I a mind reader. I talked to someone the other day who said to me, "I don't believe I'm saved." Some people who think they are saved, are not saved. God knows the hearts and minds of all men. If He could make it open and public who is saved and who is not saved, we would be so shocked, we would never get over it. It might almost drive us to insanity. Some people think they are saved who are not. Some people think they are lost who are not. Some do not know where assurance comes from. I know where a lot of people think it comes from. "Assurance is when you feel good inside." That is not it. Assurance comes from faith in the Word of God. "So then faith cometh by hearing, and hearing by the word of God" (Rom. 10:17). "Verily, verily, I say unto you, He that heareth my word, and believeth on him that sent me, hath [present possession] everlasting life, and shall not come into condemnation; but is passed from death unto life'' (John 5:24). Who said that? God.

How does one get assurance? By believing what God said. When someone tells me, "I believe God's Word, what it says about me being a sinner, about Christ as a Saviour, and the efficacy of His death on the cross; I believe in Christ as my Saviour"—I believe that one is a child of God. If you believe that in your heart, you are a child of God—not in your head, but in your heart.

Rahab believed the Word. These men said, 'When we come back, if we see a scarlet line in your window, you will be spared.' What hope did she have? After they had left, perhaps as she sat in her home in the evening, her mother and father questioned her: "Daughter, how do you know we're going to be rescued? Do you have some proof? Is there anything visible? Is this more than a wish or a hope? Is there some reason on which we can base the fact that you say we are going to be saved?"

The daughter answered, "Yes, I have their word. They promised."

"Is that all?"

"That's all I have."

And that is all you have—the Word of the eternal God. That is all I have. But, hallelujah! That's all I need! It's all I want! It's all I have ever looked for! This Book says I am saved and that I am going to be saved from judgment.

Boats have different levels. One part is called the hold. You are on a boat. Somebody says, "The only way we can ride the storm out is to throw out the anchor." Suppose you take the anchor and throw it down in the hold of the ship.

The captain comes by and asks, "Did you throw out the anchor?"

"Yes."

"Well, we are still reeling and rocking and tossing on the stormy sea."

"But I threw out the anchor."

"Where did you throw it?"

"Down in the bottom of the ship."

Astonished, the captain says, "That will never do. We have to do something more than that which is related to what is within us. Throw it overboard!"

They throw it overboard. The big anchor sinks beneath the waves. It grabs hold of the weeds and rocks at the bottom of the sea, steadies the boat and anchors it through the storm.

I have an anchor. It is not within—that would do me no good. I have the witness of the Spirit within. I have an anchor that reaches right up, knocks on Heaven's door, gains entrance, walks right up to the presence of God, lays hold upon the honor of God, and says, "You said it. I believe it."

I am saved forever because Jesus said it in His Word.

Rahab's faith was in the Word.

4. Faith Accompanied by Works

Her faith was accompanied by works. That is what James was talking about when he said, "...faith without works is dead" (James 2:20). Even James goes back to the book of Joshua for an example of a woman who was saved: "Likewise also was not Rahab the harlot justified by works, when she had received the messengers, and had sent them out another way" (2:25).

Some say that Paul said we are justified by faith. He did. James said that we are justified by works. Some people say these two men are not together, that they contradict each other. No. Paul was talking about justification before God when he said, "You are justified by faith." James was talking about proving it, showing it, demonstrating it before men when he said, "It takes works to do that."

You come every Sunday morning and sit in a soft, comfortable pew with a padded seat; but your works justify your faith before men. There are Christians who have been justified before God who give no evidence to justify their faith before men. Faith is to be accompanied by works for justification before men.

I would not exchange the peace I have in my heart and soul for all of this world. That is not an expression, not just talk, not just preaching. It is a deep feeling that wells up within me, that I would rather have the peace that I enjoy and the comfort I have in being a Christian, than to have everything this world can give.

But being a Christian is not all a bed of roses. There is ridicule and persecution. There is the responsibility to live before God. There is chastisement. There are losses.

It cost Rahab something. One day when her house crumbled, Rahab said, "We have a home in Heaven, not made with hands, an eternal home." Hers was faith accompanied by repentance. It was a saving faith, and she perished not.

Out of chapter 2 of Joshua there are three tremendous things I would like you to notice. I cannot help but think of the word *gratitude* when I read that chapter.

Two men went across the Jordan to spy out the land. Their presence in Jericho was detected. The rulers of the city came to the woman and said, "Bring forth the men that are come to thee, which are entered into thine house: for they be come to search out all the country." The king wanted to kill them. Rahab had hidden them up on her roof, hidden them beneath the stalks of flax. These two men, who had been sent to spy, were grateful. They promised her that, when Jericho was destroyed, her life would be spared.

Don't let the weeds of selfishness choke the flower of gratitude in your heart. Romans 13:7 reads, "Render therefore to all their dues: tribute to whom tribute is due; custom to whom custom; fear to whom fear; honour to whom honour." If somebody along the way has blessed you, be grateful for it. Don't be reluctant to show your gratitude. Churches are filled with ingrates—those who show no gratitude. Some are disloyal to the one who won them to Christ. I thank God every day for that man who led me to the Lord. And I thanked him before he died. When I get to Heaven, one of the first things I want to do is to thank Brother Campbell for leading me to Christ. You owe gratitude to somebody. "Owe no man any thing, but to love one another" (Rom. 13:8). An old saying is, "They can't smell the flowers after they are dead." If you owe somebody something, give it to him while he is alive.

I cannot help but think of *reward* when I read chapter 2 of Joshua. Here is Rahab, a woman who had heard of the fame and blessing of God upon the children of Israel. These two spies come into the city. She hides them, saves their lives, and God rewards her for it by saving her and all her family.

God rewards people. Jesus said that not a cup of cold water given in His name will go without reward.

I think of you who drive buses. You do not get much thanks for your hard work. I think of you who devote hours to the little folks, caring for them and teaching them. You are going to be rewarded. I think of you faithful people who are loyal to God in your tithes, your offerings, and by your presence and prayers. You who support the work of God are going to be rewarded. God's Word teaches that God will honor in Heaven those with rewards who do something for Him here. Even a cup of cold water, if given to a thirsty soul, will be rewarded in Heaven.

I cannot help but think of the certainty of *judgment* and condemnation. All through the Pentateuch—the first five books of the Bible—the destruction of Canaan was determined by God, set by God. It had to come to pass because God said it would. What judgment God describes that shall come upon the unsaved and the godless nations of the world, must and will come to pass.

I have talked about Rahab's faith; now I want to talk about

II. JOSHUA'S PREDICAMENT

Joshua was in a terrible predicament when he allowed this woman and all her family and kindred to be saved. It might have been a large group. You think that was a wonderful thing to do. Yes, but in Deuteronomy 7:2 the Lord gave specific instruction to the children of Israel as to what they were to do when they crossed that Jordan and entered into Canaan and came to those cities: "And when the Lord thy God shall deliver them before thee; thou shalt smite them, and utterly destroy them; thou shalt make no covenant with them, nor shew mercy unto them." This is important. God said, "When you cross Jordan and enter into Canaan, you set about to destroy the Canaanites—seven mighty nations; you make no covenant with them but utterly destroy them. Show no mercy unto them."

In light of this, how are you going to explain the mercy shown to a whole family, a whole family wonderfully saved and delivered out of the overthrow of the city of Jericho? Did Joshua and the people violate the Word of God? Or is this somehow in God's plan? Let us put it a different way. Let us apply it to you and me.

We read in Ezekiel 18:4, "...the soul that sinneth, it shall die." Have you ever sinned? Every person would have to say, "Yes, I have sinned and sinned and sinned." Though you are not lost because of what you do, you are lost because of what you are. Every one of us is a sinner. The inexorable law of God says, "...the soul that sinneth, it shall die."

You are here, and I am here. We are not dead in the spiritual sense but alive and enjoying life in Christ. Explain this dilemma.

Joshua had a dilemma. He was commanded to destroy them all, yet he spared some. God has the dilemma that all have sinned, and the soul that sins shall surely die; yet God has spared some.

This has been discussed by theologians of all ages. It is talked about in the Pauline writings. For instance, Romans 3:26: "...To declare, I say, at this time his righteousness: that he might be just, and the justifier of him which believeth in Jesus." A different way to say it is: "...That God might be just through the Justifier." How can God, who said, 'The soul that sinneth shall surely die,' save us and be just? God is just. And a just God must keep His Word. Then how can God be just and declare you and me as righteous as if we had never sinned? That is God's dilemma, and I speak reverently.

Of course it takes place because that judgment was poured out on Another. That is what we mean by vicarious suffering—the Innocent suffering for the guilty, the Just for the unjust, the perfect One for the sinful one. Because of the death of Christ, God can be just and the Justifier of them that believe. Thank God for justification!

I am glad justification is something man cannot tamper with. "Therefore being justified by faith, we have peace with God through our Lord Jesus Christ" (Rom. 5:1). You and I have nothing to do with justification. We cannot fool with it. It didn't take place within me. Justification is not something that, when you came forward, shook a preacher's hand and believed in Christ, you got! You got regeneration when you were saved, but not justification. Justification takes place in the perfect mind of an eternal God. God sees you and me in Christ and says, "He is as righteous as Christ is righteous because he is clothed in the garments of the Lord." So God can be just and still be the Justifier of them that believe.

Let me demonstrate. Each time there is a court case tried, there is a judge and a criminal. The judge says, "I find this man guilty/or innocent of the crime he is charged with." That judge has to be just, and he has to be justified. There has to be some reason to

RAHAB'S FAITH AND THE SCARLET CORD

say, "You're guilty," or some reason to say, "You're innocent."

What justification has the judge in saying, "You're not guilty"? He has to justify his declaration.

So does God. Thank God, He does! He justifies it in the death of His Son. He declares it in the death of His Son. He declares us justified because we have the righteousness of Jesus Christ.

There is a beautiful thing here. When Rahab got ready to let down the two men over the wall, they said, "...bind this line of scarlet thread in the window which thou didst let us down by...." It was the scarlet rope which she had used to let the men down. It is called the scarlet line.

There is a scarlet stream in the Bible. It starts with the lamb of Abel and the shed blood of the animals with which God clothed Adam and Eve. It runs through the Bible like a never-ending stream. It sometimes goes out of sight, then shows up again. It finally shows up for the last time in the book of Revelation.

A scarlet stream runs from Genesis to Revelation—the scarlet cord. It speaks of the blood of Jesus Christ. When she let them down over the wall, it was with the scarlet cord. They turned back and said to her, 'When judgment comes to Jericho, hang this scarlet cord out the window. When we see this scarlet cord, when we see the blood of Christ, we will spare you.' That is exactly the meaning.

That happened in the book of Exodus. When the blood was put upon the lintel and the doorposts, God said, "When I see the blood, I will pass over you." It is old-fashioned teaching now. Thank God, it came from an old-fashioned Bible and an old-fashioned, eternal God. It is just as pertinent and as necessary today as it ever was. This Bible declares that no one will ever be saved apart from the blood of Jesus Christ. "In whom we have redemption through his blood, the forgiveness of sins, according to the riches of his grace" (Eph. 1:7).

Had you been in Jericho, you might have seen a scene something like this. Thousands of people were destroyed—men, women and children. It was a gory, ghastly holocaust of killing and blood. Here is a family protected as if they were already in Heaven. Here is a scarlet cord hanging out the window. "Why are you being spared? What is the difference? You have been a harlot, Rahab. You have been a sinner, Rahab. Why are you spared and we condemned?" I think these words would have come from her mouth: "Because of the scarlet cord!"

That is the only way anybody is saved. The only difference between one who will spend an eternal separation from God in Hell and one who will spend an eternal bliss with God in Heaven is the scarlet cord—the blood of Jesus Christ.

I would like you to see a few things about

III. RAHAB'S SALVATION

1. God Saves Bad People

Some folks think God does not save bad people, but He does. He does, He has, He always will.

You see the Lord dying upon the cross. You hear a malefactor say to Him, "Lord, remember me when thou comest into thy kingdom." You hear Jesus say, "To day shalt thou be with me in paradise." You see the Lord walk the streets of this very city hundreds of years after the destruction. You see the Lord walk down the streets of Jericho (Luke 19). Crowds were gathered to see this miracle-working Man. A little crooked politician, who had robbed, cheated, stolen and lied in order to get his treasure, climbed up a tree to see the Lord Jesus. Jesus came under that tree. He called his name. He knew it like He knows your name and mine. "Zacchaeus, come down. To day I must abide at thy house." Jesus and Zacchaeus make a beautiful picture—the Saviour walking arm-in-arm with a little, crooked politician. They walk down the street to Zacchaeus' house. Here they break bread.

The Lord saves bad people! Society can't do that. All of the government handouts can't do it. Jail can't do it. Penal institutions can't change people. They can punish them, but they cannot change them.

It is like the maniac of Gadara. They bound him with chains and fetters, but he was no better. One day the Lord Jesus came along. The maniac was naked and bleeding. He dwelt among the tombs. Jesus saw him. This man fearfully cried out. The Lord saved him. Now you see him sitting and clothed and in his right mind. He says to Jesus as meekly as a little child, 'I want to follow Thee.' The Lord said, 'If you want to follow Me, go home to thy family and thy friends and tell what great things the Lord hath done for thee.'

When the people saw the maniac clothed and calm, they wondered what had happened to the maniac. Did a term in jail change him? Did the binding with the chains change him? No, not one bit. It was Jesus who changed him. He is the only way anybody can ever be changed.

Different things may help. You can take a coat down to Egypt, put it on the prodigal, and it will warm him but will not save him. You can take him a pair of shoes to warm his feet, but you cannot save his soul without the blood of Jesus Christ.

God saves bad people.

2. They Have an Immediate Testimony

Here is something wonderful. I don't understand it, nor need to. Christians say, "I don't have a testimony with my loved ones." Many a Christian has said to me, "Would you talk to my loved one? Somebody outside the family can talk to them better, you see." No, I do not see. When God saves a man, he has a testimony right then, immediately.

We see Jesus and the woman at the well in Samaria. She already had had five husbands. 'The one you are living with now is not your husband,' Jesus said.

I have often thought of that lady. Pardon me, but I am not trying to be sacrilegious or irreverent. She must have been a pretty nice-looking lady. No one who is as ugly as homemade sin is going to have five men, then a sixth one. She must have been a nagger, mean, for she couldn't keep any of them. Her reputation as a dissolute character was known throughout the whole countryside.

When she met Jesus, she set her waterpot on the well and never filled it. She left an empty waterpot after the Lord had said, "Whosoever drinketh of this water shall thirst again; But whosoever drinketh of the water that I shall give him shall never thirst" (John 4:13,14). She drank of the well of salvation. She left her waterpot and ran into the city. You see a cloud of dust as she gathers up her skirts and starts running. She says, "Come, see a man, which told me all things that ever I did."

The Lord sees a big crowd. Who are they? Men to whom she has witnessed.

They believed her. They had confidence in her. She had an immediate testimony.

Rahab had a testimony right away, too. Her family believed her when she said, "The Lord will save us. The blood will keep us from destruction."

What happened to Rahab is one of the most beautiful things in the Word of God. She is mentioned in Joshua, Hebrews and James. She is beautifully mentioned at the very beginning of the book of Matthew, in the genealogy of Jesus Christ. Five women are mentioned there. One is a Moabite; one is the virgin Mary. We read of a woman named Thamar who gave birth to twins by her father-in-law; then we read of Rachab (Rahab); then Ruth, both mentioned in verse 5. Bath-sheba is in verse 6. The fifth is Mary, a virgin and a wonderful woman.

RAHAB'S FAITH AND THE SCARLET CORD

Here is what is beautiful to me. The Bible tells us that a man by the name of Salmon (not Solomon), a prince in Israel, married Rahab. They had a child whose name was Booz (Boaz). Boaz was a well-to-do man. When Ruth and her mother-in-law Naomi went back into the land of Israel, Boaz saw this young woman Ruth and gave her a great bundle of grain, which she took to her mother-in-law.

In the providence and will of God, Boaz married Ruth. She became the grandmother of David. Then out of that marriage, Jesse was born, the father of David.

Think of it! Here is the harlot Rahab out of Jericho. She marries a prince. She becomes a great-great-grandmother of David, the sweet singer of Israel.

That is not all. When God's holy Word recorded the genealogy of Jesus Christ, the name of Rahab is one of five women. Thus she became an ancestress, humanly speaking, of Jesus Christ.

That is grace reaching down, grace lifting up and grace honoring a born-again child of God.

3. Her Salvation Was an Individual Matter

Her salvation was an individual matter. It has never been any other way. No one is going to be saved because his family is saved. This started, as it were, with God and Rahab. It was an individual matter. Watch—this is a solemn thought: It became a family matter. Rahab wanted all her household saved, and God saved every one of them. The night the Philippian jailer got saved, Paul and Silas said to him, "Believe on the Lord Jesus Christ, and thou shalt be saved, **and thy house.**"

If you are one of those dear people of God with lost ones in your family, then you have not let God do for you all that He wants to do.

I used to hold many revivals, sometimes for a week, sometimes two weeks, sometimes three weeks. Many were revivals, but some were just meetings. There is a great difference. I saw revival. I saw people come by the hundreds. I saw people come until the altar was filled and emptied, filled and emptied again.

I never saw a revival but that people were interested in their families being saved. I have heard them shout, "That's Daddy at the altar!" or, "That's my mother!" or, "That's my wayward boy!" or, "That's my daughter!" or, "That's my husband!" or, "That's my wife!"

God is interested in families getting saved.

If you would get tuned up with God, God would give you your loved ones.

My mother is sitting in this place. She knows this to be true. I was saved as a country boy down in Alabama. I had gotten the use of a country school, and I began to preach. Our loved ones were saved, literally by the dozens. It was in that meeting that I saw my own sweet grandparents, arm-in-arm, come down the aisle of that little schoolhouse.

If you were to ask me, "Do you have a near kin who has never been saved?" I would have to say, "Not that I know of." One of the sweetest things I can think of is that God saved my family and my loved ones.

He saved Rahab out of Jericho. The Bible says they went and dwelt in Israel. God is not just saving people out of Hell; He is saving us into Heaven.

Thank God, He is still in the saving business as He was when He saved Rahab!

"And Joshua saved Rahab the harlot alive, and her father's household, and all that she had; and she dwelleth in Israel even unto this day; because she hid the messengers, which Joshua sent to spy out Jericho."—Josh. 6:25.

"By faith the harlot Rahab perished not with them that believed not, when she had received the spies with peace."—Heb. 11:31.

Chapter XV

"According to Your Faith"

(Preached at the Emmanuel Baptist Church, Sunday morning, February 17, 1963)

READ: Matthew 9:27-38

"Then touched he their eyes, saying, According to your faith be it unto you."—Matt. 9:29.

This message is directed primarily to Christians. I will bring to your mind one passage of Scripture that will make you know how important the faith of a Christian really is. In chapter 22 of Luke, we find two tremendous verses, verses 31 and 32:

"And the Lord said, Simon, Simon, behold, Satan hath desired to have you, that he may sift you as wheat: But I have prayed for thee, that thy faith fail not: and when thou art converted, strengthen thy brethren."

Everything about Simon Peter failed except his faith. It could not fail because his faith was involved in the prayers of Jesus Christ: "But I have prayed for thee, that thy faith fail not."

If the faith of Peter was so important that Jesus made it a matter of prayer, then the faith of the Christian of this day and hour is also tremendously important to the Lord.

Some expressions in the New Testament cause us to know how important the faith of a Christian is. Romans 14:23: ". . . for whatsoever is not of faith is sin." That is a strong statement, isn't it?

Hebrews 11:6: "...without faith it is impossible to please him." That would lend importance to faith. Nothing could possibly be more important than the faith of God's children.

First John 5:4: "...this is the victory that overcometh the world, even our faith." If a Christian's faith overcomes the world and gives him victory, then how important is faith to a Christian!

"Believe" in the Bible deals with heart faith. Jesus asked these two blind men, "Believe ye that I am able to do this?" They answered, "Yea, Lord." Jesus, touching their eyes, said, "According to your faith be it unto you."

What a wonderful expression from the lips of the Lord Jesus Christ! That is like saying, "Write your own amount on the check you draw upon the bank of Heaven." These two blind men were going to receive "according to their faith." They would not receive more than they believed and asked for.

On another occasion, Jesus made a similar statement about an individual's faith. A centurion had asked the Lord to heal his sick servant. He demonstrated great faith when he told the Lord He didn't need to come to his house to heal the servant but just "speak the word only" and it would be done. It was done, and from that very hour the servant was made well.

Notice how the Lord puts emphasis upon the faith of the centurion when He said, "Go thy way; and as thou hast believed, so be it done unto thee. And his servant was healed in the selfsame hour" (Matt. 8:13).

Jesus is saying, 'You will receive "as thou hast believed" or "according to your faith."'

So very much depends upon our faith. If we ask small, we can expect to receive small. If we ask large, we can expect to receive large. Jesus said it is "according to your faith."

I will apply the expression "according to your faith" to five realms of our Christian lives.

I. THE REALM OF SALVATION

The Bible puts, perhaps, more emphasis on this subject than on any other, that salvation is by faith. In Luke 7:50 is this statement by Jesus: "Thy faith hath saved thee; go in peace." Jesus made that statement a number of times. Some four or five times He said almost these exact words to different people: "Thy faith hath saved thee; go in peace." Here He said it to a woman of dissolute character, one who came to Jesus with a little box of costly ointment worth a year's wages. She broke the box and anointed the feet of Jesus and wiped them with her long tresses of hair. She mingled her tears with the ointment. She kissed His feet, working from behind Him. She dared not get where she could look in His face. Jesus complimented her, then said to the Pharisee, "Thou gavest me no kiss. My head with oil thou didst not anoint." But to the woman He said, "Thy faith hath saved thee; go in peace." The box of ointment did not save her. What else she did for Jesus did not save her; her faith saved her and sent her away in peace.

This is a truth few people ever really see from the Bible: We are saved by faith, and faith alone. You know those familiar verses in Ephesians 2:8 and 9, "For by grace are ye saved through faith; and that not of yourselves: it is the gift of God: Not of works, lest any man should boast."

From one end of that expression, "...through faith; and that not of yourselves," I drew two little arrows and wrote at the top, "a great contrast." When it comes to being saved, the greatest contrast that could be imagined is between these two things, "...through faith; and that not of yourselves." That takes out baptism. That takes out good works. That takes out giving. That takes out church membership. According to your faith, you are saved or lost.

Notice again Romans 5:1: "Therefore being justified by faith, we have peace with God through our Lord Jesus Christ." No one can be declared righteous in God's sight but by faith. No wonder Jesus said to those two seeking men, "According to your faith be it unto you."

"So then faith cometh by hearing, and hearing by the word of God" (Rom. 10:17). I inserted in that verse two words for my own thinking: "...faith cometh by hearing"—*not seeing*—"and hearing by the word of God." It is not by sight, not by feeling. It is not physical but spiritual. "Faith cometh by hearing, and hearing by the word of God." Not seeing, but believing.

Jesus said, "Blessed are they that have not seen, and yet have believed" (John 20:29).

Dr. William Edward Biederwolf had a wonderful illustration of salvation by faith. He said that he witnessed in the western country during a time of great drought how they were trying to conserve all the water they could.

The cattle were walking in the little ponds of water, muddying them all up, and much was being wasted. The cattlemen devised a special trough with an opening in it and anchored it around the edge of the little ponds of water they were trying to conserve. It took a good many pounds to press that trough down into the water. But when the weight of the cattle pressed it down, the water would come through the open place, and they could drink.

Dr. William Biederwolf said that he saw the cattlemen trying to get the cattle to walk out onto it. There was a trough but no way for the cattle to get water until their weight was placed on it. The cattle, seeing this trough, would turn their heads with a quizzical look. Finally one big steer ventured out and put his weight on the little platform. When he did, the trough filled with water. He bent down his head and drank. Then the others soon followed suit.

The salvation described in this Bible, bought with the blood of

Jesus and made a reality in us by the Holy Spirit of God, can only come when we, by faith, step out on the eternal promises of God. Then the Fountain of Life will open and the water of salvation will freely come.

"According to your faith be it unto you."

II. THE REALM OF ASSURANCE

The Lord not only wants us to be saved, but He eagerly wants us to know we are saved, wants us to have assurance. He wants us to have what the Bible speaks of as spiritual rest. He wants us to have a confidence in Him that makes us know that the salvation He has given is as eternal as God's Book, as everlasting as God's throne and as immortal as God Himself.

Notice Hebrews 10:22: "Let us draw near with a true heart in full assurance of faith...." Assurance comes in only one way—by faith in the promises of God's holy Word.

How much assurance do you have? How much do you need? How much do you want? Jesus said, "According to your faith be it unto you." You will have just as much assurance as your faith demands from the promises of God.

Peter, who knew what it was to backslide, who knew what it was to curse, swear and deny the Lord, wrote in I Peter 1:5, "Who are kept by the power of God through faith unto salvation ready to be revealed in the last time." A Christian's faith brings him that eternal assurance.

It is said that a group of students of botany discovered a little plant growing over the side of the cliff. They wondered how they could get that plant. One suggested that the only way would be by letting someone down with a rope; then he could pull it out of the crevices of the rock.

They said to one little boy, "Son, we need that plant for our study. Would you let us put this rope around you, then let you down over the cliff so you can pluck the plant, then let us pull you up? You are not too heavy, and for you to do that would help us greatly."

The little boy thought for a moment, then answered them, "I'll do it on one condition."

"What is that?"

"That my father hold the rope."

So Daddy held the rope as they let him down over the cliff so he could pluck the plant from the crevice.

There is no one whose faith Satan has never assailed. He has mine. Satan has dangled me over the fires of Hell. But, thank God, according to His Word, my Father holds the rope!

"And I give unto them eternal life; and they shall never perish, neither shall any man pluck them out of my hand. My Father, which gave them me, is greater than all; and no man is able to pluck them out of my Father's hand."—John 10:28,29.

How I thank God that He holds the rope! We can have assurance by believing and having faith in the promises of God.

Sometimes one of God's children gets out of fellowship. You folks call yourselves Bible believers; but at the first problem you face, you get about as shaken up as if you had never seen a Bible. A Christian can get out of fellowship, but you are never out of the Father's care. He is the Shepherd of the souls of all who are saved. When fellowship is broken, it doesn't mean the family ties of God are destroyed. Here is an illustration.

David's children grieved him terribly in a million ways. One was Absalom who was slain in battle as he sought to usurp David's own throne from him. Absalom had been banished by his own daddy. He was told to leave Jerusalem and go to Hebron. David instructed, "Don't come back until I send for you."

Close to three years went by. One day a woman said to the king, "Yet doth he [talking about God] devise means, that his banished be not expelled from him.'' In other words, 'David, God wouldn't keep His children separated from Him.'

I would like to preach a sermon on the "means" God uses to bring back His children. He has many ways. He does it sometimes at the side of a little baby's crib. He does it sometimes out in a lonely cemetery. He does it sometimes in the darkness and silence of your bedroom. God has means of bringing back His children.

This woman said, 'David, God never lets His own stay banished.' She said, "For we must needs die, and are as water spilt on the ground, which cannot be gathered up again; neither doth God respect any person: yet doth he devise means, that his banished be not expelled from him" (II Sam. 14:14).

After that, David sent for Absalom and brought him back.

This old Book teaches that whatsoever God doeth, He doeth it forever. When we are born the second time and have imparted unto us a new nature and our body becomes the temple of God's Holy Ghost, He puts us into His family, and those ties are never, never broken.

"According to your faith be it unto you."

III. THE REALM OF PRAYER

Jesus plainly teaches in His Word that what we get in answer to prayer is "according to [our] faith."

In Matthew 17:20 we read, "...for verily I say unto you, If ye have faith as a grain of mustard seed, ye shall say unto this mountain, Remove hence to yonder place; and it shall remove; and NOTHING SHALL BE IMPOSSIBLE UNTO YOU."

Jesus was here talking about moving mountains, and He said that there is nothing impossible unto you—"**IF** you have faith as a grain of mustard seed...."

The smallest seed a Jew had ever seen was a mustard seed. You could take a handful of mustard seed and plant an area as big as this auditorium; then you would gather up literally wagon loads from that one little handful of seed. Jesus Himself describes this seed in Matthew 13:31,32:

"The kingdom of heaven is like to a grain of mustard seed, which a man took, and sowed in his field: Which indeed is the least of all seeds: but when it is grown, it is the greatest among herbs, and becometh a tree, so that the birds of the air come and lodge in the branches thereof."

Jesus said, 'If you have faith as a grain of mustard seed, the least of all seeds, you can move mountains.'

You say, "Well, that doesn't say you have to have a lot of faith." No, you don't have to have a lot to get things from God.

If I were to ask this morning how many of you ever had a prayer answered and were surprised when the answer came, hundreds of you would say that has happened to you.

When Simon Peter was jailed, the church met to pray for him. "Peter therefore was kept in prison: but prayer was made without ceasing of the church unto God for him" (Acts 12:5). Then when he got out, they didn't believe it. A little girl, like a lot of folks, was not paying much attention to the praying. She heard a rattle at the gate and went out to see who it was. It was Simon Peter. She didn't open the gate but ran back and told how Peter stood before the gate. They said, "Rhoda, you have gone mad. You are seeing visions. Sit down and quit disturbing this prayer meeting."

She excitedly announced, "Simon Peter is shaking the gate and wants to get in."

But Rhoda "constantly affirmed that it was even so"—that Peter was at the gate. Those in there praying argued that it was his angel. But when Peter continued knocking, they opened the gate, saw him and were astonished! The Lord had answered a prayer that they did not think He would answer.

"ACCORDING TO YOUR FAITH"

I wonder how little the average Christian cashes in on his great avenue of prayer to the throne of grace! "According to your faith" God will answer prayer.

James 5:15: "And the prayer of faith shall save the sick, and the Lord shall raise him up...."

The prayer of faith has saved a lot of things. It has saved many a soul. It has saved many situations. It has saved many churches. It has saved many testimonies. The prayer of faith has saved many other things.

A good many times I have thought about how some three or four years ago the Lord laid it upon our hearts to build the school building. We could not operate without it. We had hundreds of children in here five days a week. We were trying to operate a church and Sunday school and were running over one another. We could not possibly continue to grow under the circumstances.

The Lord led us into the building of that school building as much as He has ever led us into anything. This church launched out on faith as much as any other church that I have ever known of in America anytime, anywhere. With absolutely nothing, we undertook a building program of two-thirds of a million dollars. Many times on Sunday evenings we would call for a season of prayer. The pressure was great, the burdens heavy. Many nights my eyes were as wide open as they are now; I was praying, thinking, leaning on God and trying to strengthen my own faith. I have seen little groups of Christians go over to that acreage that God, by a miracle, gave this church; I have watched them, with the cold winds blowing and the snow flying, pray as the tears of cold and misery fell from their faces. I have seen them in near zero weather huddle in a little group out on the barren, frozen ground and pray.

The other day I looked at that school building and said, "Thank You, God! This stands as an answer to prayer."

If you have faith as a grain of mustard seed, just that much faith can put mountains out of your way.

"According to your faith" your prayers will be answered.

IV. THE REALM OF SOULS SAVED

How many of you today have a lost loved one? Mark 2:5 tells how four men had brought the palsied man to Jesus—up the stairways, breaking through the roof, the crowd standing aghast, saying, "Why are you doing it this way?" But here they come with this man. People were saying, "In all the history of spiritual things, we never saw it done this way." But the four broke up the roof and let the palsied man down. There he lay on the floor before Jesus, a broken, crippled paralytic. Jesus looked up. He saw four faces through the broken roof. "When Jesus saw **their faith** [not his], he said unto the sick of the palsy, Son, thy sins be forgiven thee." He did not just say he was healed; He said he was saved. Why? "THEIR FAITH"—the faith of four men—got that man saved.

I say to you, people are lost and on their way to Hell because God's people don't believe God is able to save.

"According to your faith." Jesus saw their faith and said, "Son, thy sins be forgiven thee." I would like to have seen him get up, grab that bed, throw it over his shoulder, press through that crowd, go outside and wait for those four to come off the roof!

We see five men leaping down the street and shouting praises to God! Why? Because one day four men said, "If we get our sick, lost neighbor to where Jesus is, that will be all there is to it." They said, "We have but one problem—to get him where Jesus is. If we can do that, Jesus will do the rest."

My friends, if God could bore into the souls of some of you this morning the faith to believe that God will save your loved ones, what a great hour this could be for your home and family!

Something else we are losing in our day, and losing fast. It is easy for us to lose our compassion. When we lose that, we have

"ACCORDING TO YOUR FAITH"   245

lost something. "They that sow in tears shall reap in joy," promises Psalm 126. You can have all the theology in the world, you can be as fundamental and straight as a gun barrel; but you will not win your loved ones without tears. "They that sow in tears shall reap in joy. He that goeth forth and weepeth, bearing precious seed, shall doubtless come again with rejoicing, bringing his sheaves with him."

When God breaks up these dry hearts and they are melted with the fire of the Holy Ghost, our loved ones will be saved.

A woman came to a preacher and said, "I have listened to you preach. I have three lost boys who are on their way to Hell. I want them saved. And I do not know why they are not saved."

"Do you know you are saved?" the preacher asked.

"Certainly. I never knew anything any more in my life."

"Are you a separated Christian?"

"As best as I know, I am. I have separated my life and dedicated it to God. I am the superintendent of the intermediate department of my church. I read my Bible every day. I love the Lord. But my three boys are lost."

The preacher looked at her. Her eyes were as dry as the back of my hand. He said, "Lady, the reason your three boys are on their way to Hell is that your eyes are dry." Not to be mean but because he wanted her to get the lesson, he turned and walked away.

She stood there aghast. She said to herself, *They are! They are! My boys are on their way to Hell, and my eyes are as dry as a chip!*

She went home that day from church and up to her room. As she turned the key in the bedroom door, she said, "Lord, in this room I will stay until You give me the assurance that my boys will be saved."

In a few hours there came a knock at the door and an inquiry from the oldest boy: "Mama, are you sick?"

"Yes, in my heart."

"What do you mean?"

"Because you and your two brothers are lost. I would rather have you saved than anything else in this world."

She unlocked the door, and he fell on his face by her side and said, "Mama, I want you to tell me again how to be saved. Right now I will give my life to the Lord."

He was saved right there by her side, on the bedroom floor.

The next morning see the scene at breakfast. The oldest looks at his plate, then at his two brothers, then says, "We have broken our mother's heart because we have not been saved. I trusted Christ last night. Now you ought to get saved." Then he gets up out of his place, goes around to the other side of the table and leads his two younger brothers to Christ.

There is no soul winning without tears and compassion. "They that sow in tears shall reap in joy."

V. THE REALM OF HEAVEN

You say, "Brother Tom, that's strange." No. The Apostle Paul even said it took faith to lay hold on Heaven and to believe in its reality. When he deals with the subject of moving out of this body to a new one in Glory, Paul said in II Corinthians 5:1, "For we know that if our earthly house of this tabernacle were dissolved, we have a building of God, an house not made with hands, eternal in the heavens." Then he said in verse 7, "(For we walk by faith, not by sight.)" He told the Corinthians, 'To believe in the glory and in Heaven takes faith.'

You read it of Abraham in Hebrews 11:9,10, "By faith he sojourned in the land of promise.... For he looked for a city which hath foundations, whose builder and maker is God." Abraham never found it on earth. But one day he found it—now he is in it!

One day God will let that City down out of the sky.

"ACCORDING TO YOUR FAITH" 247

"And I saw a new heaven and a new earth: for the first heaven and the first earth were passed away; and there was no more sea. And I John saw the holy city, new Jerusalem, coming down from God out of heaven, prepared as a bride adorned for her husband."—Rev. 21:1,2.

The Bible says it is 1500 miles cubed. If you put one corner of it in the city of New York, the other corner would reach to the city of Miami. One would reach all the way from there to Denver, Colorado. And it would be 1500 miles high.

Jesus said, "In my Father's house are many mansions: if it were not so, I would have told you. I go to prepare a place for you." There is a mansion there for me because by faith I have laid hold of the hope of Heaven.

The doctor came to the little sick boy, who had lain sick for days. He was a Christian and from a Christian home. Missing his Sunday school, he said, "Doctor, I would like to go to the Lord's house next Sunday."

The doctor took his pulse, checked his little body—as he had done every day—looked in his eyes and said, "Son, you are going to the Lord's house very soon now."

In a few hours the lad died. He was in the Lord's House the next Sunday!

Many of us have loved ones over there. We have stood at the River of Life and watched them one by one go over. Some of us stand and look both ways, on this side and "over there," and we feel almost as Paul felt—"in a straight betwixt two." So many are "over there," making it where we don't know which way we would rather go—stay here or go There.

"According to your faith" is how real Heaven is going to be.

Heaven was real to Paul: "For I am in a straight betwixt two, having a desire to depart, and be with Christ, which is far better" (Phil. 1:23).

Heaven was real to John. He wrote that Jesus said, "And if I go and prepare a place for you, I will come again, and receive you unto myself; that where I am, there ye may be also" (John 14:3).

Heaven was real to Abraham. Hebrews 11:9 says "he sojourned in the land of promise, as in a strange country, dwelling in tabernacles" (tents). He knew that the promised land was not the permanent land, so "he looked for a city which hath foundations, whose builder and maker is God" (vs. 10). He believed that there was an eternal city called Heaven, whose Architect and Builder was God.

Heaven was real to Peter. He spoke of an inheritance "reserved in heaven for you" (I Pet. 1:4).

The intensity of our faith will not change Heaven, but it will change our perception of Heaven and make it real to us. Our faith will not change our "hope which is laid up for you in heaven, whereof ye heard before in the word of the gospel" (Col. 1:5), but it will make that hope alive and burning in our hearts.

"...*According to your faith be it unto you.*"—Matt. 9:29.

Chapter XVI

Trusting in the Lord

"It is better to trust in the Lord than to put confidence in man."—Ps. 118:8.

This verse is said to be the middle verse of the Bible. There are 31,174 verses, and this is the 15,587th verse. I don't know whether or not that is important. If it were at the beginning of the Bible or at the end or anywhere else, it is still the Word of God.

In a very general sense this may be said to be the general theme of the Bible: trusting in the Lord and not in man.

This psalm has a great setting or background. It was evidently used in singing and praise when the foundations were laid for the rebuilding of the Temple at Jerusalem about 536 B.C. The great and beautiful Temple, built by Solomon about 1005 B.C., had been destroyed. God's people had been in captivity for seventy years, then had been released from heathen lands to go back to Jerusalem to rebuild the house of God. Ezra and Nehemiah particularly, and other books less specifically, give the account of the return of the Jews to Palestine and the rebuilding of the Temple. Ezra 3:10,11 gives the account of the laying of the foundations for the Temple to be reconstructed:

"And when the builders laid the foundation of the temple of the Lord, they set the priests in their apparel with trumpets, and the

Levites the sons of Asaph with cymbals, to praise the Lord, after the ordinance of David king of Israel. And they sang together by course in praising and giving thanks unto the Lord; because he is good, for his mercy endureth for ever toward Israel. And all the people shouted with a great shout, when they praised the Lord, because the foundation of the house of the Lord was laid."

The expression, "giving thanks unto the Lord; because he is good, for his mercy endureth for ever," is the same expression found in the first and last verses of Psalm 118. Many students of the Bible believe that the psalm was not only used when the foundations of the Temple were laid for rebuilding but on other festive occasions as well.

It is believed that the psalm was for many years sung as a part of the thanksgiving rendered after the observance of the passover. It was probably sung by Jesus and eleven of the disciples at the end of the institution of the Lord's Supper the night before Jesus was crucified. It is a blessed and wonderful thought that Jesus might have sung the word of the text of this message a few hours before He was crucified.

"It is better to trust in the Lord than to put confidence in man" does not mean that we are never to have confidence in another person. Jonathan and David so loved and trusted one another that they literally placed their lives in one another's hands. It does mean that in the essential matters of our faith concerning our salvation and our walk before the Lord, our trust must be in the Lord and in the Lord only.

I want to apply this glorious text to five important areas of our lives.

I. IN DELIVERANCE (SALVATION)

Sometimes in the Bible "salvation" means "deliverance." The words are used synonymously in many instances.

TRUSTING IN THE LORD

"Deliverance," as it is used numerous times in the New Testament, means "to free from," "to release," "to set free" or "make free," to rescue by "delivering," "to save." The word denotes redemption and release from bondage.

I am speaking about being saved. It is better to trust in the Lord for deliverance and freedom from the penalty of sin than to put confidence in man.

"Fear ye not, stand still, and see the salvation of the Lord," exhorts Exodus 14:13. The Bible says it is "the salvation of the Lord." The Lord is the Author of salvation, the One who planned it. Man had absolutely nothing to do with it.

"Salvation belongeth to the Lord" (Ps. 3:8), not to man. Man has no plan of salvation or scheme of redemption except that which belongs to God and is clearly set forth in the Word of God. All of us know that we can lead one another to Christ, but we also know that God is allowing us to tell someone about God's own plan of salvation. It belongs to God.

"Neither is there salvation in any other: for there is none other name under heaven given among men, whereby we must be saved" (Acts 4:12). Man cannot make you to be saved, and neither can man keep you from being saved.

I wonder how many millions have been taught that men can control salvation and say who gets saved and who must remain lost. Salvation does not belong to a church or religion, but to God. How futile to trust in man or man's creed or religion for salvation!

"It is better to trust in the Lord than to put confidence in man."

Ephesians 2:8 tells us, "For by grace are ye saved through faith; and that not of yourselves: it is the gift of God." The expression, "and that not of yourselves"—what does it mean? I know that it does not mean that God only saves the elected few and refuses to give any other lost sinner the chance to be saved. The invitation to be saved is to "whosoever will."

Some argue that the expression means salvation itself is not of ourselves, while others say that faith is not of ourselves. It surely means that salvation is not of man or by man. It is the gift of God to those who believe.

Martin Luther called Psalm 118 "My Psalm." He said this psalm could do more for him than all the kings and princes combined.

At the *Shrine of the Scala Sancta* (or "Holy Stairs") at Rome, the glorious truth of justification broke in upon his soul; and Luther walked back down the steps, trusting Christ alone for salvation, and he was saved. Martin Luther no longer trusted in man and his creeds, catechisms or dogmas, but in the Lord to be delivered from sin and its penalty. He was the father of the Reformation.

II. IN DOCTRINE

We must be sure that our doctrinal position is absolutely true to the Word of God. It is amazing how much of the so-called doctrine of religious bodies cannot be substantiated by the holy Scriptures. Jesus spoke about His doctrine and said, "My doctrine is not mine, but his that sent me. If any man will do his will, he shall know of the doctrine, whether it be of God, or whether I speak of myself" (John 7:16,17).

Doctrine means "teaching." Jesus clearly stated that His doctrine was of God, not of man. I would never teach anyone anything about the Christian faith that could not be easily substantiated by Scripture.

A preacher friend of mine came to me one morning after I had finished speaking on the radio. He told me he had just tried to witness to a man on the street who was a church member but obviously not saved.

Finally he asked the man, "What do you believe?"

"I believe just like my church believes."

"Well, what does your church believe?"

"My church believes just like I believe."

The preacher then asked me, "Do you think he knows what he believes or what his church believes?" I told him I didn't think so.

Millions of people in the world have embraced a system of religious teachings which is not of God. Jesus said of the scribes and Pharisees of His day, "But in vain they do worship me, teaching for doctrines the commandments of men" (Matt. 15:9).

People were astonished at the doctrine of Jesus. At the close of the longest recorded sermon of Jesus, the Sermon on the Mount, He talked about the two ways of life and illustrated it by the two builders.

He said those who heard His sayings and did them were like the man who built his house on the rock. No storm nor rain nor floods nor winds could destroy it.

He said those who were foolish and refused to listen to Him were like a man who built his house upon the sand, only to see the storms and winds utterly destroy it.

When Jesus had ended these sayings, "the people were astonished at his doctrine" (Matt. 7:28).

Sometimes people are astonished at our doctrine. When we teach there is a Hell for the lost and a Heaven for the saved, they are astonished. When we teach that salvation is in a Person and by grace through faith and never ends, people are astonished. That is why we must be sure our teaching is founded upon the Word of God.

When I think of doctrine, or what a person believes, there are some very important questions I would like to ask:

1. Is it built upon the Word of God?
2. Has it changed your life?
3. Could you recommend it to a dying man?
4. Will it stand the test of the fires of the judgment day?

III. IN DUTY

I don't want there to be any doubt about my Christian duties. I ought to be sure about how I serve the Lord so as to please Him. I need to know what I am supposed to be doing.

It is not only our privilege to lead souls to Christ, but it is our duty, and it is a sin to neglect it. There are scores of verses about soul winning, but one makes such a forceful impression on my heart: "And he saith unto them, Follow me, and I will make you fishers of men" (Matt. 4:19).

This statement of Jesus is plain and simple. It can be understood by every believer and is directed to every believer. God wants every Christian to be a soul winner. The reason so many churches are dead or dying is not that the preacher does not preach the Bible nor stand for something, but it is because his members do not win souls. A church can be orthodox and not win souls. And a Christian can be separated from the world and never win a soul to Christ.

"The fruit of the righteous is a tree of life; and he that winneth souls is wise."—Prov. 11:30.

"He that goeth forth and weepeth, bearing precious seed, shall doubtless come again with rejoicing, bringing his sheaves with him."—Ps. 126:6.

Our Christian duty is to win souls.

I think of the duty of fellowship, by which I mean the assembling of oneself with the people of God. Many take this duty and privilege lightly.

"And let us consider one another to provoke unto love and good works: Not forsaking the assembling of ourselves together, as the manner of some is; but exhorting one another: and so much the more, as ye see the day approaching."—Heb. 10:24,25.

A preacher recently said, "Nothing is said in the Bible about Wednesday night meetings."

The Bible does not say, "Meet together on Wednesday night," but it does teach the fellowship and assembling of the saints. If we had church every night of the week, every week of the year, it would be scriptural, for the Bible teaches fellowshiping and meeting together: "And they continued steadfastly in the apostles' doctrine and fellowship, and in breaking of bread, and in prayers" (Acts 2:42).

The Bible certainly teaches the duty of stewardship or giving unto the Lord. This is God's way of funding the work of God and sending the Gospel to the ends of the earth. There are scores of verses in the Bible on tithes and offerings. No honest Christian would want to deny this teaching, nor disobey it.

A lady once said to me, "If you'll stop talking so much about money and death, I'll start coming back to your church."

I said to her, "When people stop dying, I'll stop mentioning death. And I'll not stop talking about giving to the Lord as long as there is one lost soul in the world who needs to have the Gospel brought to him."

A child of God ought never feel that giving to the Lord is such a hard duty, such a burden. Rather, giving is a wonderful privilege and a happy part of a Christian's life.

"Give, and it shall be given unto you; good measure, pressed down, and shaken together, and running over, shall men give into your bosom. For with the same measure that ye mete withal it shall be measured to you again."—Luke 6:38.

I had certainly rather take God at His Word and trust Him about giving than to put confidence in man's way of dealing with material things.

"It is better to trust in God than to put confidence in man."

IV. IN DISTRESS

"I called upon the Lord in distress: the Lord answered me, and set me in a large place."—Ps. 118:5.

The writer of that psalm knew the meaning of distress. It is a part of the fallen nature to feel pain and anguish of body and mind. As long as we are in this earthly body we shall know the meaning of distress. The wonderful thing about it is to know what to do in times of distress. The psalmist knew. He said he called upon the Lord in his distress, and the Lord heard him.

Jacob knew what it meant to trust the Lord in a day of distress and have God take care of his problem. Jacob fled from Esau who had bargained away the wonderful birthright. Angry Esau threatened to kill Jacob.

On Jacob's first night away from home he had a great encounter with God. God made a promise to Jacob, and Jacob made a vow to God. The beautiful record of this experience is found in Genesis 28:10-22.

The opening verse of the following chapter says, "Then Jacob went on his journey, and came into the land of the people of the east." Jacob did not know he would be gone from home twenty years. When the twenty long years had passed, he set out with his large family and great herds of cattle he had accumulated in Haran. He must, however, meet Esau, who had threatened his life, and a brother he had not seen for twenty years. He meets Esau, and a peaceful settlement is reached between the two brothers.

However, his daughter Dinah is defiled by Shechem, and Jacob's sons scheme to kill all the males of Shechem's city and take all their wives and children and all their possessions as spoil.

Jacob was in great fear and distress, but now he has learned to call upon the Lord in times of trouble and anguish.

"And God said unto Jacob, Arise, and go up to Bethel, and

dwell there: and make an altar unto God, that appeared unto thee when thou fleddest from the face of Esau thy brother. Then Jacob said unto his household, and to all that were with him, Put away the strange gods that are among you, and be clean, and change your garments: And let us arise, and go up to Bethel; and I will make there an altar unto God, **who answered me in the day of my distress,** *and was with me in the way which I went."*—Gen. 35:1-3.

Jacob went back to Bethel where before God had answered him in distress; now Jacob will meet with God again. Jacob learned that God is greater than all human anguish and distress. He learned that to trust in God means more than all human help.

"It is better to trust in God than to put confidence in man."

V. IN DEATH

Statisticians say that more than 600,000,000 people die every year around the world. The Bible says, "And as it is appointed unto men once to die, but after this the judgment" (Heb. 9:27). I know "we shall not all sleep" when the Lord Jesus comes to receive us unto Himself. Except for that believing few who will be alive when the Lord comes, death is inevitable.

One of the problems now facing society is what to do with the dead. Many cemeteries have no more room, and have closed. I recently read of a large South American city which built a mausoleum thirty-nine stories high because there was no more room on the ground to bury the dead. This skyscraper will provide a burial place for 147,000 people. The building has a heliport so that bodies can be flown in by helicopter. Great Britain now cremates more bodies than it buries under the ground. Some believe that as many as three billion people might have died at one time, when God destroyed the world with a flood.

All men must meet God. It is an appointment that will not be cancelled. Are you trusting in God now for the time when you must die and leave this world?

Paul said that "to die is gain." Paul had no fear of death; and as his time approached, he was more than ready: "For I am now ready to be offered, and the time of my departure is at hand" (II Tim. 4:6).

He was ready to die because he was saved and knew it. "I know whom I have believed, and am persuaded that he is able to keep that which I have committed unto him against that day" (II Tim. 1:12).

The Apostle John, exiled on the Isle of Patmos, was taught the wonderful truth about dying in the Lord: "And I heard a voice from heaven saying unto me, Write, Blessed are the dead which die in the Lord from henceforth: Yea, saith the Spirit, that they may rest from their labours; and their works do follow them" (Rev. 14:13).

Dr. Bob Jones, Sr., told of a man who asked a Christian, "When you die, what if you find out that you were all wrong and that there was nothing to Christianity and the Bible was a lie?"

The Christian replied, "I will have lost nothing. Believing in Christ has made me most happy and secure. And I have thoroughly enjoyed my life."

Then the Christian asked this question: "But what if you, when you die, find that the Bible is true, that Christ is the only way to Heaven, and you find you have been completely wrong about Christianity?"

The man's reply was, "Well, then, I will have lost everything, including my soul."

It is better to trust in the Lord and be saved and secure, than to put confidence in the vain philosophies of men.

Years ago I was listening by radio to a speech by Vice-President Alben Barkley. It was the keynote address at the convention of his political party. I almost felt as if I were listening to an old-fashioned preacher. With great eloquence he spoke of God and His goodness. He extolled the virtues of living in a nation that believed in God. He lifted aloft the highest virtues of decent human beings. I did not know whether the man was saved or not, but I felt that one would almost have to be trusting in God to speak as he spoke.

Some years later I read how this same man died. He was speaking at Washington and Lee University. In his address he made this statement: "I had rather be a servant in the house of the Lord than to sit in the seat of the mighty." Those were his last words. He died on the spot.

How wonderful to die trusting in the Lord Jesus Christ! But how sad to die and meet God at the judgment throne and be lost forever!

"It is better to trust in God than to put confidence in man."— Ps. 118:8.

Chapter XVII

Faith for Miracles

(Preached in the Emmanuel Baptist Church, October 27, 1968, Anniversary Sunday)

READ: Mark 9:38-41

"But Jesus said, Forbid him not: for there is no man which shall do a miracle in my name, that can lightly speak evil of me."—Mark 9:39.

I want to speak on "Faith for Miracles" because I believe Emmanuel Baptist Church is a miracle. I have been thinking of the miracles God has wrought, a supernatural work of the Lord, in the Emmanuel Baptist Church these past twenty-six years.

Notice the words, "a miracle in my name."

God has given us these many years faith for miracles. This is what Jesus had in mind when He spoke to the father of the lunatic son: "If thou canst believe, all things are possible to him that believeth" (Mark 9:23). This distraught father needed a miracle. His son was completely submerged in the power of Satan and his demons. His very life was in jeopardy. He needed a miracle, and that is what he received. Jesus lifted him up and changed him.

Only the power of God could do that; only faith can lay hold upon that miracle-working power. The father had faith. "Lord, I believe; help thou mine unbelief" (Mark 9:24). He believed that a miracle could take place, and God honored his faith. God's miraculous power has been upon us here in at least seven ways.

I. THE MIRACLE OF ORIGINATION

First, I think of the miracle of origination. If you are as well acquainted with it as some of us are, you would know also that it was a miracle of God that this church began in this particular place twenty-six years ago.

A verse comes to mind when I think of the miracle of the origination of this church, John 2:11: "This beginning of miracles did Jesus...." The very beginning, the origination, of this work of God is a miracle of God.

This work was not started in desperation, nor in opposition, but started in vision, enlargement, expansion and in evangelism, reaching men and women for Jesus Christ.

This church actually began about the time our daughter Joy was born twenty-six years ago the tenth day of October. One day before our first baby was born, my wife and I had gone out to eat at a little drive-in. It was a drive-in then; now it's a beautiful, large restaurant called Ted's Restaurant. The drive-in had a large sign on it that read, "The World's Longest Hotdog." Back in those days we were looking for bargains when it came to something to eat. So we sat in the automobile and had a little something, then started back to our apartment. As we drove away from that drive-in restaurant, Mrs. Malone said, "Why don't we go home another way?"

In these twenty-six years, thousands have "gone home another way." They have come here lost and gone away saved. They have come here in need and gone away with their needs met. So with one turn of the wheel, we started home another way.

We came up Telegraph Road to this subdivision where there was a small settling of houses. On the corner was an empty building. There was another building, the Castle Inn building. I was told that thirteen different kinds of businesses had been in the Castle Inn building, and all had failed. There it sat empty. In it one time was a road house. The policemen of this city of Pontiac told me that many nights back then they were called to the Castle Inn building, knocked in the doors, loaded people in cars and hauled them away. In it was a den of infamy. There was a dance floor and a band shell. It was a house of amusement, the Devil's workshop.

As we drove along by this subdivision, we saw the sign in front of this Castle Inn building, FOR SALE. I got out of my car, parted the weeds that had grown up around the building and looked in the window. God seemed to lay it upon my heart, "This is the place."

We went home. My wife and I and her mother got down on our knees and prayed. An hour later, standing in the midst of that dance floor, I signed the papers to buy that building.

We had spent the last cent we had at the drive-in. We invested all the money we owned in two "World's Largest Hotdogs." Now I was so sure that God wanted us to have that building that I willingly signed the papers, knowing I had no money.

I borrowed a hundred dollars and mortgaged all our furniture for the down payment. So I can say from first-hand experience the very origination of this church was a miracle of God. Jesus began a miracle in this place.

The very location was as ordained of God as my salvation or yours. God put this church here. He said, "This is the spot. This is where this work of God is to begin."

I think of what the Lord said one day to the Prophet Elijah: "I have commanded the ravens to feed thee there" (I Kings 17:4).

Elijah might have said, "Where, God?"

"Back *there* in the woods," God answered.

"It is an unlikely place," Elijah might have said.

"Elijah, back *there* at the brook, back *there* in obscurity, back *there* in an unknown place—*there* is where I am going to feed you, train you and use you."

I believe with all my heart this is God's "there" for the Emmanuel Baptist Church. For twenty-six years I have enjoyed the wonderful satisfaction to believe that this work of God was begun under His direction.

Had it not been for that knowledge, in the difficult hours I might have gone under. But I have always had the conviction that God began this work, and what God starts, God will always finish.

II. THE MIRACLE OF PRESERVATION

The second miracle is the miracle of preservation. This church these years has withstood all the guns of Hell that have been trained against it. We have stood in spite of all our weaknesses, all our failures, all our mistakes. For twenty-six years God has preserved this work of His. It is a miracle of preservation.

In Philippians 1:6 the Lord says, "Being confident of this very thing, that he which hath begun a good work in you will perform it until the day of Jesus Christ."

I say again, "What God starts, God will finish." Some works may look religious, look spiritual, but perhaps they are not.

I read in II Thessalonians 3:3, "But the Lord is faithful, who shall stablish you, and keep you from evil."

What is Paul talking about in this letter? A verse or two previous to that, we read, "Pray for us...that we may be delivered from unreasonable and wicked men." I think of the wicked men of modernism, the wicked men of unbelief, the wicked men of evil intentions. God has delivered us from them all and has preserved this work.

God has delivered us from personal mistakes, from attacks of the Devil and modernism.

FAITH FOR MIRACLES

People have asked me—and I almost laugh when they do—"Dr. Malone, I don't suppose you have ever seen a good quitting place?" I feel almost like answering, "I have not even found a good starting place yet!" It has been an uphill battle. The Devil has always been at work, but there has always been the preserving, keeping grace of the blessed Son of God.

An uprising in a church is a purifying measure. It's a humbling thing, a heart-searching thing, but God never allows it to destroy His work.

I remember one time when a little group was having a "prayer meeting" here—a prayer meeting to get rid of the preacher! It was a "I-hate-Tom-Malone" prayer meeting.

I thought, *Well, it's a prayer meeting in the church. I'm the pastor, so I ought to go.* I went. I got down beside a lady who was no "humpty-dumpty." She was smart. She was well-groomed. She was a good speaker. She was educated. She had been in the work of the Lord for awhile. But she had joined the "Let's-Get-Rid-of-Tom-Malone Club."

Let me tell you, friends, this was an experience! She prayed, "God, I want you to kill that man. I want you to destroy him."

Have you ever knelt beside someone and heard that one pray, "God, kill him"? Usually when I am kneeling with others in prayer, I join in! I help them lay hold on the throne of grace. As they pray, I say, "Amen! Do it, Lord!" I say, "Praise the Lord! Thank God!" But I didn't say any of that this time!

She prayed, "I want this preacher killed. He's a devil and a liar. He has got to be removed. Kill that preacher!"

I thought, *This is no place for me! Why, the Lord might answer that foolish woman's prayer!* So I got up from my knees and walked out of the room with a broken heart, with fear and trembling. Listen, I didn't know but what God might answer that prayer. I was trying to walk in the will of God. Now people were praying for God to kill me!

I do not speak with any bitterness. What do I have to be bitter about? The goodness of God, the multiplicity of blessing, the thousands of victories—how could one be bitter in the face of such goodness and the grace of God!

A man stood one time and said, "This will all come to naught. This will all fail. This is all done, all wrapped up." He didn't know what he was talking about! That man had never learned the miracle of preservation.

I have seen the times when, humanly speaking, I thought it was true. One such time was when we got ready to build this auditorium. I didn't have much business ability. (Some of you are thinking, *He doesn't have any now.* But then I had less than I do now.) We had no money, and we have never had much of it.

We didn't have any money, and we wanted to build this auditorium, 80 feet wide, 3 stories high and 100 feet long.

I think that they estimated the cost at about $222,000 to build years ago. I didn't know we had to get a permit. When we went to the building fund to get a check to buy the permit, it was $222! We paid every dollar we had in the fund to get a little card to tack up on the job somewhere saying that we were permitted to build.

Well, we had the permit but no money with which to build. We had nothing but our trust in God.

We began to build. There is not a block nor brick in this building that I have not handled with my own two hands.

A man from Alabama said, "I have an old truck, and I want you to take it." I kept it all winter. I would preach on the radio in the morning, then haul bricks and unload them. I climbed up and down scaffolds. I couldn't lay blocks, but I could surely take care of the men who could. A fellow said one time, "Tom Malone is the best tender I have ever had. He can mix mortar the best, get it on the scaffold the quickest of anybody we have ever had on this job." I grew two inches! Good night, I was somebody! I was a tender now!

FAITH FOR MIRACLES

One day the old Devil made up his mind that this auditorium was not going to be built. The work stopped. And about that time there came a snow. I don't mean ankle-deep snow, some little sprinkling, a few flurries! I am talking about falling snow, hip-deep snow—not overshoe weather but hip-boot weather.

Everything was exposed. Walls were open. Nothing was put away. No one seemed to care. Everyone had gone; some had left for good!

God bless colored people! Sometimes in the darkest hour, I have had them stand with me. A colored man came, and we were working together. I was standing in snow up to my waist. He was up on a scaffold taking down tools so that they could be covered.

We had built some large scaffolds, "jacks" we called them, out of 2 x 6's. The "jacks" were 6 feet high, 6 feet square, and very heavy. He turned one loose from up there, and it hit me right on the back of my head and knocked me flat on my face, literally burying me in the snow. I can feel that colored man now digging down in that snow trying to find a preacher with his brains knocked out!

He finally got hold of me, picked me up and brushed the snow off. The back of my head throbbed. Standing waist deep in the snow, I was dizzy and sick.

Then that fellow asked me the most foolish question: "Did it hurt?"

Man, I didn't even know where I was! Standing there waist deep in the snow, head throbbing, I began to cry. I asked, "O God, is this the ministry?"

I asked the black man, "Are you hungry?"

"I'm always hungry," he answered. We went to a restaurant about fifty yards away for some coffee and to get warm. We ordered, and I said to him, "Are you a Christian?" He replied, "No, I've never been saved." I showed him the Gospel, and he trusted Christ as his Saviour. I said to myself, *This is worth all the heartache and the "headache" too.*

Then there came from the battlements of Heaven the assurance from God, "This I started; this I will finish."

The miracle of preservation.

III. THE MIRACLE OF MULTIPLICATION

From a little dance floor, God has multiplied this testimony. I have seen the results of this testimony literally around the world.

Acts 2:47 reads, "And the Lord added to the church daily such as should be saved." This church has multiplied. We have had here, in one year, over 1,600 first-time professions of faith in the public services. This is the result of the ministry of visitation in the hospitals, in homes and elsewhere. One year there were over 1,800 professions of faith.

If there were 25 saved in the 1,352 weeks (26 years), that would mean in this church 34,800 boys, girls, men and women said, "I will take Christ as my personal Saviour."

Those people have gone to every corner of this nation. God has multiplied this work. Pastors are preaching while I am preaching who once walked these aisles as sinners. They were saved by God's grace. They were called by His Spirit. These preachers got their training in this place and have scattered out to preach the unsearchable riches of Christ.

There are missionaries on the foreign fields who once walked these aisles—the miracle of multiplication. God has given us buildings and land; God has sent out missionaries, pastors and Christian workers.

From many states people have said, "Brother Malone, our church was dead. We had no soul-winning program, no visitation. But one day a family moved to our community who were trained in your school and attended Emmanuel Baptist Church.

This family literally revolutionized our church."
The miracle of multiplication.

IV. THE MIRACLE OF SANCTIFICATION

By sanctification I mean what God means—that great spiritual process, immediate, progressive and ultimate—the work of God in sanctifying the believer, His work of making us Christlike.

"That he might sanctify and cleanse it with the washing of water by the word."—Eph. 5:26.

"For whom he did foreknow, he also did predestinate to be conformed to the image of his Son...."—Rom. 8:29.

For twenty-six glorious years the work of God has been to make this church like Christ, to make believers Christlike, "conformed to the image of his Son."

Think of every experience—even if it is a result of your own failure—as the work of God to make you more like Christ. That is the meaning of Romans 8:28,29:

"And we know that all things work together for good to them that love God, to them who are the called according to his purpose. For whom he did foreknow, he also did predestinate to be conformed to the image of his Son...."

Some people don't understand the election of saints. They think they are elected to go to Heaven. That is not what you are elected for, not what you are predestinated for. You are going to Heaven if you are saved. You are just as certain of it as if you were already there. What is election? What is predestination? That you might be like the Son of God. "Beloved, now are we the sons of God, and it doth not yet appear what we shall be: but we know that, when he shall appear, we shall be like him; for we shall see him as he is" (I John 3:2). To make people Christlike—that is the work of God, that is sanctification.

These twenty-six years of joys, victories, laughter, tears, broken hearts, remorse, burdens all lead to one thing: Christlikeness for the believer.

I read a story of two chemists at work. One was an old veteran; the other, a beginner. The beginner had an element in a test tube over a burner. He asked the elder chemist, "How hot shall I heat it? How long shall I leave it on the fire?" The elder replied, "Heat it! Heat it! Watch it! Watch it! When it gets so hot that you can see the reflection of your own image in it, then turn it down."

Sometimes the Christian cries, "O God, how long shall the fires of trial burn?"

God answers, "Until I see in you the image of My own Son."

The miracle of sanctification.

V. THE MIRACLE OF PREPARATION

The miracle of preparation has gone on in this work.

God said to His preachers in II Timothy 2:2, "And the things that thou hast heard of me among many witnesses, the same commit thou to faithful men, who shall be able to teach others also." That is the work of the Lord.

Some preachers pay no attention to that command. They care not whether anyone else has a church to pastor. They care not whether anyone else is called into the ministry. Out of this church here has gone a constant stream of Christian workers. "And the things that thou hast heard of me among many witnesses, the same commit thou to faithful men...."

Oh, the stories that I could tell about the Frank Holmans, the Wilfred Robinsons, the Charles Whitefields, the Harry Metros, and the scores of others—those who in this place came to know the Lord in all His glory and felt that divine urgency to launch out into His vineyard and to win souls. I could mention so many.

Preachers have come to me with a college education and sadly said, "Preacher, I have an education, but I don't know how to pastor a church." I have had them say, "I am a college graduate, but I don't know how to baptize." "I have never served communion." "I don't know a thing about visitation." "I don't know what to do with a Sunday school class"—college graduates, I remind you! They weren't saved here, they weren't trained here, as scores of others have been; they had an education but no practical knowledge.

One such is now in a neighboring state. He is in a great association of Bible-believing churches and is pastoring a great church. He came and sat like a new convert. He watched and observed. Then he began to work and go visiting. He prayed and worked in the Sunday school and brought people down the aisles. He learned and prepared for the work of the Lord.

Thank God for the miracle of the work of preparation!

I thank God for the privilege this church has had to have a little hand in a Bible college. This church has carried a great burden because of it. This church has given the most of itself for it. Sometimes we are prone to think that we have missed something as a result.

Men of God who know what they are talking about have said, "Tom, if you had never been in school work, the Emmanuel Baptist Church would have been twice as large as it is." Maybe that is true, but Jesus said for every cup of cold water we give in His name, we will not lose our reward. At the day of rewards for the people of God, the Emmanuel Baptist Church will be rewarded.

What care we about the earthly plaudits of men if we can have the "well done" of Jesus in the most glorious hour of the church!

The miracle of preparation.

VI. THE MIRACLE OF MOTIVATION

What motivates this work? What keeps it going? Why does it continue? How can you explain its progress?

It is motivated by a deep and sincere love for Jesus from this great church family. Yes, we serve one another because we love one another, but we continue to serve the Lord because we love Him. "For the love of Christ constraineth us."

We are motivated by the fact of Hell, the holiness of God, and the terrors of the judgment day. "Knowing therefore the terror of the Lord, we persuade men."

We are motivated by the judgment seat of Christ. We must meet Him; we must stand in the white light of His glorious presence; we must render up an account to Him at the judgment seat. "For we must all appear before the judgment seat of Christ."

We are motivated by His Holy Spirit within us. We have a fire in our bones, a flame in our hearts, a spiritual gleam in our eyes. We are driven, urged, led and energized by His presence within. As long as there is a lost soul to win, as long as there is one broken heart to heal, one unconquered demon to conquer, we shall go on. If we are not spectacular, we are determined to be steadfast. We have a mission to accomplish, a plan to execute, a work to do, a Saviour to please. Our hearts shall know no rest until we have done His whole bidding. We shall never sheath our sword as long as there is an enemy of God left on the battlefield.

We cannot fail; we have the equipment; our orders are clear: Take the Gospel to every creature, to the ends of the earth. We have confidence in our Lord Jesus Christ, our Commander-in-Chief, so "let us go on."

Until we breathe our last or hear the shrill trumpet of the coming King, we will enjoy the work because it is His work. The result is inevitable, for "we are more than conquerors through him that loved us."

The miracle of motivation.

VII. THE MIRACLE OF SALVATION

I have seen in this place the miracle of salvation. I gave an estimate earlier in my message of these twenty-six years when over 30,000 people have made a first-time profession of faith.

Here is a church with an active membership of over 4,000. Hundreds have been saved in this place whom God has taken elsewhere. Hundreds have been saved here who are now in Heaven. Only God knows how many thousands have been saved and baptized and have joined this church in twenty-six years.

We have seen drunkards saved. In these twenty-six years we have learned, experimentally, that God can separate a man from the demon that is in the bottle.

We have seen in this church convicts saved. The outcasts of society have come forward for salvation. We have seen men from behind bars walk these aisles, their lives change. We have seen God put them back in the social structure to have a testimony for Jesus Christ.

We have seen poor people saved. I love them because that is where I classify myself—a country boy in overalls and tennis shoes when God saved me. God said, 'The poor you have with you always.' Don't ever forget that. God has given me a special love for poor people. I greet them with open hands. I greet them with an open heart.

We have seen professional people saved. We have seen those saved that we wonder if any church in all the world would want. We have seen them with their physical presence—so unsightly, so unlovely. They weren't dressed like angels, had no halo, wore dirty, filthy clothes; but they were angels of God.

There was Mr. Arthur McVean, an old man, whose sister lay dying. He called and said, "Brother Tom, I've been listening to you on the radio. From childhood my sister and I have been members of [he named a big downtown church]. My sister has been a schoolteacher all of her adult life. We asked people from our church to come visit, but they never came."

I went to see them. I led his sister to the Lord two weeks before she died. I had the joy of leading him to Christ also.

What a man *has*, has never meant anything to me. It is what a man *is*. That is where God puts the premium. He is a soul! We don't minister to people for what they can do for us. We minister to people because we have the answer to their needs.

That man was well-to-do. Years later he said to me one day, after he had put $20,000 in this work, "There are 32 1/2 acres of land around the corner from the church. Your church ought to have it."

I said, "We have no money."

He handed me $5,000 and said, "Go buy it." We went and bought it.

Today we have 45 acres of land because of a little unkempt man whom no one seemed to want except Jesus.

Jesus said, "All that the Father giveth me shall come to me; and him that cometh to me I will in no wise cast out."

The miracle of salvation.

When we come to the close of the Bible, it seems the Holy Spirit of God says, "John, don't stop here. Write one more thing: 'And the Spirit and the bride say, Come. And let him that heareth say, Come. And let him that is athirst come. And whosoever will, let him take the water of life freely' (Rev. 22:17)."

Anyone can come. God loves all people. We have seen people from all walks of life saved.

I have been in this city about twenty-nine years. I was pastor of a Sunday school called the Marimont Baptist Church. The first ones saved under my ministry were a barber and his family. And they were the first people I ever baptized in Pontiac.

The Lord took from their home some years later their beautiful little daughter. I preached her funeral, stood with them in the hour of sorrow.

From that Ballard family, saved twenty-nine years ago, some have gone into the Lord's work. Some of the children went to Bob Jones College.

Thank God, they weren't the last. They have come from the little shacks by the railroad; they have come from the mansions; they have come from the offices; they have come from the mills; they have come from the fields. "For God so loved the world, that he gave his only begotten Son, that whosoever believeth in him should not perish, but have everlasting life."

That is why I believe in miracles.

"For there is no man which shall do a miracle in my name, that can lightly speak evil of me."—Mark 9:39.

For a complete list of books available from the Sword of the Lord, write to Sword of the Lord Publishers, P. O. Box 1099, Murfreesboro, Tennessee 37133.